The Military Campaigns of Lieutenant-General Chaffee

By permission of Pirie MacDonald

ADNA ROMANZA CHAFFEE, LIEUTENANT GENERAL, U.S.A.

The Military Campaigns of Lieutenant-General Chaffee

The Civil War, Indian Wars, Spanish-American War, Boxer Rebellion & Philippine Campaign

ILLUSTRATED

The Life of Lieutenant-General Chaffee
William Harding Carter

Some Observations on the Pekin Expedition
by William Crozier

LEONAUR

The Military Campaigns of Lieutenant-General Chaffee
The Civil War, Indian Wars, Spanish-American War, Boxer Rebellion & Philippine
Campaign
The Life of Lieutenant-General Chaffee
by William Harding Carter
Some Observations on the Pekin Expedition
by William Crozier

ILLUSTRATED

FIRST EDITION IN THIS FORM

First published under the titles
The Life of Lieutenant-General Chaffee
and
Some Observations on the Pekin Expedition

Leonaur is an imprint of Oakpast Ltd

ISBN: 978-1-917666-18-3 (hardcover)
ISBN: 978-1-917666-19-0 (softcover)

http://www.leonaur.com

Contents

Foreword   7

Chapter 1: Early Life and Characteristics   11

Chapter 2: Enlistment for the Civil War   13

Chapter 3: At the Front: The Peninsular Campaign   17

Chapter 4: Antietam and Fredericksburg   20

Chapter 5: Picketing the Rappahannock; Stoneman's
Raid; Gettysburg   22

Chapter 6: Sheridan's Raid to Richmond   29

Chapter 7: With Sheridan in the Shenandoah Valley   35

Chapter 8: Five Forks; Sailor's Creek; Appomattox   37

Chapter 9: Frontier Service in Texas   40

Chapter 10: Frontier Service in Kansas and Indian Territory 50

Chapter 11: Frontier Service in Arizona   55

Chapter 12: Indian Agent at San Carlos   59

Chapter 13: Frontier Service in Arizona (Continued)   63

Chapter 14: Frontier Service with Crook's   68

Chapter 15: Frontier Service in New Mexico   73

Chapter 16: End of the Indian Wars   80

Chapter 17: War With Spain   83

Chapter 18: The Santiago Campaign 90

Chapter 19: The Siege and Surrender of Santiago 98

Chapter 20: El Caney—The Official Report 107

Chapter 21: The Return to Cuba 111

Chapter 22: China Relief Expedition 118

Chapter 23: The Capture of Pekin 125

Chapter 24: Allies Assume Control in Pekin 135

Chapter 25: Winter Quarters in Pekin 145

Chapter 26: The Evacuation of Pekin 155

Chapter 27: Philippine Service 161

Chapter 28: Homeward Bound 176

Chapter 29: Chief of Staff 181

Some Observations on the Pekin Expedition 191

Foreword

We pride ourselves in America upon the fact that the door of opportunity is never closed to genuine merit. Yet it has remained for the present generation to witness the solitary instance in which a soldier risen from the ranks of the Regular Army has been honoured with the highest military office in the gift of the nation. Not for this exceptional fact, but because of his long and remarkable career in arms, the life-work of Lieutenant-General Adna Romanza Chaffee deserves to be made of record, that future generations of Americans may comprehend what men of his time endured for the nation's sake. His rise from the lowest to the highest rank in the American Army was due to no extraneous influence, but came as a just reward for meritorious achievements in competition with an exceptional body of men.

When the old flag was lowered at Sumter, the gauge of battle was thrown down and there was naught to do but prepare for the coming struggle. The early calls for volunteers did not indicate, in the light of subsequent events, any very decided or comprehensive plans beyond preparations for battle. No one could base a calculation upon the experience of the past. There was grave misunderstanding between the sections as to their relative strength: the southerners were strangely vain of their individual prowess; the northerners were more phlegmatic, slower to move, but once they were aroused neither defeat nor disaster could swerve them from their purpose.

General Chaffee was one of two million young men and boys who during the fratricidal conflict volunteered with only one thought—to save the Union. The vast majority of them have gone to their tombs, and the Grim Reaper, from whom none escapes, is rapidly gathering the survivors to their last bivouac. The world goes on, and the kaleidoscopic course of modern events seems to leave no time for reflection upon the deeds of those young patriots, yet their fame and glory are secure in the hearts of the nation, and the story of their achievements will survive when all the bronze and marble monuments now standing to mark their conquering pathway in war have crumbled to dust and passed back to Mother Earth.

We are coming more and more to recognise that truthful history of the great forward movements which have characterised the nation's rise and progress is best deduced from the journals, diaries, and reports of the men who have rendered the state some service. General Chaffee's life was an open book to his comrades, but now that he and they have passed over the great divide it is no easy matter to uncover the earlier trail of half a century and to do justice to his modest, fearless, and successful career.

Volumes have been written upon the fortunes of individual soldiers, and hero-worship has ever been more or less blind in the adulation bestowed upon successful commanders. It is the fate of nations to witness the rise and fall of popular military idols, for truthful history disposes of ephemeral reputations. The history of war is not always the story of success, but American manhood has often been exalted by defeat as well as by victory. There is no pride akin to that which comes of a knowledge that one's ancestors have rendered the state some service, and as long as there remain upon the pages of history the stories of Valley Forge, of Yorktown, of Mexico, of Chickamauga, of Gettysburg, of Santiago, and of Pekin, so long will children lisp with proud mien the stories of their fathers' swords.

In the preparation of the life-story of General Chaffee it has been the constant endeavour to present an honest and unpretentious representation of his service, as substantiated by the records, and to avoid entirely the tempting realms of speculation. With the lapse of years dangers are forgotten and the memory of hardships is mellowed; yet when the country was supposed to be in a state of profound peace the little frontier garrisons, which made the settlement of half a continent possible, unostentatiously went about their work of carving the path of an empire without expectation of other reward than a consciousness of duty nobly done.

During the quarter-century of Indian wars following the close of the Civil War no officer was more uniformly successful than General Chaffee. His subsequent military career in Cuba, China, and the Philippines served to fill some of the most interesting pages of his country's history. His civil career subsequent to retirement rounded out the closing years of a well-spent life.

The public is apt to exaggerate the merits of some at the expense of others. Opportunity and influence must be reckoned with by all who have ambitious dreams of military fame. History shows a trail of broken hearts and wrongs which will never be righted, in the wake of every war. The Civil War and the war with Spain have both left their scars in the uneven distribution of rewards. General Chaffee did not suffer from lack of appreciation, yet none was more worthy. His personal papers record that his sincerest wish, in every recognition of his own services, was that he might share his good fortune with comrades whom he knew to be worthy. His last act before retirement establishes the fact that his wishes were sincere.

No discussion of military matters is ever allowed to proceed far in America without some congressman or editor delivering a homily upon the evils of aristocracy in our army. General Chaffee's career is not only a complete refutation of all such assertions, but should be an inspiration to every young man whose tastes and qualifications suggest the army as a career. Throughout his military life General Chaffee numbered among his most devoted friends and sincere admirers the graduates of West Point who were associated with him. This was natural and eminently fitting, for not the least of the things cherished in that incomparable school on the Hudson is appreciation of military merit.

CHAFFEE JUST BEFORE
ENLISTMENT

CHAFFEE AS SECOND LIEUTENANT,
SIXTH CAVALRY

THE OLD HOME

CHAFFEE AS FIRST LIEUTENANT,
SIXTH CAVALRY

CHAFFEE AS CAPTAIN
SIXTH CAVALRY

Chapter 1: Early Life and Characteristics

Adna Romanza Chaffee was born in Orwell, Ashtabula County, Ohio, on April 14, 1842. His father was Truman Bibbins Chaffee and his mother was Grace Hyde Chaffee. Truman Bibbins Chaffee was a descendant, in the seventh generation, of Thomas Chaffee, who emigrated from England and was living at Hingham, Massachusetts, in 1683. Grace Hyde was descended from Humphrey Hyde, who emigrated from England and settled at Fairfield, Connecticut, about 1650.

Truman and Grace Hyde Chaffee were the parents of twelve children, three of whom entered the United States military service at the outbreak of the Civil War in 1861, a fourth, Orestes P. Chaffee, entering the Confederate service. The last-named son, the oldest of the four, had moved from Ohio to Alabama some years before the war, and, like many other planters of northern birth residing in the South, he joined forces with the section of his adoption in the struggle. Orestes P. Chaffee served through the war and then went to South America, where he resided for many years.

Upon his return to the United States, he accepted a civil position under the War Department and rendered many years of service. One brother, Truman Everal Chaffee, Fourteenth Ohio Battery, was killed at the battle of Shiloh, April 6, 1862. Sherburn Howard Chaffee served through the Civil War in the Sixth Ohio Cavalry and was mustered out on June 27, 1865.

Adna Romanza Chaffee enlisted in the Regular Army on July 22, 1861, and continued in the military service until his death, at which time he held the rank of lieutenant general, then the highest grade in the army.

The early life of General Chaffee was similar to that of the average healthy, robust boy of the Western Reserve of Ohio. His mother was a woman of cultivated mind. She had been a school teacher in her early life, and endeavoured to guide and direct her children along lines which would induce them to seek further education. The wife of a farmer and the mother of a large family, she found many duties to occupy her time, but her loving guidance and influence remained always in General Chaffee's mind and led him to constant endeavour at self-improvement. As to his early school life we have the words of one of his teachers, Mrs. Elizabeth Dyer:

It was in a little brown schoolhouse, a mile south and a mile east of Orwell, Ashtabula County, Ohio. The schoolhouse was frame and had long benches running from one end to the other. There were short seats with desks behind them on each side. Seats and desks were cut up with notches, for nearly every boy carried a jack-knife and, proud of them, loved to cut the benches when the teacher's back was turned. I think the very best boy in my school was little Adna Chaffee. He was always obedient and never tried to play smart. His lessons were well learned.

My teaching was done in the old days when the schoolteacher boarded round, and I stopped at the Chaffee home a large portion of my time. I was only fourteen years old when I began to teach and got homesick pretty often. Mrs. Chaffee could comfort me at such times as no other person could, and I often went to her for sympathy. I liked the whole Chaffee family. They were truthful and honourable in all their dealings.

The foundation of Adna Chaffee's education was laid under the guidance of his parents in the comprehensive and insistent manner usual in those families which had removed from New England to the Middle West. At an early age he began to develop qualities of leadership and was usually selected as the captain of their hunts and sports by his boyhood friends, by one of whom it is related that at that early period he had already announced his desire to become a soldier. He was always very firm of purpose in all he undertook about the farm, in the woods, or at school, a characteristic which he retained through life.

During the period just preceding the Civil War an old sergeant came to Orwell and from among the boys of the neighbourhood formed one of the "Wide-Awake" companies and instructed them in the rudiments of drill. The drills not only proved of value as practical military instruction, but aroused the deep enthusiasm of the lads to such an extent that it needed but little to fan the flame to intense patriotism in 1861. Nearly all of these boys volunteered at the first call of President Lincoln, including, of course, Adna Chaffee.

During the youthful and formative period of his military life he was engaged in most active and arduous service in the field, where he absorbed the practical lessons so essential to the finished soldier.

He clearly recognised that the fate of the nation hung in the balance many times during that critical period, and that each great crisis demanded men of sterling, uncompromising character. He was unerring in his judgment of those whom he regarded as having rendered the nation services of a high order.

The subtleties of diplomacy made no appeal to this straightforward and plain-spoken man whose principles admitted of no compromise with truth and frank dealing. To be found wanting in the hour of need was unpardonable in his eyes, and his whole life was one of preparation to meet the obligations and duties of the next higher call. Scarcely had the smoke of battle dissolved at the close of the Civil War when he undertook to perfect his knowledge by a study of history and the art of war, which served him to good purpose later when he was called to high command. He accepted as worthy models only those whose patriotism, unflinching courage, and high professional attainments were beyond question. Men of that type do not abound, but every great crisis brings them forward, and they thrive and grow with the responsibilities thrust upon them.

As the story of General Chaffee's career unfolds, it will be recognised that he earnestly and steadfastly hewed to the line of high endeavour, according to the principles which he had inherited and standardised for his guidance through life.

Chapter 2: Enlistment for the Civil War

When the crisis of secession arose in 1861, President Lincoln, without awaiting the sanction of Congress, directed that the Regular Army be immediately increased by one regiment of cavalry, one regiment of artillery, and eight regiments of infantry. At that time there were five mounted regiments in the army—two of dragoons, one of mounted rifles, and two of cavalry. The new mounted organisation was designated as the Third Cavalry. In order to simplify matters for the large volunteer army being organised at the time, Congress voted, on August 3, 1861, before the organisation of the new regiment had been completed, that all mounted regiments should belong to the cavalry, and on August 10, 1861, the recently created regiment was designated as the Sixth Cavalry.

General Chaffee was one of the original members of the regiment, and for twenty-five years, through the Civil War and the Indian wars, he followed its fortunes and had no small part in moulding its character and sustaining its well-earned reputation. The regiment was engaged in sixty battles and combats while in the Army of the Potomac, during the Civil War, and, except when disabled by wounds, General Chaffee was constantly with it. The history of the regiment in the Indian wars revolved in no small degree around General Chaffee. During a quarter of a century there was little of hardship or victory that he did not share with the regiment; hence in tracing its story by flood and field during that period General Chaffee's trail is readily followed.

The Sixth Cavalry was recruited mainly in western Pennsylvania, New York, and eastern Ohio, in the summer of 1861, at the same time that volunteer regiments were being organised in those regions. Among the officers appointed to the regiment from civil life, and sent to recruit it in Ohio, was Charles Russell Lowell, a nephew of James Russell Lowell. At that time Captain Lowell was twenty-six years of age. He had graduated with the highest honours at Harvard, had travelled much in Europe, had engaged in railroad construction in Iowa, and, at the outbreak of the Civil War, was manager of the iron works at Mount Savage, Maryland. When the call for volunteers was issued by President Lincoln, young Lowell hastened to Washington and had little difficulty in securing an appointment as captain to fill one of the vacancies reserved in the new regiment for candidates from civil life.

The newly appointed captains were sent immediately to recruit their organisations. In regard to this duty Captain Lowell wrote from Franklin, Pennsylvania, on July 15, 1861:

> I am just in from a ride of thirty-four miles—have averaged twenty-five for the last eight days. We have about twenty recruits secured—a very good beginning; now that a nucleus is formed, I think they will collect rapidly. I shall start on Wednesday for Warren, Trumbull County, Ohio; this is the Western Reserve, and I believe is settled by Yankees.

Later, on July 20, 1861, Lowell wrote:

> I am located, or stationed I believe is the proper word now, in what is called the Western Reserve; a glorious place to recruit it must have been two months ago, but unfortunately all the young men were too patriotic to wait for a chance in the Regular Cavalry and went off in the Volunteers—three companies went from this little town.

In a letter two days later, Lowell said:

> I write out of sheer dullness; a mounted officer without a horse, a captain without a lieutenant or a command, a recruiting offic-

er without a sergeant, and with but one enlisted man, a human being condemned to a country tavern and familiar thrice a day with dried apples and "a little piece of the beefsteak"—have I not an excuse for dullness? I am known here as the agent of that cavalry company—and the agent's office is the resort of half the idle clerks and daguerreotype artists in town—but those fellows don't enlist. . . . . I am afraid the colonel will object to many of my recruits, that they are too youthful, but I cannot help the tendency. I have a perfect longing for young things.

On the day that Lowell wrote this letter Adna Chaffee was on his way to enlist in a regiment of volunteers in which some of his boyhood friends had already enlisted. In later years, writing of his change of plans, General Chaffee said:

I was *en route* from my home to Columbus, Ohio, to enlist in the 23rd Ohio Volunteers. Walking along Main Street, in Warren, I observed a recruiting poster on the wall of a building, with a picture of a mounted soldier. I stopped for a moment to take in the situation and read, "Recruits wanted for the United States Army." Standing in a nearby door was a fine-looking man in uniform, and he said to me, "Young man, don't you wish to enlist?" I told him of my intention to join the 23rd Ohio. He at once set forth the advantages of the cavalry service *and the Regular Army* in such fascinating terms that within fifteen minutes I determined to accept his opinion of what was best for me to do. I enlisted in his troop—K, Sixth Cavalry—and served as an enlisted man until May 12, 1863. While I was not the first, I was one of the first dozen enlisted by Lowell at Warren, Ohio, in the summer of 1861, my hand being held up on the 22nd of July.

A former sergeant of K Troop, Sixth Cavalry, writing of that period, said:

Captain Lowell was recruiting for K Company, Sixth United States Cavalry, one of the new regiments that Congress had authorised to be raised for the Regular Army, and Chaffee, along with several other young men of that community, myself included, was attracted by the enticing handbills which the enterprising captain had caused to be scattered broadcast over the surrounding country. Accordingly, he climbed a rickety pair of rear stairs in a two-storey building to the recruiting office, being conducted thither by a little dry-goods clerk, with a bald spot the size of a teapot lid a little back of the crown of his head. This little clerk was always conveniently at hand to offer himself as an escort to the would-be recruit, as there was a fee of two dollars a head for as many as he could thus conduct to the recruiting officer occupying rooms over the store in which the little clerk was employed.

The squad of twenty-five or thirty young men that had been gathered up at the Warren recruiting office started for Pittsburgh, Pennsylvania, August 5, 1861, being hauled in heavy farm wagons to Salem, Ohio, whence we were to go by rail to Pittsburgh. While on the way for Salem a heavy rain drenched us to the skin. Had some prophet foretold that in one of the three heavy wagons that were rumbling along the road to Salem on that sultry day there was a future Major-General and a hero, none would have guessed that the quiet and unassuming Chaffee would win such honours.

Captain Lowell exercised a great influence over the career of young Chaffee, who looked upon him as a cultured gentleman and a model soldier. In expressing his opinion of his former captain, General Chaffee said:

For self-control, personal courage, daring exposure to wounds or death in battle, I did not see his equal during the war. For bravery he is yet, after forty years of experience in the army, my ideal—*the brave officer*. As he was viewed *from the ranks*, he seemed unconscious that he possessed bravery in larger degree than usual with men. He was not one to do anything for mere show. Captain Lowell was always kind to his men, duly considerate of all faults and failures on their part; he was, nevertheless, strict in his discipline.

There are many of Chaffee's comrades in arms who can with entire justice and candour make the identical statement concerning Chaffee himself, for he was all of that and more, as will be recognised as the story of his career is unfolded.

The regiment having been ordered to assemble at Bladensburg, Maryland, Chaffee and his fellow-recruits left Camp Scott, near Pittsburgh, under a lieutenant, but were overtaken by Captain Lowell at Baltimore and conducted by him to the camp of the regiment at Bladensburg, arriving at midnight in a pouring rain, without tents or overcoats. The organisation of the regiment was begun at this camp.

Despite his youth private Chaffee was made a lance corporal, but served as such only a few days, when he was promoted to the grade of sergeant, on October 1, 1861.

The troop to which Sergeant Chaffee belonged remained at Bladensburg until October 12, 1861, when the regiment was assigned to the camp of instruction east of the Capitol at Washington. It remained at this camp through the winter, the men undergoing instruction regardless of whether, in preparation for the work in the field, which began with the Army of the Potomac in March, 1862, and terminated three years later, when they returned to Washington to participate in the Grand Review, the closing and spectacular ceremony of the Civil War. Lowell's Troop K was the first in the regiment to receive horses. In writing of the camp east of the Capitol he said:

> I don't know whether the newspapers, which have so many facts to telegraph, have said anything about the rainy, muddy thaw which has been the most important fact in the Army of the Potomac since the first of January. It is particularly hard on cavalry, encamped on a clay bank—the horse splashed with wet clay after three hours' drill is not a cheerful spectacle to the recruit who has to clean him—it opens his eyes to some of the advantages of infantry. Our fellows, however, are kept in spirits by the constant hope of an "advance"—an advance where, or upon what, they do not stop to think; for more than three weeks they have had orders to be in readiness at a few hours' notice.

In the organisation of the Sixth Cavalry, it was provided that two-thirds of the troop officers should be appointed from other regular regiments. Among these were some of the most talented officers of the army, and some excellent drill sergeants, promoted from the dragoons to be lieutenants in the new regiment. Under these instructors Chaffee received his first systematic training in the practical duties of a soldier and in the code of military ethics. He had been brought up on a farm and was familiar with horses. His adaptability and sterling character attracted attention and won immediate recognition, for he was employed in assisting with the instruction of new recruits, so essential in moulding men into a dependable fighting machine.

Chapter 3: At the Front: The Peninsular Campaign

After more than six months of constant drilling and instruction Sergeant Chaffee, in common with one thousand other martial spirits, welcomed the order to abandon their cantonment in Washington. Proudly they rode down Pennsylvania Avenue, in column of platoons, and, crossing the Long Bridge, entered Virginia, upon whose soil young Chaffee and his Ohio comrades were destined to undergo an experience in warfare which entitled them to recognition as veterans while yet boys in years.

The regiment moved forward to Centerville and Manassas Junction, where Confederate pickets were encountered for the first time. After more than a week of reconnaissance and screening in the vicinity of the historic battlefield of Bull Run, Sergeant Chaffee found himself at Alexandria about to embark for the seat of war on the Peninsula.

Arriving in York River, the command to which Sergeant Chaffee belonged disembarked and became the advance guard of the Army of the Potomac, moving on Williamsburg after the enemy had evacuated his lines about Yorktown. The leading squadron came up with the rear guard of the enemy about two miles from Williamsburg. The regiment then moved forward to occupy a strip of woods, which was the centre of the battlefield of the following day, and came unexpectedly upon an enclosed earthwork occupied by the Confederates.

As the regiment moved to the attack a supporting force of Confederate infantry and cavalry was discovered. In attempting to withdraw, the regiment encountered a morass, and while it was effecting a crossing the Confederate cavalry closed on the rear of the column and captured several men. The rear squadron wheeled about and charged the enemy; the squadron to which Sergeant Chaffee belonged supported the charge, causing the enemy to abandon the pursuit.

A few days later, May 7, 1862, the regiment led the pursuit of the enemy from Williamsburg and reached Slatersville on May 9. Coming up with the Confederate cavalry, Lowell's squadron was sent to make a detour of the town and cut off a detachment which had been observed. Reinforcements for the enemy arrived, and Captain Lowell led his squadron to the charge. The enemy retreated in the direction of some buildings from which a heavy fire was poured into Lowell's squadron as soon as the retreating foe had passed them. Another squadron of Confederates then came up on the flank.

The regiment being still in column on the road. Captain Sanders led his troop through a gap in the fence and boldly charged this squadron and forced it to retreat. Still another squadron of the enemy now came in sight, advancing rapidly, but Captain Sanders quickly rallied his men and led them against the enemy who had last come upon the field, threw them into confusion, and compelled a retreat. It was now clearly apparent that the advance guard had encountered the enemy in force and was greatly outnumbered.

The recall was sounded and Captain Sanders withdrew his men. Captain Lowell had pursued through the town beyond the sound of the recall, but by prompt action he managed to withdraw before the enemy had recovered sufficiently to recognise the smallness of the opposing force. The loss in this action was four killed, eight wounded, and three missing, a baptism of cavalry fighting for this new regiment. Our young Ohio boy absorbed the lessons of this combat to the full and forever after held Sanders and Lowell in memory as his ideals of cavalrymen.

★★★★★★★★★★

Captain William P. Sanders and Captain Charles R. Lowell emerged from McClellan's peninsular campaign with high reputations which led to larger fields of usefulness. Both reached the rank of Brigadier-General of volunteers. General Sanders was killed at Knoxville and General Lowell received his mortal wound while leading the Reserve Brigade to the charge at the Battle of Cedar Creek in the Shenandoah Valley, the Sixth Cavalry being one of the regiments of that brigade.

★★★★★★★★★★

There was no lack of opportunity for Chaffee to get military experience in this campaign. The regiment to which he belonged led the advance up the Peninsula, engaged actively in the efforts to capture Stuart during his celebrated raid around the Army of the Potomac, was under the personal command of General Stoneman during the Seven Days' Battle, and acted as rear guard when the cavalry withdrew down the Peninsula to Fort Monroe. The regiment then returned by transports up the James to Harrison's Landing and covered the withdrawal of the Army of the Potomac, the Sixth Cavalry comprising the extreme rear guard after having led the advance up the Peninsula.

In recommending that authority be granted the Sixth Cavalry to inscribe "Malvern Hill, August 5, 1862" upon its colours, General Pleasanton said:

The Sixth Regular Cavalry, the Eighth Pennsylvania Cavalry, the Eighth Illinois Cavalry, Robertson's battery of horse artillery, and Benson's battery of horse artillery were the only troops that were actually engaged with the enemy on that day; the only troops that followed in pursuit, and were the last to leave the field when the army was withdrawn. They victoriously closed the fighting of the Army of the Potomac on the Peninsula.

The evacuation of Harrison's Landing by the Army of the Potomac having been completed on August 18, 1862, Sergeant Chaffee marched with his regiment, as rear guard of the army, through Charles City Court House and reached Yorktown on August 20, 1862.

In this brief but arduous campaign the regiment had earned the right to emblazon upon its colours the names of ten battles and combats in which it had participated with honour, and in all these Sergeant Chaffee had borne well his part, as attested by those in authority over him as well as by those comrades who had had their baptism of fire with him.

The regiment had repeatedly engaged with the flower of the Confederate Army, Stuart's cavalry, which was made up of young men who furnished their own horses and had been accustomed to the saddle from childhood. During the campaign Sergeant Chaffee won the highest praise for capturing the wagon train of General Winder's brigade.

Chapter 4: Antietam and Fredericksburg

General Lee's movement from Richmond to the north, to carry the war into the enemy's country, caused an immediate and urgent demand for the return of the Army of the Potomac. The Sixth Cavalry was hurriedly embarked on transports at Yorktown on August 31, 1862, and arrived at Alexandria, below Washington, the next day. The regiment was disembarked at once and moved forward to overtake the Confederate forces, which were marching northward and already threatening Washington. The enemy's cavalry was encountered within a few miles, at Falls Church, and in the combat which took place there the regiment lost four men killed and wounded.

The near approach of General Lee's forces to Washington caused the withdrawal of the regiment across the Potomac during the night of September 5, 1862. The passage of the stream was effected at the Aqueduct Bridge, and the regiment moved rapidly through Tennallytown and Darnestown to Dawsonville before halting for rest. Passing through Barnesville, it sent scouting parties toward Point of Rocks and found the enemy at Sugar Loaf Mountain. Reinforced by two guns, the Sixth Cavalry, under command of Captain Sanders, moved to the attack and attempted to dislodge the enemy. The attack failed, and after some casualties had been sustained the action was suspended, to await the arrival of reinforcements. Two days later the regiment reached Middletown and sent detachments to guard the fords of the Potomac from the mouth of the Monocacy to Knoxville.

Stuart crossed the Potomac on September 10, on his raid into Maryland and Pennsylvania, and crossed back into Virginia, under the fire of Pleasanton's guns, on September 19, 1862, after having passed around the entire Federal Army. The service of the cavalry under General Pleasanton had been most exhausting, and, while the men were getting a splendid war experience, the horses were broken down by long hours under the saddle and continued lack of forage. General Pleasanton, reporting on these operations, said:

> The services of this division (cavalry) from the 4th of September up to the 19th were of the most constant and arduous character. For fifteen successive days we were in contact with the enemy, and each day conflicts of some kind were maintained, in which we steadily advanced. The officers and men have exerted themselves to ensure the success of every expedition, and these efforts have been fortunate.

Captain W. P. Sanders and five other officers of the Sixth Cavalry were mentioned for gallant services. In the midst of operations of great armies individuals are of small moment so long as they perform cheerfully and courageously the arduous duties imposed upon them. It is of some interest, however, in recording Sergeant Chaffee's services at this time, to note that so well had he played his part that, although only twenty years of age, he was promoted to first sergeant of Troop K, Sixth Cavalry, on September 26, 1862.

When Lee's army crossed back into Virginia, after the Battle of Antietam, the cavalry of the Army of the Potomac was badly in need of recuperation, but no time for rest was available. The ensuing weeks were filled with activity for the command to which First Sergeant Chaffee belonged. Many engagements occurred with the enemy before the regiment finally reached its stations on November 24, 1862, along the Rappahannock River. During this period the enemy had been engaged at Charlestown, Philomont, Union, Upperville, Barbee's Cross Roads, Little Washington, and Corbin's Cross Roads before reaching the Rappahannock River.

The regiment continued picketing the fords of the Rappahannock until daylight on December 12, 1862, when it withdrew and marched to the Phillips House, near Fredericksburg, to participate in the battle about to begin on that historic field. The army had begun crossing below Fredericksburg, while a pontoon bridge was being constructed immediately opposite the city. This bridge was completed about noon, and at 3:00 p.m. a squadron of the Sixth Cavalry, composed of D and K troops, was ordered to cross and make a reconnaissance of the enemy's works. First Sergeant Chaffee was at the head of K Troop.

The squadron marched through the town and thence to the foot of Marye's Heights and the adjoining ridges. The advance guard was allowed to approach the Confederate positions from which the main attack of the magnificent Army of the Potomac was soon to recoil in defeat. When the squadron had approached as near as the Confederates deemed it advisable to permit, firing began. The squadron turned to the right and galloped along the front of the enemy's lines and developed the infantry fire. Although it was in rapid motion, two men and eight horses were wounded before the squadron again reached the bridge, which was recrossed in good order, under fire. This incident is the subject of a virile picture by the celebrated artist De Thulstrup.

The Battle of Fredericksburg which followed was an infantry and artillery fight of great magnitude, and, although unsuccessful, the Army of the Potomac could not well afford to efface from history the record of its defeat, for the valorous assaults on Marye's Heights could have been repulsed only by soldiers of the highest type. When the situation was reversed at Gettysburg, the same Confederate Army was defeated by the same Army of the Potomac, but Pickett's charge added a page of history beside which the "Charge of the Six Hundred" pales almost into insignificance.

During the Battle of Fredericksburg, following the recrossing of the squadron, the Sixth Cavalry was posted in the rear of Falmouth in support of the batteries guarding the right flank, and remained there in position until the evening of December 13, when it was withdrawn.

Chapter 5: Picketing the Rappahannock; Stoneman's Raid; Gettysburg

After the Battle of Fredericksburg, the regiment went into camp near Falmouth, where it remained through the winter and until April 13, 1863, performing picket duty along the Rappahannock at United States, Richards' and Banks' fords above, and Corbin's Neck below, Fredericksburg.

The regiment had been for some time under that excellent officer, Captain W. P. Sanders, and, although originally recruited in the same manner as the volunteer regiments, it had won fame in its recent campaigns and had become Regulars in fact as well as in name. While it was posted along the Rappahannock, General Wade Hampton, one of the able and energetic Confederate cavalry commanders, selected detachments from his division and crossed the river at Kelly's Mill, entered the Federal lines, captured pickets to within a few miles of Falmouth, and returned safely across the river. In his report he says:

> A part of my plan was to have cut off the forces at Richards' Ferry, but, though I got completely in their rear, I was forced reluctantly to abandon my design. The Sixth Regiment of Regulars was on post there, and I had to leave them for another time.

The cavalry had exhibited magnificent fighting qualities on many fields of battle, but the true uses of that arm, and its capabilities when it was properly handled, were not appreciated at that time by anyone powerful enough in council to rectify abuses and stop the enormous waste of horses.

Side-lights of war are always of interest. One of Sergeant Chaffee's comrades of the Sixth Cavalry occupied himself one Sunday morning with writing this letter:

Banks of the Rappahannock, Virginia
Sunday morning

Dear Mother:

Being very hard off for paper and ink and something to write on, I take one-half of the sheet of paper you sent me and sit down to answer your welcome letter which I received this morning. At present I am on picket duty only a short distance across the river from the rebel pickets. We are in sight of each other. I am writing this on the butt of my carbine. There is another man on post with me; he is a Scotchman. He keeps me in good humour all the time telling stories. He is talking to the Secesh all the time. They asked him to what regiment he belonged. He told them it was the 1st Dublin. We don't fire at one another unless someone attempts to cross the river.

The weather is very pleasant at present, but the nights are cold. We get along very well. We have a fire to warm ourselves. I like to stand picket in good weather; but it is very nasty work in bad weather. We are going to have a good dinner. One of the boys has killed a hog, so we will have pork steaks today. We get plenty of corn cakes from the farmers. We have to stop out here eight days. We are out six now. I wish the war was at an end. As soon as the war is over, I shall quit the service for good and settle down . . . . . Your affectionate son,   James

It will be remembered that young Chaffee, now twenty years of age, had been advanced to the rank of first sergeant during the Antietam campaign in the autumn of 1862. The position is one of the highest importance and is concerned with the discipline and efficiency of the army at its very foundation. Usually, men are selected as first sergeants in the Regulars from those of long experience. Those were war times, however, and men learned rapidly the essentials and discarded the nonessentials. Every effort was made to complete the equipment and perfect the instruction of men and horses while they were in the camp at Falmouth, and First Sergeant Chaffee, vigorous, earnest, and patriotic, received the finishing touches which qualified him for further promotion.

There had been much to contend with, but when "*boots and saddles*" sounded on April 13, 1863, for the "Stoneman Raid," the Sixth Cavalry turned out six hundred and sixty-one men mounted and well equipped for the expedition. Stoneman's Raid stands out unrivalled in the annals of the Civil War for hardships and discomforts. Starting from their camps at Falmouth, each trooper packed thirty pounds of grain on his horse, besides his own rations. Each troop had six pack mules.

Owing to improper packing and the necessity for keeping the packs on for long periods in very bad weather, the mules were quickly disabled by sore backs. From May 2 until May 8 the command was out of supplies, except such as could be obtained by foraging parties while marching rapidly in a country already despoiled of provisions. Ninety-three horses gave out, fifty-one were killed, and seven captured by the enemy. The regiment captured twenty-nine horses and thirteen mules—not enough to make an appreciable showing as compared with the loss. No good results attended this raid commensurate with the labour involved and the breaking down of horses and men.

The Battle of Chancellorsville was fought during the absence of Stoneman's command. The presence of Stuart's cavalry with Lee's army aided much in making a success of the great flanking movement which brought the Army of the Potomac to the verge of ruin.

The conduct of First Sergeant Chaffee during Stoneman's Raid, April 29 to May 7, 1863, and prior services attracted most favourable comment in the regiment and brought about recommendations for his promotion to the rank of second lieutenant, which occurred on May 12, 1863, in time for him to participate as an officer in the next movement against Stuart's cavalry, which resulted in the severe Battle of Beverly Ford, June 9, 1863.

★★★★★★★★★★

The order for the promotion of First Sergeant Chaffee was written by Secretary of War Edwin M. Stanton on an official envelope, which is still preserved at the War Department and of which the accompanying illustration is a photographic copy.

★★★★★★★★★★

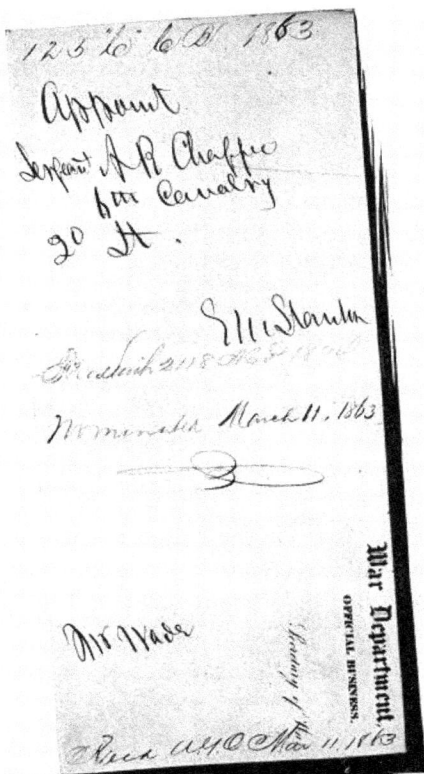

PHOTOGRAPH OF SECRETARY OF WAR E. M. STANTON'S ORDER
FOR APPOINTMENT OF SERGEANT CHAFFEE TO BE
A SECOND LIEUTENANT

The regiment lost one-third of its officers in this battle, which raged all day in the forests and clearings bordering on the Rappahannock. Until this battle took place Stuart's cavalry divisions had held those of the Army of the Potomac in great contempt, so far as mounted fighting was concerned. The men not only showed an unflinching readiness to follow their officers in every charge, but when, through the losses of battle, three troops were left without officers, the sergeants gallantly led them in the fray, which throughout was the long-hoped-for test of strength between the Cavalry Corps of the two armies. The Federal cavalry had boldly crossed the river, captured Stuart's headquarters, developed Lee's march toward Pennsylvania, and fearlessly engaged their opponents, fighting mounted or dismounted as occasion demanded.

An incident of this battle remained always fresh in the mind of General Chaffee and his comrades. Lieutenant Ward commanded one of the squadrons which twice charged when the enemy attempted to flank the line of Federal skirmishers. The enemy was driven away with loss by both charges, but in the last Ward fell at the head of his squadron while endeavouring to seize the enemy's battle flag. It was believed that Ward was not mortally wounded, and he was carried on the regimental returns as a prisoner in the hands of the enemy. He had been seen by a sergeant to fall, shot through the breast, but still alive. The day after the battle the enemy gave notice that an officer of the Sixth had been killed in the charge, and later officers of the regiment held in Libby Prison in Richmond sent word that Ward had never been with them.

During January, 1864, when the cavalry was again encamped at the scene of the battle of June 9, 1863, a farmer living in the vicinity recognised the insignia of the Sixth Cavalry and informed the men that he had assisted in burying one of their officers. General Pleasanton's headquarters were then on the hill over which the regiment had charged and where Ward was seen to fall. The spot was located and the body disinterred and identified. Many years after the author received a package of papers containing Ward's commission, recovered from his effects by one of his comrades, but no trace of any of his relatives was ever obtained.

When Hooker effected the passage of the Army of the Potomac across the Rappahannock the previous month, Lee had good cause to fear for the safety of his army. With Jackson's wonderful flank attack, where success was achieved at the terrible cost to the Confederacy of his valuable life, Lee was relieved of immediate anxiety concerning Richmond and made plans to carry the war to the north. This having been disclosed by the cavalry attack at Beverly Ford, Hooker proposed to the President that Lee be met by such other troops as could be assembled to confront him, while he, Hooker, should move on Richmond with the Army of the Potomac. President Lincoln had been the victim of superabundant advice, but had developed into a strategist himself. His reply was characteristic:

I think Lee's army, and not Richmond, is your objective point. If he comes toward the upper Potomac, follow on his flank and on his inside track, shortening your lines while he lengthens his. Fight him, too, when opportunity offers. If he stays where he is, fret him and fret him.

The race for the north began. The cavalry, moving on Lee's flank and covering Washington, kept constantly in contact with the enemy. Lieutenant Chaffee and his comrades had many fights during the campaign. The first occurred at Benton's Mill, June 17, 1863, while they were on the road from Aldie to Middleburg, Virginia. The Sixth Cavalry remained near the scene of the combat until June 21, when it joined General Gregg's command and had a running fight between Middleburg and Upperville, in which nearly all the cavalry of both armies finally engaged.

The Sixth Cavalry returned to Aldie on June 22, and marched thence, *via* Leesburg, and crossed the Potomac at Edwards' Ferry, and the Monocacy, near its mouth; thence *via* Point of Rocks, Maryland, and Mechanicstown.

The Sixth Cavalry, as part of General Merritt's command, remained on the flank during July 1 and 2, 1863, while the battle of Gettysburg raged and approached its zenith. Then General Merritt detached the regiment to Fairfield, on the road leading to Gettysburg from the northwest, to capture a wagon train, while the rest of the brigade moved toward Gettysburg by way of Farmington. Fairfield was reached at noon, where two troops were sent along the base of the mountain, while the regiment continued on the main road to Gettysburg.

About a mile from Fairfield the enemy's pickets were met and forced back to their supports. As the regiment pressed forward, the Seventh Virginia Cavalry was encountered and driven back to the forks of the road from which two Confederate brigades of cavalry, commanded by Robertson and Jones, could be seen by the Sixth Cavalry, which was close enough to hear the command, "Draw sabres!" as the enemy came forward to the charge.

The two advance squadrons of the Sixth United States Cavalry were in the road between post and rail fences and could not form line or join those in the fields before they were charged by the Sixth Virginia Cavalry, supported by the two brigades. The regiment was caught in a bad plight far from any help from Merritt's column, but remained firm and continued firing until literally ridden down.

The squadron near the foot of the mountain charged the enemy to relieve the pressure upon those in the road, but when the squadron commander, Captain Cram, was captured, the next in command retreated, fighting his way back in the direction of Mechanicstown, and rejoined the brigade. The regiment lost heavily in this fight, but interrupted the operations of the two brigades of Virginians endeavouring to get to the rear of the Federal army. The Sixth Cavalry went into this fight, known as Fairfield, with less than four hundred men and lost two hundred and thirty-two killed, wounded, and captured. The regimental commander, Major Starr, and Lieutenants Tucker, Wood, and Chaffee were wounded. In attempting to cut his way out with a few men Lieutenant Balder was killed. Chaffee was among the captured.

The Confederate commander endeavoured to parole Lieutenant Chaffee, but he refused to accept a parole on the field, in obedience to a recent War Department order, issued some months earlier when Mosby's men slipped in between the Sixth Cavalry camp and General Buford's headquarters, and, concealing themselves in a grove through which the road ran, captured the commanding officer of the Sixth Cavalry and several officers and men. Fearing that they could not make their way out with the prisoners, the guerrillas paroled them and escaped capture themselves. As a result of his refusal to be paroled Lieutenant Chaffee was abandoned with the other wounded. For his gallant and meritorious services in this fight he was brevetted First Lieutenant on July 3, 1863.

The remnant of the regiment, after the fight at Fairfield, had just rejoined the brigade when it was engaged again at Boonsboro and the day following at Funkstown. The regiment then had lost all but a few officers and men and was ordered to corps headquarters for escort and courier duty. By the end of August many men had found their way back to the regiment, and when Lieutenant Chaffee was able to rejoin early in September, he found eight officers and four hundred and sixty men ready to take the saddle again.

On September 12, 1863, Lieutenant Chaffee, in command of his troop, marched with the regiment to the Rappahannock River, crossed the following day, and engaged Stuart's cavalry at Brandy Station. After driving the enemy across the Rapidan the regiment withdrew with the Cavalry Corps to Culpeper and remained there for a month, when the Confederate Army advanced in force.

On October 11 the Sixth Cavalry withdrew toward Brandy Station and took its position on the right of the road, and some distance from it, fronting toward Culpeper. The skirmish line in front was held by the Harris Light Cavalry, which withdrew and passed to the rear, leaving the Sixth Cavalry exposed to attack from flank and rear, its position being at the extremity of a field bordered on three sides by dense undergrowth. The commanding officer, Major Morris, finding himself thus isolated, was in the act of withdrawing from the position when a column of Confederate cavalry made its appearance on the opposite side of the field. It was of the greatest importance to gain the road and go around the point of undergrowth before the Confederates should cross the field and gain that point and block escape.

A rapid gait was taken, and as the point of undergrowth was turned a severe fire was poured into the head of the column, by mistake on the part of the Harris Light Cavalry, which had taken a position behind the timber. Lieutenant Chaffee, commanding the leading troop. Surgeon Forwood, and one private were wounded and Sergeant Ellsworth killed. While the head of the column was being fired on by friends, the rear was charged by the Confederates and two privates were captured. This unfortunate incident was brought vividly to mind, thirty-seven years later in Lieutenant Chaffee's career, while he was commanding the American forces engaged in the operations for the relief of legations in Pekin, China, when a number of his men were killed and wounded by the fire of European Allies.

Lieutenant Chaffee was again invalided by wounds; but with an exceptionally robust constitution he soon recovered and rejoined his troop in November. The regiment had been engaged during his absence, but without suffering any losses.

The regiment took up its old line of march back toward Brandy Station, went into camp on December 1, 1863, and began the erection of huts and stables for the winter. By the end of December thirteen officers and six hundred and fifteen men were present. The regiment remained in this cantonment for five months, and during that period its efficiency was greatly increased by the issue of Sharp's breech-loading carbines and new-model Colt revolvers. The Cavalry Corps which emerged from winter quarters and fell under General Sheridan's command had become infinitely more self-sustaining in its dismounted fighting by reason of the opportunity for instruction during the period of rest from active operations.

Chapter 6: Sheridan's Raid to Richmond

General Sheridan assumed command of the Cavalry Corps of the Army of the Potomac on April 6, 1864, and immediately set about having the cavalry relieved from the arduous and harassing picket duty which had been its portion under General Meade and other commanders of that army. This afforded an opportunity to give a brief rest to the horses and to fit out the various commands for the active operations about to commence, with the object of breaking Lee's communications and defeating Stuart's cavalry.

There had been a lamentable loss of power in the Army of the Potomac from the very beginning of the war, because the great value of concerted cavalry action was not appreciated. Notwithstanding the excellent account which that arm had given of itself on every field, it had immediately been returned to picket duty, much of which could have been performed readily by infantry, and the horses might have been thus saved from the semi-starvation incident to being scattered along the banks of streams where it was impossible to deliver forage. It was therefore with universal satisfaction that the authority was received to cease guarding trains and picketing the infantry camps and to go after Stuart's cavalry. Many of the senior officers of the Sixth Cavalry had been advanced to higher rank in the Volunteers, and to the young juniors fell the privilege of taking the regiment through under Sheridan to the closing scenes at Appomattox.

Lieutenant Chaffee's troop was fit and ready for action when the regiment was sent from winter cantonments to reconnoitre Germania Ford, Mine Run, and United States Ford on May 4, 1864, and then to Chancellorsville in time to go with the Cavalry Corps to Todd's Tavern and participate in the encounter at that place.

Then began preparations for Sheridan's Raid toward Richmond, around Lee's army, which was a very different operation from that of Stoneman. The Sixth Cavalry marched May 9, 1864, on the Fredericksburg and Richmond Pike, crossing the North Anna River after dark. The clouds of dust attracted the attention of the enemy, who took up the pursuit and opened with artillery fire on the corps headquarters at daylight. However, the march was promptly resumed toward Beaver Dam Station, the enemy frequently attacking the rear guard. Stuart realised the full danger of the situation and hastened his force at a killing pace to head off Sheridan's troops and put his own between the enemy and Richmond.

At Yellow Tavern, six miles from Richmond, Stuart turned and struck Sheridan. A severe engagement took place, resulting in the defeat of the Confederates and the death of their famous commander, J. E. B. Stuart. This was a disastrous action for the Confederate cavalry, which was never again the same important factor it had been in the past. Stuart's corps practically ceased to exist, and the cavalry divisions were assigned thereafter to duty under General Lee's personal direction.

Sheridan continued his march after the battle, and at daylight the next morning, May 12, 1864, the column reached the bluffs overlooking the Mechanicsville Pike, where Sheridan massed his command between the first and second lines around Richmond. Shells had been buried in the road, and one of them exploded as the Sixth Cavalry passed over it. It became evident that the column could not pass between the Confederate fortifications and the Chickahominy. Custer's brigade was then detailed to repair Meadow Bridge and force a crossing, which was attempted under a heavy fire from the enemy posted on the opposite side.

Merritt's division was finally sent in to accomplish what appeared to be too much for a brigade. The bridge was floored with rails and planks and a column pushed across. The defeat of the Confederates intrenched opposite this bridge, and the repulse of the two brigades which came out from Richmond, ended their hopes of doing anything to impede seriously Sheridan's cavalry.

Lieutenant Chaffee's troop remained with the column until it arrived at Bottom's Bridge, when his regiment was detached and ordered to Fort Monroe to hurry forward supplies. The regiment marched to Williamsburg the first day—a distance of fifty miles—and with little or no delay for rest continued the march to Fort Monroe, arriving the next day and delivering General Sheridan's dispatches. The Sixth Cavalry marched back and met the Cavalry Corps at the White House. After receiving the much-needed supplies Sheridan resumed the march and rejoined the Army of the Potomac on May 22, 1864, near Chesterfield Station on the Richmond & Fredericksburg Railroad.

This expedition had fulfilled Sheridan's expectations and knitted together the force with which he was later to deal the final blow to the Army of Northern Virginia. To the young lieutenants of Chaffee's generation, it was an inspiration and a never-ending source of reminiscence in after-years at the camp fires of the frontier. At the time of the occurrences there was little opportunity for reflection and exchange of views, for scenes were changing rapidly.

The regiment participated in the general advance of the Army of the Potomac on the Pamunkey. Crossing on the pontoon bridge at old Hanovertown, the regiment proceeded to the vicinity of Hawe's Shop, where a severe cavalry engagement took place on May 28, 1864.

Pushing on to Cold Harbor, the regiment effected the capture of that important point after a hard fight against both cavalry and infantry. The regiment to which Chaffee belonged was on the left on June 1 and did not participate actively in the fighting between the two armies on that day. Following the battle the regiment moved next day down the Chickahominy to the vicinity of Bottom's Bridge, the Confederates being on the opposite side.

On June 7, 1864, the Sixth Cavalry, provided with three days' rations to last five days, and with two days' grain on the saddles, started with General Sheridan on the raid to Trevilian Station to cut the Virginia Central Railroad near Charlottesville. The advance was continually contested by the enemy until Trevilian Station was reached on June 11, when a severe battle took place with Fitzhugh Lee's and Hampton's cavalry divisions, resulting in their defeat. The return march was begun on June 12, and it was not until the North Anna had been crossed that the horses were unsaddled and allowed to graze. They had been without food for two days and were nearly famished.

On June 15 the Cavalry Corps crossed the Mattapony on the pontoon bridge where the Sixth Cavalry was posted to await the arrival of detachments left behind. After all had crossed, the bridge was taken up on June 18, and the regiment rejoined the corps the next day. On June 21 the regiment crossed on the railroad bridge and marched to New Baltimore and thence to the James River, arriving at Willcox's Landing on June 26. The river was crossed in boats on June 28 and the enemy was engaged at Dabney's Mills the next day.

On June 30 the regiment returned to the vicinity of City Point, Virginia. The Cavalry Corps had now been marching and fighting for fifty-six consecutive days, and was placed in camp near Light House Point to rest and refit. The loss of horses had been serious throughout the war. The hard riding and lack of forage during this period had played havoc, and nearly six thousand unserviceable animals were turned in at City Point for recuperation under the cavalry bureau.

A kinsman of Lieutenant Chaffee who was a surgeon in the Sixth Ohio Cavalry, writing of Sheridan's Raid to Richmond, says:

> Early on the morning of the 9th we were in motion, the object being to get away from Lee's infantry before meeting Stuart's cavalry. It was early spring, and a cloudless sky and clear invigorating atmosphere contributed to render the day nearly perfect. Our regiment, the Sixth Ohio, brought up the extreme rear, and the beauty and quiet of the day was still upon us, when,

as we made a turn through a stretch of wood, the advance was startled by the well-known Confederate yell, accompanied by rapid firing. The colonel commanding, turning in his saddle, saw the rear of his regiment scattering in every direction closely pressed by the attacking party. In an instant everything was in the utmost confusion. The artillery, pack-train, and forming bodies of troops seemed to be inextricably mixed, and the writer found himself in a sort of pandemonium, separated from every familiar face, and uncertain which way to turn, to avoid the increasing fire, or to find a post of duty. Just then a staff officer galloped past, and with a shout, "You are wanted this way. Doctor," he swept by and I followed on.

In a moment a position was attained enabling me to witness the rare sight of cavalry fighting hand to hand with sabre and pistol. The excitement was too great to allow the details to be firmly fixed in mind. A swaying mass of horsemen, and the roar of a section of artillery in the rear, were the main impressions made. Only one distinct act can be recalled at this day. The adjutant of the regiment, whose death occurred but a short time subsequently, had just received the ineffectual fire of a Southern soldier. With horses careering side by side, he had grasped the Confederate by the collar of his coat with one hand, and with the other was in the act of striking him from his saddle with the butt of his pistol.

One poor fellow was lying upon the turf bleeding and pale, and dismounting, I gave the reins of my horse to an attendant who had just joined me. It was anything but a pleasant time or place for the exercise of the gentle ministrations of the healing art. Bullets were whistling through the air on every side, and it needed only the ear to assure us that the enemy was in close proximity. The wounded man was too weak to lift his head from the ground, and as I was intently examining the arm, through which a bullet had passed, the startling cry of "Here they come!" was heard.

We were in a ploughed field, and in looking up a body of Confederate cavalry was seen, not over a hundred yards away, coming toward us as rapidly as the nature of the ground would permit, firing their carbines and with all manner of exclamations. Not one of us stood on the order of his going. The orderly gallantly led the flight, followed by the surgeon, who was in turn followed by the wounded man. He, poor fellow, had not feigned anything, as he lay there apparently unable to rise. It was only the stimulus of imminent danger that enabled him to leap unassisted to his feet and to his saddle. My own horse, left to himself, started, and there was only time to grasp him around the neck and throw one leg over the saddle. The efforts of the thoroughly terrified horse, as he plunged through the soft earth, were frantic enough, but not more so than my own as I strained every nerve to retain my hold and right myself.

Success finally crowned these efforts, and our speed was further rewarded by the welcome sight of a fine of our own forces just ahead. These were flanked, and as we came to a halt the wounded man was close at our heels. In a sudden attack such as this there could be no very satisfactory or permanent alignment. The scene constantly shifted; hence no sooner had we alighted, and stretched the almost fainting man upon the ground, than we had the extraordinary experience of being exposed for a second time in five minutes to the enemy's charge, and were compelled to fly once more; this time we did not halt until we had safely outdistanced that persistent body of rebels.

Referring to the withdrawal from Trevilian Station, the same surgeon said:

After midnight the withdrawal was successfully accomplished, and with entire secrecy, and a backward march began, which in some respects was more painful than anything we experienced before or after. We had captured six hundred prisoners, who had to be guarded, and were encumbered with nearly the same number of wounded men. We were far from our base of supplies, and five hundred helpless men, suffering from injuries of almost every conceivable character, had to be transported for days, over rough roads, in ambulances, and in army wagons without springs, and in the heat and thick dust of summer.

Look not for the extremest horrors of war upon the battlefield, however awful the carnage or cruel the adversary, but find it rather in some of the experiences of prison life and the unutterable and prolonged agonies of a retrograde march, such as ours of eight days' duration.

From sunrise to sunset the long cavalcade of canvas-covered vehicles toiled along with jar and jolt, enveloped in clouds of dust and eliciting from the wretched sufferers a continuous succession of groans and heartrending cries. Soldiers in general know little of such scenes as these. The excitement and danger of the battle over, the resultant suffering is quickly removed and left to its proper care.

Lieutenant Chaffee and his comrades were not destined to enjoy a prolonged rest. General James H. Wilson's division had been attacked by both cavalry and infantry during a detached operation and forced to withdraw by a circuitous route. General Sheridan made a rapid march from Reams Station to Wilson's relief and took the Sixth Cavalry with him.

Chapter 7: With Sheridan in the Shenandoah Valley

General Sheridan was relieved from duty with the Army of the Potomac on August 1, 1864, and assigned to the command of the Middle Military Division and the Department of the Shenandoah Valley. L Troop, Sixth Cavalry, accompanied the general as his escort, and on August 12 the remaining troops of the regiment embarked on transports at Light House Point, and disembarked the following day at Giesboro Point, the great remount depot of the Civil War, opposite the present Army War College, Washington. Three days were spent here exchanging horses, and on August 15 the regiment marched over the familiar route of the Antietam campaign—Rockville, Frederick, and Harpers Ferry—and thence to Berryville in the Shenandoah Valley, where the Cavalry Corps was assembled.

The regiment remained in camp until September 19, 1864. At 3:00 a.m. that morning the call to arms was sounded, the regiment went into position on the front and left, and the battle of Winchester then took place. The Confederates were defeated and retreated up the Shenandoah Valley; the pursuit was begun the next morning. The Confederates took up a new position at Fishers Hill, but were driven out of it, the battle of that name taking place on September 22, 1864. The enemy continued to retreat up the Valley, the Sixth Cavalry reaching Harrisonburg on September 24. The return march down the Valley was the occasion for destroying everything in the way of forage, wheat, and corn and for driving off all the livestock to prevent the Confederate forces from relying upon that section for any further supplies.

The Sixth Cavalry went into camp near Cedar Creek on October 12, 1864. About 4:00 a.m. on October 19 the army was attacked and thrown into considerable confusion. The regiment saddled in haste and got into line. At break of day, it was discovered that the left had been taken by surprise and involved the whole line, which doubled back from left to right. Soon after daylight the Confederate army obtained possession of the camps and all they contained. The troops retired on the Sixth Corps, and a new line was selected about two miles to the rear of the first position on Cedar Creek.

The advance of the Confederates ceased here. General Sheridan arrived on the field from Winchester about three o'clock. Soon after his arrival the advance was sounded, the tide of battle turned, and the Confederates were routed with the loss of their captures of the morning, much of their own artillery and trains, and fifteen hundred prisoners. At the conclusion of the fight the Sixth Cavalry returned to its old camp.

At this battle General Charles Russell Lowell, United States Volunteers, whose regular rank was captain of the Sixth Cavalry, and who, it will be remembered, enlisted young Adna Chaffee for his troop, was killed under pathetic circumstances. General Sheridan had given him command of the Reserve Brigade, then composed of the First, Second, and Fifth Cavalry, Regulars, and Lowell's volunteer regiment, the Second Massachusetts. His brigade had been moved to the left, where it took up a position at the village of Middletown. A Confederate battery in the vicinity was troublesome, and sharpshooters on the roofs of buildings in Middletown constantly fired at his skirmishers, who were posted along a stone wall.

Lowell rode forward to reconnoitre, when he was struck with great force by a rifle ball which probably glanced from the stone wall. While the ball did not penetrate, it caused faintness and loss of voice. He was laid on the ground and covered by the overcoat of one of his staff, where he waited for his strength to return, as he had determined to lead when the advance was ordered. General Torbert urged him to leave the field, but he declined to do so.

When the order to advance was given, Lowell was helped into his saddle—thirteen horses had been shot under him during the war—and formed his brigade, whispering his orders to his *aides*. He drew his sabre and took position with the line of colonels in front. The bugles sounded and the line moved rapidly forward. Almost immediately Lowell was struck by a bullet and fell. He was carried forward in the rear of the advancing cavalry to the village of Middletown, where he was taken into a house and laid upon a table. He had been shot through from shoulder to shoulder, the ball cutting the spinal cord and paralyzing the lower part of his body.

He had been recently married, and as his strength failed the surgeon of his volunteer regiment placed a scrap of paper on a piece of board and held up his arm so that he might write a few words of farewell. His mind was perfectly clear. He knew he had no chance of living, yet while his strength lasted, he dictated private messages and gave directions about his command. As day dawned, he ceased speaking and passed away. He died at the age of twenty-nine. His commission as Brigadier-General had been signed, but had not yet reached him, although he was exercising the command.

The Sixth Cavalry remained at its camp on the field of battle until the middle of November, when it was withdrawn to Kernstown, near Winchester. It was during this period, on November 11, that Chaffee was appointed regimental adjutant. Only a few months later, on February 22, 1865, he was made first lieutenant.

The regiment accompanied General Merritt's command on the expedition into Loudoun Valley, returning on December 10, 1864. On December 19 the regiment comprised part of General Torbert's command in the raid to Gordonsville, returning to its Kernstown camp the last day of the year. On February 27, 1865, the camps about Winchester were broken up, and the Sixth Cavalry marched with General Sheridan up the Shenandoah Valley, on the way to join the Army of the Potomac for the closing scenes of the war. The Cavalry Reserve Brigade at that time consisted of the Sixth Regulars, the Sixth Pennsylvania, the First Rhode Island, and the Second Massachusetts.

Chapter 8: Five Forks; Sailor's Creek; Appomattox

The Cavalry Corps joined the Army of the Potomac, near Petersburg, on March 27, 1865, and two days later went to Dinwiddie Court House, Virginia, engaged the enemy there on March 30 and 31, and drove them into their works at Five Forks. For his services in this battle Chaffee was brevetted Captain on March 31, 1865.

The Sixth Cavalry occupied the extreme right in the memorable battle of Five Forks, April 1, 1865. The Cavalry Corps took up the pursuit next day and continued to harass the enemy until April 6, when they were compelled to make a stand to save their trains. With the Cavalry Corps pressing hard on the flank, awaiting a favourable opportunity to attack, Lee's infantry was forced to interrupt the march and form for battle. The delay enabled the Sixth Corps to arrive. The

Cavalry Corps proceeded to the attack, the Third Cavalry Division executing the charge, supported by the other two divisions. This action is known as the battle of Sailors Creek and resulted in the capture of about ten thousand of General Lee's forces.

During this battle the remnant of the Sixth Cavalry was ordered to dismount and drive the enemy from some log huts. The regiment had become so reduced that the few men left in the ranks hesitated. They knew that the war was practically over and that the collapse of the enemy's opposition was at hand, but when Lieutenant McLellan, a veteran of the Mexican War, faced them and said, "Men, let us die like soldiers," they rushed for the huts under a shower of bullets and gained them with a loss of only three men wounded.

The pursuit was pressed until far into the night, and while the little band bearing so bravely the standard of the Sixth Cavalry was trying to force a passage across a creek in the dark a shell exploded in its midst, wounding three men, one of whom died the next day. The march was resumed in the morning and continued through the following day to Appomattox Station, where important captures were made. The day following, April 9, 1865, the Confederates made a desperate attack upon the cavalry at Clover Hill, but the arrival of infantry supports about 9:00 a.m. relieved the cavalry, which at once proceeded at a gallop to the enemy's left with a view to charging that flank. On nearing the Confederate lines, however, the cavalry met the bearer of a flag of truce, requesting a cessation of hostilities, as General Lee had decided to surrender. At 4:00 p.m. the surrender was announced.

Between May 5, 1864, and April 9, 1865, the day on which Lee's Army of Northern Virginia surrendered, the Cavalry Corps captured and sent to the War Department two hundred and five battle flags, taken in battle from troops as brave and determined as ever faced a foe. The number of battle flags nearly equals the total sent in by the combined armies of the Union during the entire period of the war. The fire action of the Cavalry Corps had been so enormously increased by the issue of breech-loading magazine carbines that no hesitation occurred in engaging superior numbers of infantry still dependent upon the muzzle-loading rifles.

The Sixth Cavalry was now depleted to a shadow of the full organisation which so proudly marched down Pennsylvania Avenue three years previously. At the Battle of Sailor's Creek, the regiment had become reduced to two officers, Lieutenants McLellan and Chaffee, and less than one hundred men present for duty.

Upon the surrender of Johnston's army in North Carolina the regiment marched *via* Richmond to Alexandria, where it was reviewed by General Sheridan on May 21, 1865, and then went into camp near Bladensburg, where it had been first assembled as recruits to be organised into a regiment. Again, the regiment marched down Pennsylvania Avenue, in the historic Grand Review, held May 23, 1865, before the President and the assembled army commanders.

The salient features of Sixth Cavalry service during this eventful period of our nation's history have been traced from its organisation until it formed for the last charge at Appomattox. Many of its officers were appointed to higher grades in the Volunteers—Generals Hunter, Emory, Kautz, Carleton, the two Greggs, Sanders, Lowell, and others—and rendered admirable service. As their places in the regiment, under our military system, remained vacant, the duty and privilege of bearing the standard of the Sixth Cavalry eventually devolved upon a small group of officers, rarely exceeding a dozen in number at any one time, who fought with the regiment through its sixty engagements. Eight officers were killed; fifty-three men were killed in action, seventeen by accident; fifty-three died of wounds and disease, and one hundred and twenty-two were wounded.

Many of the engagements in which the regiment participated were historic battles. For each battle there should be credited weeks and months of outpost and picket duty, weary marches, and fruitless scouts that try the strength and spirit of troops. Brave officers and men constantly returned from hospitals, southern prisons, and camps for dismounted men to fill the gaps left in the ranks. Life in the cavalry of those days was strenuous and hardships continuous.

Of the group of young officers and men who remained with the regiment during the four years following its organisation none saw more of battle, or of hard service in campaign, than Adna R. Chaffee. With the exception of the brief periods when he was absent recovering from wounds, he shared the honour of making the war history of his regiment during its first four years of existence. The author joined the Sixth Cavalry nine years after the Civil War terminated. At that time the captains were Chaffee and some of his youthful comrades of the Civil War period. They were still young in years, but were looked up to with reverence by the younger generation as battle-scarred veterans of our greatest and fiercest war.

Around the camp fires of the prairie and mountain region of the vast Indian frontier conversation constantly drifted back to the scenes and incidents of the Civil War. The impression was borne in upon the younger officers that many of these veterans had individually proven their mettle when courage was so common a quality that its exhibition called for no special consideration. As time progressed, it was easily discernible that the younger generation was closing up under the influence of several of the veterans, and of these latter none had a more sincere and devoted following than Major Chaffee, as he was known for many years in the Sixth Cavalry.

As the story of his later services is revealed, it will be evident that the confidence of the younger generation in the soldierly qualities of Adna R. Chaffee had not been misplaced. It is regrettable that in the days of his most active and dangerous enterprises—the Civil War period—he had not yet formed the habit of keeping a journal or writing of his experiences by flood and field in the manner which characterised his later service.

Chapter 9: Frontier Service in Texas

With the surrender of Lee's and Johnston's armies the Civil War practically closed. Only sufficient troops to gather the scattered elements of opposition remaining in the field were retained, the volunteer regiments being sent to their homes as rapidly as transportation could be provided. The Regulars were ordered into camps for reorganisation. The Sixth Cavalry was sent to Frederick, Maryland, where it arrived on June 14, 1865. The regiment had dwindled sadly, as had other regular organisations. The losses could not be made up by recruiting during the war. In all our wars until the present, politics, patronage, and failure to comprehend the situation have prevented the establishment of regimental depots, where men and horses should have been concentrated and trained to meet the losses at the front.

The incomparable Reserve Cavalry Brigade, Army of the Potomac, mustered less than five hundred sabres during the closing scenes of the great drama enacted at Appomattox. The enormous bounties paid by the states for volunteers had completely paralyzed recruiting for the Regulars. It has taken fifty years of effort on the part of military men to induce the authorities to place upon the statute books a provision for regimental depots and for universal service by selective draft. Under the pressure of recent world-events the system so necessary for efficiency has been adopted.

Some of the difficulties which confronted Lieutenant Chaffee, who was the regimental adjutant at the time, may be understood by an examination of the list of officers, showing how their services were being utilized under the pressure of war. It will be observed that there was not a second lieutenant in the regiment at the time.

The stations and duties of officers of the Sixth United States Cavalry on June 30, 1865, were as follows:

Colonel:

  David Hunter, Major-General, Volunteers

Lieutenant-Colonel:

  S. D, Sturgis, Brigadier-General, Volunteers

Majors:

  J. H. Carleton, Brigadier-General, Volunteers

  R. M. Morris, commanding regiment

  S. H. Starr, on leave (had lost an arm at Gettysburg)

Captains:

  A. V. Kautz, Brigadier-General, Volunteers

  A. W. Evans, Colonel, First Maryland Cavalry

  W. S. Abert, Colonel, Third Massachusetts Artillery

  J. H. Taylor, Lieutenant-Colonel, A.A.G. Volunteers

  J. J. Gregg, Brigadier-General, Volunteers

  G. C. Cram, on leave

  J. S. Brisbin, Colonel, Fifth United States Coloured Cavalry

  I. W. Claflin, Inspector of Cavalry, Department of W. Virginia

  B. T. Hutchins, Lieutenant-Colonel, First N. Hamp. Cavalry

  H. T. McLean, with regiment

  T. Paulding, Recruiting Service, New York City

  J. B. Johnson, Recruiting Service, Cincinnati, Ohio

First Lieutenants:

  J. F. Wade, Colonel, Sixth United States Coloured Cavalry

  J. C. Audenreid, Captain, A.D.C. Volunteers

  Henry Tucker, *en route* to regiment

  J. W. Spangler, A.A.Q.M. at Headquarters, Middle Milit. Div.

  C. B. McLellan, with regiment

  Albert Coats, Lieutenant-Colonel, Sixth U.S. Col. Cavalry

  Joseph Kerin, mustering duty

  S. M. Whitside, Commissary of Musters

  Daniel Madden, with regiment

  Nicholas Nolan, with regiment

  J. A. Irwin, with regiment

  T. C. Tupper, Recruiting Service, Cav. Depot, Carl. Penn.

  L. H. Carpenter, Lieutenant-Colonel, Fifth U.S. Col. Cav.

J. H. Wood, Lieutenant-Colonel, Second N. York Mt Rifles

A. R. Chaffee, with regiment

Second Lieutenants:

None

Hundreds of recruits were received during the summer, the majority of them having seen some service in the Volunteers. A number of officers, released from service with the Volunteers, and the newly appointed second lieutenants joined during the summer and assisted in getting the regiment ready for duty on the Indian frontier. It was no easy matter, however, to reorganise and drill a regiment at a time when everyone was tired of war and the Volunteers were being welcomed home in every village and town of the north.

The reorganisation accomplished, the regiment was ordered to Texas for station. The camp at Frederick was broken up on October 15, 1865, when the regiment proceeded by rail to New York, and on October 19 embarked on the steamship *Herman Livingston*. Only a few horses were taken on the vessel, which sailed on October 20 for New Orleans. A violent storm was encountered off the coast near Hatteras, which sent many vessels, including passenger steamers, to the bottom. It became necessary to lighten the ship, and the regiment was subjected to the heart-breaking scene of throwing overboard the horses, some of which had carried their riders through the closing campaign of the Civil War and were regarded with deepest affection.

The regiment arrived without further mishap at New Orleans and went into camp to await a steamer for Texas ports. Sailing on the steamship *Clinton*, the regiment reached Galveston on November 12 and marched thence to Austin, Texas. A camp was established near Austin and named in honour of Captain Sanders, who, it will be recalled, had been killed while serving as a Brigadier-General of Volunteers. The regimental headquarters remained at this camp for nearly three years, during which period Lieutenant Chaffee was relieved as adjutant and appointed regimental and depot quartermaster at Austin on December 12, 1866. Lieutenant Chaffee continued to perform the functions of depot quartermaster until 1868—an experience of rare value to him later when called to high command.

While serving as depot quartermaster at Austin, Lieutenant Chaffee came to the conclusion that he would resign and go into business. He was not yet twenty-five years of age, a veteran of fifty battles, and enjoyed a high reputation among his companions in arms, all of whom urged that he should not quit a profession in which he had won recognition for the uncertainties of a business career. The story of this incident is best told by the official correspondence:

Austin, Texas, January 12, 1867

Adjt. General U.S. Army
Washington, D.C.

General: I have the honour to apply for a leave of absence for twelve months with permission to engage in business with a view of resigning.

Very respectfully, General,
Your ob't servant
A. R. Chaffee
1st Lieut. 6th Cavalry, Brevet Captain, U.S.A.

Hd. Qrs. Austin, Texas,
Jan. 12, 1867

Respectfully forwarded with the remark that Captain Chaffee is an officer in every way worthy of the indulgence of the government, and I hope that his request may be granted, though his loss will be very seriously felt in his regiment.

S. D. Sturgis
Lt. Col. 6th Cav., Brevet Brig. Gen'l.

Hd. Qrs. District of Texas Galveston,
Texas, Jan'y 18, 1867

Respectfully returned to Captain Chaffee thro Regimental Hd. Qrs. 6th U.S. Cavalry, for his reasons for so unusual a request as the within. As far as the private reasons existing for this indulgence can be given, they should be, in order that the indorsement from these Headquarters may be given intelligently and for the best interests of the service.

This paper to be returned.

By command. Brevet Maj. Gen. Griffin.

A. M. Taylor
2nd Lt. 17th U.S. Infantry, A.A.A.G.

Austin, Texas, January 23, 1867

Respectfully returned.

My reasons for applying for the within indulgence are, that I desire to leave the service and enter into other business, and having been in service since July, 1861, I asked the within indulgence that I might, should I fail to succeed in private business, return again to military life. I enclose herewith my resignation which I request may be forwarded instead of the within, *as I do not wish to ask an unusual indulgence from the government.*

A. R. Chaffee
1st Lieut. 6th Cavalry, Brevet Captain U.S.A.

Headquarters, Austin, Texas, Jan'y 23, 1867

To Assistant Adj't Gen'l
District of Texas, Galveston

Sir: I have the honour to enclose the resignation of 1st Lieutenant and Brevet Captain A. R. Chaffee, 6th Cav. The original request is also returned, not because Captain Chaffee wishes it forwarded (which he does not) but because the endorsement from your office requires it to be returned. The indulgence asked by Captain Chaffee in his first resignation was suggested by myself—he desired to make it unconditional—but as he is a very valuable officer and one who has served the government faithfully, I did not like his services to be lost and therefore made the suggestion to him with the remote hope that, in the end, he might change his mind; and that for the further reason that it has been the constant practice of the government (at least before the war) to grant officers, under similar circumstances, as much as two years' leave, in order that they might not go empty handed while trying their fortune in business. This was the result of a kind of paternal feeling which the government felt and exercised toward its officers, well knowing that they were not likely to have accumulated much capital to embark in business, nor was their profession one likely to induce habits of business. As Captain Chaffee has already made arrangements to enter into business as soon as his resignation may be accepted, I trust the General Commanding will forward it with his approval.

I am sir.

Very respectfully.

Your ob't servant,   S. D. Sturgis
Lt. Col. 6th Cavalry Com'd'g.

Austin, Texas, January 23, 1867

Adj't Gen'l U.S. Army
Washington, D.C.

General: I have the honour to tender herewith my resignation as 1st Lieutenant 6th Cavalry and Brevet Captain U.S. Army, with the request that it may be accepted to take effect from the 13th of March next.

    Very respectfully, General,
        Your ob't servant,

                            A. R. Chaffee
        1st Lieutenant 6th Cavalry Brevet Captain U.S. A .

Forwarded
    S. D. Sturgis
    Brevet Brig.-Gen. Comdg.

               Hd. Qrs. District of Texas Galveston,
                        Texas, Jan. 29, 1867

Respectfully forwarded through Department Headquarters recommended for acceptance, to date March 13, 1867.

                      Chas. Griffin
          Brevet Maj. Gen. U.S. A. Com'd'g.

                      Feb. 14th, 1867

Approved by command of General Grant.

                      Geo. K. Leet
                      Ass't Adj't General

                      Feb. 14th, 1867
Approved.   E. M. Stanton
                      Secretary of War

        TELEGRAM RECEIVED AT WAR DEPARTMENT
             Washington, D.C, March 12, 1867
From Austin, Texas, March 11, 1867.
Adjutant Gen'l U.S.A.

The acceptance of the resignation of Brevet Captain A. R. Chaffee, First Lieutenant and R.Q.M. Sixth Cavalry, is received. I beg to recommend that it be revoked and Captain Chaffee be retained in service. He is too valuable an officer to lose and his place cannot well be filled. I ask this with his consent further by mail. If necessary, please answer by telegraph.

                      James Oakes
        Colonel 6th Cavalry and Brvt. Brig. General

Respectfully submitted to the General-in-Chief. The resignation of Brevet Captain A. R. Chaffee 6th U.S. Cavalry was accepted to date March 13, 1867. Its acceptance was announced in S.O. 100, par. 7, Feb. 26, 1867.

A.G.O.	J. C. Kelton
March 13, 1867	Ass't Adjt. General

Approved.

Headquarters Army	U. S. Grant, General
March 16, 1867	

Respectfully submitted to the Secretary of War. The vacancy has not been filled.

A.G.O. March 19, '67	J. C. Kelton, A.A.G.

Restoration approved.

By order of the Secretary of War.

J. C. Kelton, A.A.G.

A.G.O. March 20, '67

It will be observed that the resignation became effective, in accordance with Lieutenant Chaffee's request, on March 13, and under the construction of all the laws bearing on the case he ceased to be an officer on that date. There was no authority of law for his restoration, but when General Grant and the Secretary of War intervened, his continuance in the service became effective. Upon his reaching the next grade his confirmation by the Senate terminated all previous irregularity.

General Oakes's return to the regiment, and his prompt intervention to save to the service a young officer who had displayed courage and soldierly qualities upon many battlefields, met with the warmest response from all his officers. Those were the days when regimental promotion prevailed and juniors looked longingly for promotion, but the making of a file by his juniors did not weigh in their minds with the retention in service of a young officer who gave such promise of future usefulness to the nation. Having put aside all thoughts of leaving his regiment. Lieutenant Chaffee soon after received his promotion to a captaincy, in the Sixth Cavalry, on October 12, 1867, and began immediately to add creditable deeds to its already long roll of battles and skirmishes.

Some years later, when asked by one of his kinsmen for advice as to establishing himself in business in Arizona, Captain Chaffee wrote:

It would be an unsafe thing to take my views on such a subject for it is a question I never think of or inquire into, nor would I be able to form an intelligent opinion if I should inquire. Mercantile life is always a struggle; no end to continuous planning and figuring as to how this venture or that experiment will turn out. I dare say it is fascinating work, and that the successful man derives a vast deal of comfort in witnessing a satisfactory ending to ventures he has rolled, twisted, and turned over in his mind a long time ere he decided to act.

Captain Chaffee secured relief from his quartermaster duties soon after he received his new commission, and in February, 1868, he assumed command of his troop at Fort Griffin, Texas. At this period the conditions in Texas were deplorable. Organised bands of outlaws under Lee and other *desperadoes* vied with Indians in their deviltry. Captain Chaffee had been at his new post of duty only a few days when a band of Quahada Comanches began to raid the sparsely settled country. When the Comanche tribe was induced to move to the reservation near Fort Sill, Indian Territory, the Quahada band of outlaws, made up of Comanches, *mulattoes*, and Mexicans, refused to go upon a reservation and located on the Staked Plains, where they lived on game and by stealing from the settlements. The part of the Staked Plains in which they located their village was very difficult for troops to operate in by reason of the scarcity of water.

A sawmill had been established about thirty miles from Fort Griffin to get out lumber for the quarters at the post. The wagon trains had made many trips back and forth without molestation, but the Comanches, observing one train with a small escort, boldly attacked and captured the mules, which were rapidly driven away by a few of the Indians, the others remaining for further depredations.

Within an hour after receipt of information of the attack Captain Chaffee was in the saddle with his troop and a detachment of Tonkaway Indian scouts. He left Fort Griffin at 8:30 a.m. on March 5, 1868, and, proceeding by way of Leobetter's Ranch, reached Dead Man's Creek during the night. Crossing the Clear Fork of the Brazos about twelve miles below Phantom Hill, he found the Indian trail next morning and followed it all day. The trail of the party with the mules separated from that of the war party, but was ignored and the latter vigorously followed.

Early the next morning the chief of the Tonkaway scouts came back with the word that the Comanches were in camp a short distance in advance. Captain Chaffee sent the scouts to make a detour around the Indian bivouac and led his men to the charge with pistols, killing seven of the war party, the others escaping in the *chaparral*. On the receipt of Captain Chaffee's report of the affair the post commander issued the following order:

Headquarters
Fort Griffin, Texas, March 10, 1868

General Orders
No. 19

The Commanding Officer takes pleasure in openly announcing to the troops of this command the complete success of the expedition which left this post on the 6th instant, under command of Captain A. R. Chaffee, 6th U.S. Cavalry. This short and decisive campaign has resulted in the killing of five Indians and one Mexican and one *mulatto* (both of whom were leaders), the capture of five horses, together with a large number of shields, bows, arrows, etc., and the total breaking up of an Indian camp, which had been for a long time a scourge to the people of the frontier. The casualties on our side were three men wounded, *viz.*: Privates John F. Butler and Charles Hoffman of I Troop, and Private James Regan of F Troop.

With the exception of the wounds of these men, the result is extremely gratifying, as was also the soldierly manner in which the troops bore their deprivations throughout the pursuit, suffering from the want of water, and want of shelter from the cold storm that raged throughout the entire march, without a murmur of discontent. In all campaigns where important results are achieved, and especially in operations against Indians, where the nature of the country is not well known, troops must expect to undergo hardships and deprivations, which cannot be foreseen or obviated; yet it is only the true soldiers who accept these inconveniences as necessary and unavoidable, and who, like men, maintain their spirits in spite of these.

(Signed) S. D. Sturgis
Lieutenant-Colonel, 6th Cavalry, Commanding

As a result of his efficient service in this engagement, Captain Chaffee was brevetted Major on March 7, 1868.

After the close of the Civil War, Texas was overrun with outlaws and *desperadoes* who were even worse than the hostile Comanches. Officers and men were continually called upon to guard courts of justice, assist revenue officers, supervise elections, pursue outlaws and murderers, aid in the execution of convicted criminals, and, in general, to establish the due processes of law where anarchy reigned. Many soldiers were assassinated for their devotion to law and order, and nothing but incessant vigilance and unflinching courage prevented the lawless element from controlling the border counties of the state. Captain Chaffee, with his troop, was moved from place to place with great frequency between the time he left Austin and the date the regiment was relieved from duty in Texas and ordered to Kansas. His men hunted down outlaws with a persistency that gained for them among the lawless element the name of "Chaffee's Guerrillas."

During this period Captain Chaffee commanded the post at Sulphur Springs from September, 1868, to March, 1869; Canton to July, 1869; Tyler to January, 1870; Corsicana to May, 1870; Fort Griffin to September, 1870, when he took station at Fort Richardson. He had been at his new post only a few weeks when he again took the field in pursuit of Indians. He left the post on November 12, 1870, and upon going into camp, two days later, observed some cattle in the distance running as though being chased. While the troop stood to horse a Tonkaway scout was sent to ascertain the cause of the commotion among the cattle. The scout had scarcely disappeared behind a slight elevation when a shot was fired and he rushed back and announced that he had seen five Comanche Indians on the other side of the ridge. Captain Chaffee started immediately and, in a few minutes, struck the trail.

The five Indians were soon joined by seven others. The pursuit, mainly at a gallop, continued for about fifteen miles. Just as the Indians were overtaken darkness set in and they scattered, rendering further pursuit futile. The troop returned to camp and the next morning went to the scene of the chase and found seven ponies and two saddles which had been abandoned by the Comanches in their flight.

Ordered direct from the scenes of the great Civil War to the distant frontier to combat Indians unexcelled in ability, cunning, and cruelty by any other tribes save perhaps the Apaches, officers and men found themselves in a community imbued with the hatred and bitterness left by the Civil War in the hearts of the people who had not been called upon to suffer from the presence of armies as had been the case in other southern states. Many ex-Confederate soldiers, on that distant frontier, had succumbed to the inevitable with bad grace, and the more lawless of them encouraged a hostile feeling toward the very men who were daily exposing their lives in protecting the settlements from Indians and outlaws. When, after ill treatment and murder of comrades, the men came to realise the contempt in which they were held, there was little leniency shown the lawless bands which had assembled in many parts of Texas whenever they came in contact with the troops.

Chapter 10: Frontier Service in Kansas and Indian Territory

There was little regret in the regiment when it was notified of a contemplated change of station to Kansas. At no time during its service in Texas had the regiment been provided with barracks and quarters, except the rude shelter constructed by the men. The scattered troops were assembled at Fort Richardson and began the march northward on March 20, 1871. Upon reaching Fort Sill the troops were dispersed to various posts in Indian Territory and Kansas. Captain Chaffee continued the march to Fort Riley, Kansas, where he took station until the following winter.

On January 28, 1872, Captain Chaffee was detached with his troop to duty at Oxford, Mississippi, a university town. The South was still undergoing reconstruction, and the presence of troops was not acceptable to the people. The inhabitants of Oxford soon realised that the young veteran was a high type of soldier, who, having fought the armies of the Confederacy for four years, was disposed to preserve order in strict accordance with his instructions but with an entire absence of sectional feeling. When Captain Chaffee was relieved from command of the post at Oxford in December, 1872, the citizens presented him with a silver cup in appreciation of the exemplary conduct of his command while there. The presentation address was made by Hon. L. Q. C. Lamar, then a professor in the university at Oxford, and who later represented his state in the Senate of the United States until appointed as one of the justices of the Supreme Court.

Upon Captain Chaffee's return to the regiment, he was ordered to take station with his troop at Fort Harker, Kansas, but conditions in Indian Territory were growing unsatisfactory, and early in April he was moved to Fort Supply, Indian Territory. Settlers were venturing into Kansas far beyond the safety line, and unprincipled skin-hunters were decimating the buffalo herds and arousing the resentment of the Indians. The preservation of peace was becoming more and more difficult, but the regiment laboured faithfully with the delicate situation. To sit idly by and witness the disappearance of their meat supply at the hands of the white men was beyond the endurance of the Indians.

War parties became more bold, and once more the frontier settlements were called upon to suffer the consequences of the inevitable conflict between advancing civilization and the doomed Indians—a conflict the tides of which have rolled back and forth across plain and mountain for nearly three centuries, with here and there a success for the red men, but with the ultimate result always the same from the days of the brave Wampanoags of New England and Powhatans of Virginia down to the Sioux at Wounded Knee.

It had always been customary among the great Indian tribes to pay extended visits to one another. On March 12, 1874, a party of Southern Cheyennes, who had been on a six months' visit to the Northern Cheyennes and Arapahoes, reported at Fort Dodge, Kansas, on the way back to their reservation. Before they reached Fort Supply some white men stole thirty or forty of their ponies. It was certain that the Indians would retaliate, and troops were immediately ordered out as a precautionary measure. A few days later the Cheyennes began their depredations near Sun City, not far from Fort Dodge, and ran off twenty horses and mules and a herd of cattle. Then began a series of attacks on mail parties, isolated ranches, and small detachments escorting trains from post to post. From day to day reports came from widely separated localities of theft, rapine, and murder. Trains were attacked, ranches looted, and women and children carried away into captivity. It had now become evident that desultory scouting and chasing war parties were equally unprofitable. The disaffection among the Indians became widespread, and expeditions were organised for the beginning of the campaigns which terminated only when the power of the Indians for sustained hostilities was permanently broken.

During August, 1874, eight troops of the Sixth Cavalry, including Captain Chaffee's, took the field and joined the force commanded by General N. A. Miles in the operations later known as the Indian Territory Expedition. On the evening of August 26, a fresh trail was discovered near the Sweetwater, which rapidly grew larger through accession of war parties joining from the agencies. Abandoning the wagon train, the command pushed rapidly ahead, and on the morning of August 30, 1874, while crossing the prairie about twelve miles from Red River, the advance guard was charged by about two hundred Indians, who came so close that one man was wounded by a lance thrust. When repulsed, the Indians retreated to a line of hills and joined the main body, numbering about six hundred warriors, who then took up a position along a broken line of bluffs interspersed with deep ravines.

The troops were deployed in line, with a small reserve, and moved forward to the attack, advancing from crest to crest and driving the Indians from every position they took up. Captain Chaffee, in the advance, led his troop in a gallant charge, using pistols. The Indians at first showed some tenacity, but the determined nature of the attack forced them to retire rapidly out of range. They attempted a final stand on a high bluff, on the right bank of Red River, but when the bugles again sounded the advance and the troops moved up the ascent the Indians fled. The fight had lasted over five hours, the Indians contesting various positions for about twelve miles.

As they finally abandoned the fight, the smoke of their burning villages could be seen. Immediate pursuit began across Red River and through the burning villages. For more than a hundred miles their trail was strewn with broken-down ponies and abandoned property. The dead Indians, lodges, arrows, and *moccasins* found along the trail indicated that the Cheyennes, Comanches, and Kiowas had united in this war. The Indians killed buffaloes, made water sacks of the skins, and, filling them, vanished into the almost waterless recesses of the Staked Plains.

The command, including both men and horses, suffered from the midsummer heat, as well as from thirst. Little water was found, and that obtained was generally so alkaline as to be really unfit for use and caused much sickness. It was determined to continue in the field and to order forward the necessary supplies. Captain Chaffee selected Sergeant Z. T. Woodall, of his troop, to take charge of one of the two parties sent by different routes from the battlefield to Fort Supply with the orders for supplies. Sergeant Woodall's detachment encountered a large war party of Kiowas and Comanches and had an experience rare even in the annals of frontier warfare, filled always with danger. The official report of the expedition commander tells the story of this remarkable episode:

Adjutant General, U.S. Army

General: I deem it but a duty to brave men and faithful soldiers, to bring to the notice of the highest military authority an instance of indomitable courage, skill, and true heroism on the part of a detachment from this command, with the request that the actors be rewarded, and their faithfulness and bravery be recognised by pensions, medals of honour, or in such way as may be deemed most fitting.

On the night of the 10th instant a party consisting of Sergeant Z. T. Woodall, Troop I; Privates Peter Roth, Troop A; John Harrington, Troop H, and George W. Smith, Troop M, 6th Cavalry; Scouts Amos Chapman and William Dixon, were sent as bearers of despatches from the camp of this command on McLellan Creek, Texas, to Camp Supply, Indian Territory. At six a.m., on the 12th, when approaching Washita River, they were met and surrounded by a band of 125 Kiowas and Comanches, who had recently left their agency, and at the first attack all were struck, Private Smith mortally, and all the others severely wounded.

Although enclosed on all sides, and by overwhelming numbers, one of them succeeded, while they were under a severe fire at short range, and while the others with their rifles were keeping the Indians at bay, in digging with his knife and hands a slight cover. After this had been secured they placed themselves within it; the wounded walking with brave and painful efforts, and Private Smith, though he had received a mortal wound, sitting upright in the trench to conceal the crippled condition of their party from the Indians.

From early morning till dark, outnumbered twenty-five to one, under an almost constant fire, and at such short range that they sometimes used their pistols, retaining the last charge to prevent capture and torture, this little party of five defended their lives and the person of their dying comrade, without food and their only drink the rain water that collected in a pool mingled with their own blood. There is no doubt but that they killed more than double their number, besides those that were wounded. The Indians abandoned the attack at dark on the 12th.

The exposure and distance from the command, which were necessary incidents of their duty, were such that for thirty-six hours from the first attack their condition could not be known, and not until midnight of the 13th could they receive medical attendance or food; exposed during this time to an incessant cold storm. Sergeant Woodall, Private Harrington, and Scout Chapman were seriously wounded; Private Roth and Scout Dixon were struck but not disabled.

The simple recital of their deeds and the mention of the odds against which they fought; how the wounded defended the dying, and the dying aided the wounded by exposure to fresh wounds after the power of action was gone; these alone present a scene of cool courage, heroism, and self-sacrifice, which duty as well as inclination prompts us to recognise, but which we cannot fitly honour,

N. A, Miles Brevet Major-General

The Congressional Medal of Honour was awarded to Sergeant Woodall, who survived to render many years of valuable service as first sergeant of Captain Chaffee's troop, and later as ordnance sergeant, which office he held at the time of his death, in 1899, at Havana, Cuba, during the period of American occupation. The author well recalls the impression made upon him and all the younger officers and men whenever Sergeant Woodall appeared in full uniform wearing the Medal of Honor. The esteem in which he was held may well be likened to that enjoined by General George Washington when the Purple Heart was bestowed upon its first recipient:

> Now therefore know ye that the aforesaid Sergeant Elijah Churchill hath fully and truly deserved, and hath been properly invested with the Honorary Badge of Military Merit and is authorised to pass and repass all guards and military posts as fully and amply as any commissioned officer whatever; and is hereby further recommended to that favourable notice which a brave and faithful soldier deserves from his countrymen.
>
> Given under my hand and seal at the Headquarters of the American Army, this first day of May, 1783.
>
> By His Excellency,
Commander-in-Chief,
Jono. Trumbull, Jr.
Secretary

A supply train was sent back from the field and met a train coming out from Camp Supply, A transfer of the stores was made, and the trains had started on their return journeys when the loaded train was attacked on the divide north of the Washita River by a large force of Kiowa and Comanche Indians. The train was parked, rifle pits dug, and the attacks of the Indians successfully resisted for five days without water. A portion of the Sixth Cavalry made a forced march from Fort Supply and relieved the train, which had scarcely resumed its journey when Captain Chaffee was met on his way back to discover the cause of delay. He had just found and relieved Sergeant Woodall's party from their distressing predicament. The campaign against the Indians continued far into the winter.

The last movement against them on the Staked Plains was executed in intensely cold weather, the thermometer registering twenty-five degrees below zero, when Captain Chaffee, on December 1, 1874, made a night march to surprise a party of Indians reported to be on a branch of the North Fork of Red River. They had scented danger and decamped, but were pursued by a detachment and overtaken at daylight on December 2, when they were attacked and routed with the loss of their ponies, about seventy in number, most of which were saddled and packed.

During this campaign the Indians were fought by the regiment in nine engagements, and were harassed by such insistent pursuit that they were finally driven into the agencies, broken in spirit and greatly impoverished. It was this campaign that brought about the recovery of the four Germain girls, captured by the Indians near the Smoky Hill River when the rest of the family, father, mother, brother, and a sister, were killed by Cheyennes.

Captain Chaffee had previously been honoured, as before mentioned, with the brevet of Major for his brave fight with the Quahada Comanches. During this campaign, on August 30, 1874, the brevet of Lieutenant-Colonel was awarded to him for gallant service in leading a cavalry charge over rough and precipitous bluffs held by Indians on the Red River of Texas.

It was late in the winter before affairs assumed a condition which would justify sending the troops into quarters. Captain Chaffee had been in garrison at Fort Supply only a month when the order for the regiment to change stations with the Fifth Cavalry in Arizona, which had been suspended the previous year because of hostilities, was reissued.

Chapter 11: Frontier Service in Arizona

In 1875, when the Sixth Cavalry was ordered to Arizona, there were no railroads in New Mexico or Arizona. It was not deemed wise to leave Arizona without any cavalry for field operations during the long period necessary for the exchange of regiments. To provide for this, one-half of each regiment was started, with instructions to meet and exchange transportation and horses. The first half of the Sixth Cavalry was assembled at Fort Dodge, Kansas, and, proceeding over the old Santa Fé Trail, met the first half of the Fifth Cavalry at Santa Fé, New Mexico. The second half of the Sixth Cavalry, which included Captain Chaffee's troop, left Fort Dodge on August 2, 1875, and exchanged transportation and horses with the second half of the Fifth Cavalry at Fort Union, New Mexico. Captain Chaffee's troop reached its station, Fort Verde, Arizona, on October 9, 1875.

The author has a vivid recollection of this exchange of regiments.

Although a Second Lieutenant of the Sixth Cavalry at the time, he was on duty at old Fort Verde in Arizona, commanding a troop of the Fifth Cavalry, which had lost its only officer present during the previous autumn, this officer having been invalided on account of a wound received in action with a band of Apaches at Sunset Pass, Arizona. On the eve of the movement to Santa Fé of three troops of the Fifth Cavalry assembled at Fort Verde the second lieutenant of the troop returned to duty. The author was then detailed as adjutant and quartermaster, and had an unusual experience, taking a contract train of freight wagons across the mountains over the worst road then in the United States.

The wagons were of the type known as "prairie schooners," and each had a trail wagon of smaller dimensions attached. Each wagon and trail were drawn by twelve or fourteen mules. More than forty years have passed, but there still remains in the author's mind a clear picture of Sam Miller, the train-master, piloting those overloaded teams up out of the Verde River valley; across the Mai Pais *mesa*; up to Stoneman's Lake; through Sunset Pass and down grade to the Little Colorado, with its shifting, bottomless quicksands; up Lithodendron Creek and beyond where the leading wagon cut through the sand and stalled against a veritable monarch of the forest, petrified and squarely athwart our course; to Navajo Springs; to Fort Wingate; to Albuquerque, where we joined forces with regimental headquarters and three more troops; up the Rio Grande and thence to the end of our first lap, Santa Fé, New Mexico.

Here were foregathered old comrades of three cavalry regiments changing frontier stations by marching, and here keen disappointment was experienced by men of the Sixth Cavalry, who were compelled to exchange their beautiful Missouri and Kentucky horses for the California mustangs of the Fifth Cavalry, which were accustomed to field service without forage other than grazing, and were therefore better fitted for the work in Arizona.

It was at Fort Verde, a station long since abandoned, that the author's friendship for Captain Chaffee began—a friendship which lasted through forty years of service and to the end.

The duties of the cavalry in Arizona at that time were performed almost wholly by small detachments operating in conjunction with Indian scouts. In the spring of 1876 conditions had become so bad along the Mexican border of Arizona and New Mexico, owing to the proximity of the Warm Spring and Chiricahui Apache reservations, that a removal of the Indians to the San Carlos Agency was determined upon. The troops of the regiment were widely scattered, but were promptly put on the march for the rendezvous in southeastern Arizona. Captain Chaffee marched from Fort Verde by way of Tonto Basin to Fort Grant, arriving on the last day of the month. The route followed took him past the site of the present Roosevelt Dam. At that time there were no settlers for more than two hundred miles of his route because of the continuous raids of the Apaches.

Upon the arrival of all the troops several expeditions were organised. Captain Chaffee's troop accompanied the squadron sent into the San Simon Valley on the eastern side of the Chiricahui Reservation, and when it reached Horse Shoe Cañon, on the east side of the Chiricahui Mountains, the trail of a large part of the tribe was found leading toward Mexico. The trail was followed, but the Indians had already crossed the line.

The Chiricahuis consisted of four bands—that of Natchez, son of the famous Cochise, the other three under Ju, Geronimo, and Nolge. Of the four, that of Natchez was the only one which moved to the San Carlos Reservation; the others escaped into Sonora, and from the inaccessible fastnesses of the Sierra Madre Mountains began a series of raids which lasted ten years and involved the loss of hundreds of lives. Upon the completion of the movement of Natchez' band the several expeditions were abandoned. Captain Chaffee was ordered to take station at Fort McDowell, Arizona, an assignment which gave him command of a post.

It was the custom in the Sixth Cavalry to offer the recruiting detail, available every other year, to the officer longest on duty with the regiment. Captain Chaffee had been with it since its organisation and had experienced many years of hard service. The detail was offered to him, and he accepted it in the autumn and was absent during the ensuing two years. His troop was still in garrison at Fort McDowell when he returned from recruiting service, and he assumed command of the post on November 12, 1878.

For some time, there had been considerable dissatisfaction among the Indians on the reservations in Arizona and New Mexico, and there was much honest criticism at the scant meed of justice accorded them in a community whose sole thoughts at that time appeared to lie in the direction of location of mines, on or off reservations. The malodorous Indian Ring was in full power, and the dawn of the era of contentment and peace seemed far off.

The history of the Apaches is shrouded in much uncertainty. The whole face of the country is covered with the remains of villages occupied by a people of an entirely different nature and, in all probability, akin to the scattered Pueblo Indians of today. The cliff-dwellers left many strange abodes in almost every watered canyon; the foundations and walls of many of their valley locations indicate a large population in olden times. Old settlers well acquainted with the habits of the various tribes unite in the belief that the disappearance of the ancient dwellers in Arizona is traceable to the incessant warfare of the Apaches. It was against these Apaches, utterly wild Indians, that the Sixth Cavalry was pitted for more than ten years.

Arizona is an immense expanse of country, much of it covered with rough and broken mountain chains—the southern spurs of the Rockies. The western part contains immense deserts, and neither Indians nor settlers undertook to extract a living from such uninviting sand wastes. The character of the country generally was entirely in favour of the Apaches in their contest for supremacy with the whites. The Indians had learned to utilise much in nature that was unknown to the whites, being so accustomed to exposure that sudden changes from snow-covered mountains to parched sand deserts affected them but little, if at all. Traveling without baggage, and able to cover, when hard pressed, from fifty to seventy miles on foot within twenty-four hours, they constituted most formidable enemies. Their food consisted of game, baked mescal root, which is very palatable and not unlike sweet potato, grass seed, and other wild productions of that strange land.

With a supply of food which would not furnish a meal for a soldier an Apache would go on a long raid, trusting to luck and his knowledge of nature's foods to escape suffering. His ability to crawl stealthily upon his enemy, to conceal himself with a few wisps of grass, to deliver his fire and disappear as from the face of the earth, made him an enemy to be guarded against incessantly.

It became the fixed opinion of those experienced in Apache warfare that if the government had not taken advantage of their tribal animosities Arizona would have remained undeveloped for a long time. The number of attacks made upon wagon trains, stage coaches, and travellers is beyond belief. The records of the War Department show that between January, 1866, and May, 1875, when the Sixth Cavalry was ordered to duty in Arizona, two hundred and seventeen engagements had occurred between troops and Indians in Arizona.

Comparative peace had reigned while the Sixth Cavalry was taking its first stations, but soon marauding bands began their deviltry, which continued, at intervals, during all the time the regiment remained in that country and the adjoining territory, New Mexico—a period of fifteen years.

The result of an inspection of the agencies by General Hatch may be profitably examined:

> These Indians have not advanced in any manner since placed upon reservations. They plant less than when wild and seem to have devoted their energies in preparing for the warpath by theft of horses and purchase of arms and ammunition. The reservation furnishes a place of concealment for stolen property, and draws near it a disreputable class of traders. There is no discipline among these Indians; they come and go when it pleases them, raid with impunity on the neighbouring settlers in small stealing parties, and make extensive raids into Mexico. Eventually the settlers will be strong enough to resist successfully. In the meantime, a sense of insecurity will pervade the community, and I believe it is economy for the government to settle the matter at once.

Such were the conditions when Captain Chaffee was selected to take charge of the San Carlos Indian Agency, larger than all the other southwestern agencies combined and embracing among its wards all the daredevils who with their forebears had made the Chihuahua Sonora border of Mexico a barren waste.

Chapter 12: Indian Agent at San Carlos

During a long period of years, the affairs of the Indians assembled on reservations in the Far West were in a most unsatisfactory condition, especially in those localities occupied by warlike tribes. Dishonesty and incompetency were the common charges against the agents. When matters became unbearable, the Indians frequently revolted and murdered agency employees before fleeing from the reservations. The San Carlos Agency, situated on the Gila River, was no exception to the rule. The "Indian Ring," as the group of contractors and spoilsmen had long been known, seemed to have no conscience about carrying its abuses to extremes, for the army could always be called in to punish the Indians should they leave their reservations.

On July 1, 1879, Captain Chaffee received a telegram to proceed at once from Fort McDowell, Arizona, to San Carlos and assume the duties of Indian agent. There was no direct road to the agency; mounting his horse, therefore, he started in the afternoon over the mountain trails to take up the most uncongenial work that could possibly have been assigned to him. After five days of mountain trails, and under a midsummer sun, he reached his destination and was met by the refusal of the Indian agent to transfer his accountability unless his bondsmen were relieved of responsibility. As a matter of fact, no orders had been received by the agent to turn the agency over to Captain Chaffee, and the latter declined to settle the matter arbitrarily, but communicated the status of affairs to the proper authorities. Captain Chaffee expressed the view that it was for the Commissioner of Indian Affairs to secure compliance with his orders. One month later Captain Chaffee wrote:

When I took hold, Hart (the agent who had been removed) informed me that, do as I might, I would find that the old rut would prove best in the end. The old rut by no means satisfies me, and the agency employees find something else to do besides sitting in the shade. Order begins to reign in storerooms, oceans of property now assembled according to class; glassware, hardware, annuity, and other stores in order; flour, coffee, beans, salt, sugar, and soap, each in its appropriate place. To do all this I've had to direct in person, as well as to post myself in the office, and receive many stores. The traders tell their stories, the contractors theirs, and the agency folks of course are not behind.

There had been much of scandal involved in the brief existence of the San Carlos Reservation. The rights of the Indians were ignored in the most flagrant manner. The agent was accused of allowing a silver mine on the reservation to be worked as long as he shared in the profits. The reservation was curtailed several times by acts of Congress, an action brought about by men interested in the seizure of all the mineral lands of value. The Indians had received no protection from their official guardians. Just when Captain Chaffee had about concluded that life was not worth living in such a den of thieves he received a visit from the chairman of the Board of Indian Commissioners, General Fisk, a banker of New York, whom he described as a very pleasant gentleman, one of the humanitarian school, who rendered voluntary service to the Indians from pure and conscientious motives.

During October Captain Chaffee undertook to make a personal census of all the Indians on the San Carlos and White Mountain reservations and on Eagle Creek, where about one hundred and twenty were permitted to live. According to the count made, there were four thousand three hundred Indians on the San Carlos, three hundred on the adjoining White Mountain Reservation, and those living on Eagle Creek.

When Captain Chaffee took charge of the agency, he had been secretly warned that someone interested in the cattle contracts had recently carried away a set of weights belonging to the scales. Captain Chaffee made a record of this incident:

There are two scales; one in use and one in store. When I took the property, I examined closely for the weights belonging to the set in store, but, found only the 1,000-pound weight, three 2,000-pound weights being missing. I casually called Indian Agent Hart's attention to the subject and passed on. Lieutenant von Schrader was here at the time, so I took him with me to the scales at the corral, where we marked the weights in use with an iron punch. Since then, I have looked for the other weights to appear in the scales. Day before yesterday *I nailed them dead*, the weights having been put in during the past week. To show the object it is only necessary to say that the weights have been lightened by having been bored out—the old borings having been deepened.

As near as I can ascertain, each weight has been lightened about five ounces. I ascertained the result the parties would have accomplished, had they not been caught, by weighing on a Howe storehouse scale 2,000 pounds of flour, which I then took to the cattle scale. They had left the 1,000-pound weight; the knob on the beam, when shoved to the outer end, covers 1,000 pounds; thus, you see I could weigh 2,000 pounds. I put on my 2,000 pounds of flour, when the beam balanced to a hair. The two scales agreed. I then took off the 1,000-pound weight, shoved the knob to zero, and laid on one of the tampered with 2,000-pound weights, but it did not prove sufficiently heavy to balance the 2,000 pounds of flour. I shoved the knob forward till it reached the 170-pound notch, when the beam balanced and showed the difference that would accrue to the contractor every time the weight should be used.

I tested each of the weights separately and found they varied from 158 to 170 pounds. We consume here weekly about eighty head of cattle that will average 850 pounds each. On an average we weigh five head at each draft, which would call into use two of the 2,000-pound weights. One of the provisions of the contract requires the cattle to average 850 pounds from May 1 to December 1; the balance of the year 800. Of course, they want to make their small Mexican cattle come up to the average. Unless they make the average required by contract a deduction is made of one *percentum* for every five pounds and fraction thereof that their cattle are under the required average. When I discovered the weights that had been tampered with, I accused the contractor's agent with having committed the act. He of course denied it, when I lost my temper and from all accounts did not comply strictly with the commandment which forbids swearing on all occasions. At all events I scared the fellow so much that he left the reservation within an hour without taking any breakfast. I look on him and ———— as the principal rascals, though he is but an employee.

The contempt in which the rights of the Indians were held in the Far West is well illustrated by the fact that Mr. ————'s participation in this wholesale robbery of the nation's wards did not prevent his election later to the United States Senate. The whole situation was obnoxious to Captain Chaffee, and a few days after the unearthing of the plot to cheat the Indians out of part of their small rations of beef he tendered his resignation as agent and requested that his successor should arrive by December 31, 1879. In the meantime, he kept busy improving the condition of things around him by perfecting the dam and irrigation ditches, thus making it possible for the Indians to help themselves to a greater degree than had been possible previously. He had the agency buildings roofed with shingles instead of thatch and mud, thereby saving the stores from frequent drenchings, and secured the erection of a telegraph line to the nearest military post, putting the agency in communication with the outer world.

Captain Chaffee's repeated requests to be relieved did not result in early action. On February 1, 1880, he described a heavy fall of snow—about five inches—which had occurred the previous week, a most unusual phenomenon in that locality. The Indians were illy prepared for such weather, and Captain Chaffee was tireless in his efforts to relieve the situation. He wrote of this incident:

"I believe it is serving the Lord to serve the poor. Hence this has been no Sunday for me or anyone here. I have been on my feet since early morning issuing goods to the Indians. I began the work yesterday. Today the work is slower on account of having to issue through a door. Yesterday we issued in the open air where we could work to more advantage. Somehow, I felt well satisfied with the fatigue of the work; to see how much good a little can do for the suffering poor, spurred my tongue as I called off each article. The Indians lost no time in making use of the articles given them in the shape of clothing to keep out the cold."

It was the end of May, 1880, before Captain Chaffee was relieved from the duties of Indian agent, a thankless task at best for army officers, who were consistently assailed in the most libelous manner whenever they undertook to protect the Indian in his rights. There were some good and true people among the early settlers of Arizona, but there came a time when the pressure for law and order in Texas, Kansas, and Colorado drove to New Mexico and Arizona the most lawless aggregation of thieves and murderers ever assembled on our soil. The army had to contend with these as well as with the predatory bands of Apache renegades, and there was little choice between them.

Chapter 13: Frontier Service in Arizona (Continued)

During the summer of 1881 there appeared among the White Mountain Apaches a medicine-man named Nockay-det-Klinne, who proclaimed himself the Messiah. The oracle gradually inflamed the minds of the Indians and became so infatuated by his success that he appeared to believe the truth of his own weird dreams. So long as he confined himself to ordinary incantations there was no cause for anxiety. In common with more civilised charlatans, however, he had gradually mulcted the faithful believers of much of their limited wealth, and it appeared necessary for him to make a bold stroke to conceal the falseness of his own prophecies. He was growing rich through the largesse of his simple-minded followers.

To retain his power, he announced that he was restoring all the dead Apaches to life, and that they were now risen, except that their feet were held down waiting for the whites to be driven from the Indian country. Considering the length of time during which the White Mountain Apaches had been closely associated with the whites, and their general intelligence, it is inexplicable that this fanatic should have imposed upon the tribe to the extent of making large numbers of them believe that if they would rise and murder the whites, he would restore to life all their deceased kinsmen.

It is neither expedient nor profitable to discuss an aimless policy which permitted license to run riot on reservations until the Indians grew sullen and insubordinate through brooding over racial wrongs, and then threw upon the small and inadequate garrisons the work of restoring order and enforcing obedience.

The regimental commander was at Fort Apache, an isolated post in the centre of the White Mountain Reservation, with a garrison of only two small troops of cavalry and one much-depleted company of infantry. Recognising the very serious turn of affairs, he summoned the medicine-man and several prominent chiefs and heads of families and explained to them the futility of rising against the whites. The author was present at all the interviews, and in later years was much struck with the similarity of argument used by Nockay-det-Klinne in 1881, Sitting Bull and other Plains Indians in 1890, during the Ghost Dance craze, and the active and successful leader of Pulajans, Enrique Darguhob, in Samar, one of the Philippine Islands, in 1904 and 1905. The advice and warnings given Nockay-det-Klinne fell upon deaf ears, and he returned to his camp, about forty miles back in the Indian country, where he spurned the orders of the agent to report himself at San Carlos. The deluded Indians followed him, and the excitement grew widespread.

The time for parley and remonstrance ended when the agent made a formal demand that the military arm be set in motion and that the recalcitrant medicine-man be brought before him dead or alive. The story of the march, the arrest, the attempt at rescue, the hand-to-hand combat, constitutes an interesting page of the regimental history. While the medicine-man lay mortally wounded, after the rescuers had been driven off and we were preparing to bury our dead, the author examined the body and took from its receptacle the pass by authority of which Nockay-det-Klinne left the agency. The pass had expired, and the deluded messiah had repeatedly refused to return and report himself as was required of all reservation Indians.

There was a short, sharp campaign, but the failure of the messiah to come back to life, as he had promised to do if killed, cooled the ardour of the White Mountain Apaches, and they rapidly drifted back to their reservation camps. The troops of the regiment made rapid marches through all the exposed districts, gradually concentrating at and near the agency, where for some unexplained reason the wild

Chiricahuis of Ju and Geronimo, who were at the San Carlos Agency, fled toward Mexico, leaving a trail of blood and pillage to mark their hurried flight.

Other regiments were ordered in to assist in protecting the southern border, while some troops of the Sixth Cavalry, including Captain Chaffee's, were sent back to their stations, encircling the White Mountain and San Carlos Apaches to guard against further outbreak in that direction. Some troops of the Sixth pursued and fought Geronimo's band, as did those of other cavalry regiments, but the Indians again made good their escape, this time to the Sierra Madres in Sonora. The year following this outbreak was one of continuous scouting, trailing, and fighting near the Mexican border, comparative peace prevailing, however, north of the Gila until the following spring.

In April, 1882, Geronimo and a considerable number of bucks crossed the Mexican border and made their way to the San Carlos Agency, where they induced Loco's band of Chiricahuis to leave the reservation. The troops of the regiment nearest to the trail followed and fought them before they reached the line, and Mexican troops, which were fortunate enough to observe their flight, prepared an ambuscade and almost annihilated that portion of the band that remained together.

After a forced march from his station at Fort McDowell to Maricopa, Captain Chaffee's troop was entrained and sent hurriedly to Willcox, a station on the Southern Pacific Railroad, in southeastern Arizona. The direction of the flight of the Apaches was reported by other troops of the regiment to Captain Chaffee, who left Willcox at midnight and marched sixty miles without halting to cook a meal until he was on the Indian trail, which he followed to Skeleton Canyon in the Stein's Peak range of mountains, near the Mexican border. Other troops from nearby stations had taken up the pursuit and were ahead of him on the trail. Captain Chaffee therefore moved his command across to the Chiricahui Mountains and occupied a favourite border crossing of the Indians.

Serious trouble was brewing at San Carlos, which culminated on July 6, 1882, in the killing of the chief of scouts, Colvig, and three Indian policemen. For several days it was not known whether it was an outbreak of the usual kind resulting in raids or merely one of the affrays involving murder so common on the reservation. All doubt was removed, on July 8, when the Indians attacked McMillenville, an isolated mining village near the reservation. The renegades were led by Nantiatish and Sanchez, and included some of the scouts who had mutinied and deserted when the medicine-man was arrested the preceding summer and who had been in hiding since that time. They made a rapid raid north across Tonto Basin in the direction of the Black Mesa, stealing horses, and it was rumoured that they intended to go to the Navajo country.

Troops were ordered in pursuit from Forts Apache, McDowell, Thomas, and Whipple, widely separated posts with a wilderness of canyons and rough mountains intervening. The result was the most remarkable concentration of troops at a danger point ever known on the frontier. Moving for several days, over very difficult country, guided mainly by reports of outrages committed, the troops approached a common centre. Captain Chaffee, marching east, struck the trail first. Arriving at General's Springs, at the summit of the Black Mesa, on the morning of July 17, 1882, he found that the Indians had camped there the previous night. Leaving a message on a bush at the Springs and sending back a courier to notify other troops, he pushed rapidly on the trail.

The courier shortly encountered the column from Fort Apache, which had come westward and had cut the trail between Captain Chaffee's troop and his pack train, and was following it. Major Evans, who was in command of the Fort Apache squadron, at once detached the leading troop to move rapidly to the front as a reinforcement in the event the Indians should be overtaken before his main column should arrive. Captain Chaffee overtook the Indians about 3:00 p.m., and had just formed for attack when Major Evans arrived with re-inforcements. Although the senior of all the officers then in pursuit of the Indians, Major Evans generously placed his own command at Captain Chaffee's disposal and directed him to proceed with the attack as planned.

The Indians occupied a strong position on the north side of the canyon, where from a vertical wall they overlooked and commanded the trail leading across the canyon. They had built circular rifle pits of stones, and their position was impregnable from a frontal attack. Captain Chaffee formed his dismounted skirmishers along the brink of the canyon opposite the Indian position, sending troops to cross above and below the position. They were met by a fire at close range from behind pine trees and rocks as they fought their way across. The Indian position was gradually encircled, and the troops closed in as well as their limited numbers permitted. The fight lasted through the day and into the night. About 10: 00 p.m. the lines were withdrawn to bring in the wounded and get back to the canyon for water. Two officers and a number of men were seriously wounded, one of the latter dying during the night. Commands from other posts continued to arrive during the night, and the next morning twelve troops of cavalry assembled at the scene of the combat from four separate stations.

The hostiles escaped during the night, abandoning everything and leaving six wounded and sixteen dead upon the field. Seventy-three horses, twenty-four saddles, and much camp plunder were captured. Fourteen horses of the Indians were killed in action and seventeen abandoned on the trail, making their loss more than one hundred. A severe hailstorm lasting four hours completely obliterated the trail of the *moccasined* Indians, who fled on foot to the reservations, where they scattered and were hidden by their kinsmen.

While the troopers were advancing on the north side of the canyon it became necessary for them to leave cover and advance across an open space against a group of Indians concealed behind trees. The men were somewhat wary of exposing themselves, but Captain Chaffee displayed his wonderful control of men. As soon as he observed the hesitation he fairly roared in his deep and powerful voice, "Forward!" and every man instantly moved out against the enemy and drove the Indians to cover in a ravine.

This encounter took place at the Big Dry Wash, a branch canyon of Chevelon's Fork of the Little Colorado River. The country was so rough that the wounded had to be carried out on hand litters for many miles. The pursuit and assault of the Indians in a strong position selected and fortified by them reflected much credit upon the troops engaged, for it was impossible for the main body to deploy before night overtook them. The following order was issued concerning this affair:

Headquarters Department of Arizona
Whipple Barracks, Prescott, July 31, 1882
General Orders
No. 37
The Department Commander is happy to announce another success of our gallant troops against the Apaches.
On the 17th instant Captain A. R. Chaffee, Sixth Cavalry, came up with Nan-tia-tish and his whole band of desperate renegade scouts and released Cibicu prisoners.
The engagement took place on Big Dry Wash, misnamed "Chevelon's Fork" in the despatches; it lasted until nightfall result-

ing in killing 16 warriors whose bodies were found, and the capture of the hostiles' camp, saddles, and reserved ammunition (500 metallic cartridges Cal. .45), over 100 horses and mules (including those killed), and 6 squaws and children.

Too much praise cannot be accorded to Captain Chaffee and his immediate command. Troop I, Sixth Cavalry, and Company E, Indian Scouts, Lieutenant Morgan, Third Cavalry, commanding, and scarcely less to Major A. W. Evans, Third Cavalry, and his troops who came up from a remote post in good time, and fought with equal bravery, Major Evans himself generously waiving the management of the fight to his junior in rank—Captain and Brevet Major Chaffee.

Our casualties consisted of two officers, Lieutenants Morgan and Converse, Third Cavalry, wounded, one enlisted man and one Indian Scout killed, and five enlisted men and one Indian Scout wounded.

The lessons taught by this fight are first the necessity of greater precautions to prevent Indians from obtaining arms and ammunition. Second, the value of energetic and persistent pursuit, however remote and hopeless it may seem at first. Third, the importance of trailing and attacking the hostiles even with inferior numbers, and holding on to them until other troops arrive on the ground.

By order of Brevet Major-General Willcox:

H. L, Haskell
Aide-de-Camp

Chapter 14: Frontier Service with Crook's Expedition and in Mexico

It should be remembered that when the Chiricahuis were removed from their home country in the Chiricahui and Dragoon mountains, adjoining the border line, a considerable number refused to go to the San Carlos Agency and fled to Mexico, where they found a safe retreat in the heart of the Sierra Madre Mountains. They constantly passed back and forth between the San Carlos and New Mexican Indian agencies, and in nearly every instance left a trail of rapine and murder. During the outbreak of the Coyoteros or White Mountain Indians in Arizona in 1881 many of the Chiricahuis left San Carlos and made a most successful dash through a cordon of troops, fighting almost the entire way to the Mexican border, which they crossed with little loss to themselves.

When the Chiricahui Agency near Fort Bowie, in Apache Pass, was finally abandoned, the development of many rich mines in southern Arizona was undertaken, and towns of considerable size were growing rapidly in that section. The constant turmoil arising from Apache depredations kept the entire population of Arizona and New Mexico in a state of never-ending anxiety. General George Crook was still remembered by the old pioneers for the successful manner in which he had settled the Apaches on reservations ten years before, and, owing to their appeals and to dissatisfaction in Washington over the existing conditions, he was again assigned to command the Department of Arizona. The meagre force allotted to the department was distributed with a view to safeguarding the community as far as possible. General Crook personally visited the Apache villages on the reservations, and such was his influence that he succeeded in again winning their confidence and promises of their services in restoring peaceful conditions.

Attended only by an aid, a surgeon, and a dozen Indian scouts General Crook next proceeded to the Mexican border and attempted to open communication with the renegade Indians in Mexico. He was unsuccessful on the whole, but learned from two squaws, intercepted while attempting to return to the San Carlos Agency, that the Apaches in the Sierra Madres occupied an impregnable position and had sworn hostility to both Americans and Mexicans. The territory harassed by the Chiricahuis stretched over all the northern part of Sonora and Chihuahua. Ruins of depopulated and abandoned villages abounded within the radius of Apache depredations. Bottom lands which once supplied abundant crops of wheat and barley were no longer cultivated, being overgrown with a jungle of wild vegetation. Hostility between the Mexicans and Indians was intense, and constant warfare had sadly reduced the numbers on both sides.

Matters drifted along in a most unsatisfactory manner. Captain Emmet Crawford, with a body of one hundred and fifty Indian scouts, was assigned to the arduous duty of patrolling about two hundred miles of the border. No one familiar with Apache warfare was at all surprised to learn during March, 1883, that an enterprising young chief named Chatto, with a band of twenty-six Chiricahuis, had crossed the border and was raiding in Arizona and New Mexico. By stealing fresh horses, the raiders were enabled to travel from seventy to a hundred miles a day. During this raid of about eight hundred miles

Chatto's band killed twenty-five Americans and Mexicans and lost only two bucks, one being killed near the Total Wreck mine in Arizona and one being captured by American troops. The culmination of this bloody raid was the massacre of Judge McComas and his wife, prominent residents of Silver City, New Mexico, and the carrying into captivity of their little son Charlie.

All that could be done to guard the settlements was done. Troops scoured the country in every direction, hoping to overtake the marauding Indians. Direct pursuit was hopeless as long as the raiders could obtain a constant supply of fresh horses, not available to troops. The trail made by the band coming from the Sierra Madres north seemed to offer the only solution. General Crook concentrated as many of the small troops of cavalry in the territory as could be safely withdrawn from their stations around the reservation, and on April 23, 1883, moved from Willcox with seven troops of the Third and Sixth Cavalry under command of Major James Biddle, and a large body of Indian scouts.

The march was directed to San Bernardino Springs, where the command was to be joined by Captain Crawford with additional scouts and pack trains. These springs had once been the main source of water supply for large herds of cattle, but the Apaches had long since caused the abandonment of the extensive ranch building. General Crook now directed the base camp to be established at Silver Springs on the American side of the line and organised the expedition which he intended to conduct in person to the stronghold in the Sierra Madres. He had directed the captured raider of Chatto's band, "Peaches" by name, to be sent to the border. The prisoner finally consented to conduct the command to the hiding-places of the hostile bands.

On May 1 1883, the expedition crossed the Mexican line and marched down the valley of the San Bernardino. It comprised Captain Chaffee's troop of the Sixth Cavalry, with Lieutenants West and Forsyth and forty-two men; one hundred and ninety-three Indian scouts, under Captain Emmet Crawford, Third Cavalry, Lieutenant Mackay, Third Cavalry, Lieutenant Gate wood. Sixth Cavalry, and the most competent aggregation of guides and interpreters in that country, Al. Seiber, Mcintosh, Sam Bowman, Severiano, and Mickey Free. General Crook was accompanied by his personal aid. Captain Bourke, Lieutenant Febiger, engineer officer, and Doctor Andrews.

Marching down the San Bernardino to the junction of the Bavispe River, and then up the latter stream, on May 7 the expedition, led by

"Peaches," headed straight for the Sierra Madres, and in the foothills struck a trail of the Chiricahuis made recently while they were driving into the mountains cattle stolen from Mexican ranches. The trail was rocky and steep, although fresh and well beaten by ponies and cattle. It wound up the mountain, and each ridge seemed to be followed by another one higher and more difficult. Cross-trails ran in every direction, and all were littered with odds and ends of things useless to Indians, stolen from Mexicans and thrown away.

General Crook, following his accustomed plan, had decided upon a night march to pass over the open country and get into the mountains in order to escape observation by the watchful Apache pickets. Captain Chaffee was riding a favourite horse, selected for the occasion because of his great powers of endurance. The night was very dark, and upon reaching the mountains the command had to dismount and lead their horses. The trail was steep and difficult, especially so in the darkness of night. At a particularly bad place on the trail Captain Chaffee's horse slipped, lost his footing, and rolled down the mountain side. Not knowing whether it was ten or a thousand feet. Captain Chaffee held onto the bridle reins and went down with his horse. After they had rolled about twenty yards. Captain Chaffee's weight on the bridle, together with some fortunately placed bushes, enabled them to stop and recover their footing. When asked next morning why he had not let go of the reins, he replied that he did not want his pet horse Patty to be killed without an effort to save it.

All through the mountains in sheltered canyons were found the ruins of buildings, walls, and dams erected by a race long since extinct. Evidences of recent and long-continued occupancy by the Apaches multiplied. Carcasses of mules, ponies, and cattle were scattered along the trails and about the camping places. The trail finally led into a narrow, rocky gorge, which gradually widened into a small amphitheatre, which "Peaches," the captive guide, said was the stronghold occupied while he was with the Apaches, but which was now abandoned. The pack trains experienced much difficulty on this part of the trail. Five mules fell over the precipice during one day's march and were either killed or had to be destroyed. Officers and men wearily led their tired mounts up, up the steep and dangerous trails. Progress was slow and secrecy indispensable.

General Crook finally sent one hundred and fifty Indian scouts, under their officers and white guides, forward on the trail so as to keep ahead of the pack trains, guarded by Indian scouts and Captain

Chaffee's troop. For three days the white troopers and pack trains followed cautiously on the trail of Crawford and the scouts. The command constantly came upon the brush shelters, or *wickiups*, of the hostile Apaches, with *caches* of calico, clothing, dried meat, and hides.

On May 15 an Apache runner, who had come six miles through the mountains, arrived with a note from Crawford saying that he had run into two hostile Indians and doubtless alarmed the main body. At that moment firing was heard, and Captain Chaffee's troop mounted to move forward and join in the combat. The firing died away, however, and about dark Crawford came back on the trail to camp. He had found the *rancherias* of Bonito and Chatto and in the fight which ensued killed nine Indians and captured five boys and girls. This was all the damage known to have been done.

The pursuit had led across a broken country, with countless ravines, covered with scrub oak and pines. All the animals of the hostile bands were captured. Intense interest existed throughout the command concerning the whereabouts of little Charlie McComas, who, it will be remembered, had been captured in New Mexico by Chatto's raiders. One of the young squaws captured gave the information that a little white boy about six years old, called "Charlie," was in the camp. He had run away with the old squaws when the Indian scouts first appeared. His presence was confirmed by other squaws who came to camp and surrendered. Unhappily the little boy whose fate had set the whole southwestern frontier aflame was never recovered. Many of the fleeing Indians were doubtless wounded and fell in the ravines and underbrush. If Charlie escaped injury in his flight, he probably perished from exposure.

The renegade Chiricahuis seemed disconcerted when they learned that General Crook was being guided by "Peaches," and they began surrendering in squads. Among them were five utterly exhausted Mexican women, one of whom had a nursing baby, who had been captured in Chihuahua by Geronimo during his last raid. They were wives of Mexican soldiers who had been killed by the Indians. All possible kindness was shown to the women. Their gratitude was unbounded and two became hysterical from over-excitement. Altogether thirteen captives—women and children, held as hostages by the Indians—were recovered.

The return march with nearly four hundred of the surrendered Indians was only less difficult than the pursuit in that the tension of the hunter for game was relaxed. The presence of so many hostile Indians, armed with the best of modern magazine rifles, did not ensure that confidence which would justify the white troops in any relaxation of vigilance. It was with a feeling of great relief that on June 15, 1883, the command recrossed the border and went into camp at Silver Springs with the troops under Major Biddle.

Captain Chaffee was relieved from further duty with General Crook's expedition and proceeded with his troop to his old station at Fort McDowell, Arizona, having marched nearly a thousand miles during his absence in the field. After a few months of rest in garrison Captain Chaffee was ordered to proceed with his troop and take station at Fort Huachuca, a post in southern Arizona near the Mexican border.

On the crest of the hill at Arlington Cemetery a monument has been erected by his comrades to that sincere, unassuming, and accomplished soldier. General Crook, upon the front of which appears in bronze a group consisting of the General, Captain Chaffee, and the officers, guides, and chiefs who accompanied the expedition into the Sierra Madres in pursuit of the Chiricahuis.

Chapter 15: Frontier Service in New Mexico

After nine years of most arduous and dangerous frontier service, Captain Chaffee was informed that the War Department had under consideration a change of station for the Sixth Cavalry. Visions of civilization and reunited families were of short duration, however, for when the long-expected order arrived it provided for an exchange of stations between the Fourth Cavalry in New Mexico and the Sixth in Arizona. The Sixth had been privileged to look eastward at the Dos Cabezas, and now crossed the line into New Mexico and looked westward upon the same landmark, being destined to operate against the same Indians a little farther to the east on the New Mexico-Chihuahua border.

Captain Chaffee left Fort Huachuca on June 5, 1884, and marched to his new station, Fort Craig, New Mexico, arriving there on June 24. This was one of the old posts in New Mexico marked for abandonment, and a few months after its arrival the troop had another change of station, to Fort Wingate, on the Navajo Reservation. The neighbouring bands of Indians had been following the paths of peace for many years and were now well established as masters of large herds of sheep. Their women had long been held in esteem as expert weavers, and their blankets were much sought after. Among these surroundings the only war clouds to be expected would be such as might arise from impositions on the part of the whites, from which no Indians escaped.

These were peaceful dreams, rudely shattered in the spring, when on May 17, 1885, without reasonable grievance, Geronimo, Nana, Mangus, Natchez, and Colorado, with forty bucks and ninety-two women and children of the most savage element of the Chiricahui Indians, fled from the reservation near Fort Apache in Arizona. The renegades started for New Mexico over a route previously selected with a view to replenishing their supply of horses. The pursuing column from Fort Apache was in the saddle within an hour after the renegades left their camp, but the Indians travelled one hundred and twenty miles before halting for rest or food.

Immediately after the outbreak was made known troops were put in motion from all available garrisons in the effort to intercept the hostiles before they should reach Mexico. Within a few days no less than twenty troops of cavalry were scattered through the country, yet the hostiles eluded them and crossed into Mexico on June 10, notwithstanding the pursuers, men and animals, had been pushed to the limit of endurance. The Indians left more than one hundred and fifty dead or abandoned horses and mules along the trail. Captain Chaffee reached Hillsboro, New Mexico, on May 24, and on May 27 the Indians passed near that place. As soon as the trail was discovered Captain Chaffee followed it. The pursuit was continued through much rough country for five days, the command reaching Lake Palomas in Mexico on the fifth day, having trailed the hostiles one hundred and fifty miles. Numerous false reports concerning Indians in the rear caused the troop to be withdrawn across the border to scout the country.

The operations incident to this outbreak became known as the Geronimo Campaign, lasting two years. During this period Captain Chaffee's troop occupied the eastern part of the long stretch of border guarded by the troops to prevent the hostiles from crossing back and forth. For eighteen months his troop rode the line and guarded water holes, but did not have any further encounters with the Indians. Some facts concerning this remarkable campaign, although not involving Captain Chaffee personally, are cited to show the character of service required of the troops.

Captain Emmet Crawford, Third Cavalry, who had gone with his regiment to Texas, was recalled, and he reported to General Crook at Fort Bayard, New Mexico, for instructions. He was directed to assemble a large detachment of Indian scouts and proceed to the border, where he was joined by A Troop, Sixth Cavalry, which had come from

Fort Wingate with Captain Chaffee. Captain Crawford took up the main trail, with ninety-two scouts and A Troop, Sixth Cavalry, following it for more than five hundred miles into the Sierra Madres in Sonora, Mexico. During the pursuit of the Indians every known water hole along the border was guarded by troops and small detachments of scouts.

On June 22, 1885, Captain Crawford discovered a fresh trail, leading into the Bavispe Mountains, and sent Chatto and a party of selected scouts forward to overtake and hold the Indians until the main command should come up. Chatto discovered the *rancheria* next morning in such a position that it was impracticable to surround it, and he therefore made the attack at once, and in a running fight of several miles captured fifteen women and children and recovered five horses, some saddles, revolvers, belts, and other property obtained by the Indians from Captain Lawton's camp in Guadaloupe Canyon when the camp guard was attacked during the absence of the troop. The Indians were under the leadership of Chihuahua, whose family was captured.

All through the summer the pursuit of the hostiles was kept up; yet in November a party of eleven renegades slipped through the cordon of frontier patrols in New Mexico, being observed by only two scouts, one of whom was killed by the hostiles. As soon as the party crossed the border the alarm was given and the whole country was immediately on the alert. The Indians went up the valley of the Mimbres River, in New Mexico, and while passing a Mexican's ranch attacked two small boys at the woodpile, killing one and carrying the other away. This twelve-year-old boy survived the most successful, difficult, and dangerous raid ever made by Apaches and was subsequently rescued by troops far down in Mexico.

Vigilance was never relaxed, yet this band went as far as the White Mountain Reservation, near Fort Apache, where one of them was killed by a friendly Indian, this being the only loss sustained by them. They returned by way of New Mexico, waylaying and murdering at every opportunity. They actually prepared an ambush for a troop of the Eighth Cavalry scouting for them and killed Surgeon Maddox and four men riding at the head of the column in Dry Creek Canyon, New Mexico. This party of eleven Indians, under the leadership of Josanie, a brother of Chihuahua, crossed the border coming north early in November and passed back into Mexico before Christmas, carrying several captives with them and leaving thirty-eight known murders to mark their bloody trail. The difficulties of the situation can

75

scarcely be comprehended by those not familiar with the country in which the operations were carried on.

In describing the pursuit of the band during November, 1885, Captain Chaffee wrote:

We had to abandon the trail as we found no water and the scouts played out. Neither Forsyth nor myself drank a drop of anything from here (Cambray) till we got to the Rio Grande west of Fort Bliss—about seventy-five miles and thirty-six hours of time. We gave all our water to the scouts, who being on foot used a great deal—needed water to sustain them more than we who rode. At noon on the 8th they could hardly speak, they were so thirsty. I got water to them about 10:00 p.m., when three of them drank seven canteens full in less than an hour. If I could have made a night march, I feel that I could have reached the camp of the Indians, and perhaps have got some of them. But there was no moon; I was uncertain where they had gone, hence had to keep on the trail. The night, in consequence, had to be spent in camp, which served to prolong our hours without water, in idleness, when we ought to have been marching if we were to accomplish anything. The next day the trail struck out direct for the Candelaria Mountains across a desert forty miles. I knew then I could accomplish nothing, so gave it up. A hundred and fifty mile ride for nothing.

A note written at Cambray, New Mexico, December 13, 1885, recites further hardships:

I returned here last night. Nothing is known of the hostiles for a week and I am more than anxious, fearing they will be on my line before I hear of their approaching it. If they come down by Lake Valley without killing anyone or stealing stock, they may, and probably would be through my lines a half a day before we would know that they were in the vicinity. It was awful cold the night we left here at 1:00 a.m. the 10th. My moustache was a solid piece of ice by four o'clock. It was so cold we had to walk most of the way, which stiffened the men badly, some being so lame as to hardly be able to get back to camp after we had explored the canyon where the water was. The "Old Man" is quite able to down most of the young officers and the soldiers too, when it comes to hard work and fatigue. I really think it is due to my desire to do something, that enables me to forget fatigue and endure without suffering what others find so hard to bear.

The prolonged watching of the border proved a weary vigil, interspersed with many fruitless forced marches and hardships, many of them the result of false reports, as, for instance, the following:

Yesterday at eleven o'clock I got a note from Deming that a fight had occurred near Hillsboro on the 30th, the day I left there, and that on the night of that day the Indians stole twenty horses. I started over here at once with twelve men, expecting to cut the trail leading toward the border, but found no sign. On arriving here, I heard the Indians had gone north. Then a man told me that he saw ten or twelve mounted men passing along the slope of the Colorado Mountains at 11:00 a.m. yesterday. These mountains are N.E. from here—Hillsboro is N.W. I ordered Forsyth to march here today. This morning I started for the Colorado Mountains with my twelve men and could not find a sign of horse tracks anywhere in the country. A twenty-mile ride for nothing. No doubt the man thought he saw horsemen, but I think it was antelope magnified by the mirage.

After a year of border patrol Captain Chaffee made a note:

The year has flown by slowly—slipped away, day by day, as did its predecessor. It has left its mark by adding numbers of grey hairs to those in sight a year ago. Further than this I do not know that I have any special cause to complain. We know there is no such thing as applying brakes or locking the wheels of time.

During the autumn of 1885 General Crook was attacked in a scurrilous article which was copied in the press of the country. Captain Chaffee, writing of the matter, said:

The squib in the papers that the general would not allow the troops to capture Geronimo at Apache you can believe a lie. The general is not a natural born fool; the article is the mere stuff of a brainless scoundrel and liar. Anyone with a grain of sense knows better. If the general has made mistakes, it is a question of his judgment against the man who claims a mistake has been made. The general has been exceedingly patient, knowing that in that way only success can be won. The high-flyer would accomplish nothing when General Crook fails, you may be sure.

The troops continued to patrol the border from El Paso westward.

Every water hole was watched, and columns of troops and Indian scouts were kept constantly on the trail of the hostiles to prevent them from establishing themselves anywhere free from danger. Captain Emmet Crawford, commanding one of these pursuing columns, discovered the main camp of the Indians near the Arras River in Mexico, attacked, and captured all the stock and supplies of the Apaches. The Indian renegades asked for a conference, to be held the following morning. This was agreed to, and Captain Crawford's command, consisting almost entirely of Indian scouts, lay down for much-needed rest and did not exercise the usual vigilance.

Before daylight the Indian scouts, while asleep, were attacked, by one hundred and fifty Mexicans who had been trailing the hostiles. The scouts promptly took cover and opened fire in self-defence. Every effort was made to explain the true status of affairs to the Mexicans. Captain Crawford, unarmed, climbed to an exposed position on a large rock and had the interpreter make known to the Mexicans that they were firing upon American officers and scouts. It required the exertions of all the officers and civilian guides to induce the scouts to cease firing. When all was apparently over, a Mexican, who had approached within about thirty yards of Captain Crawford, without warning shot him through the head. In face of such treachery the firing was resumed, and continued until the Mexicans had lost their commanding officer and second in command, after which a parley ensued.

Captain Crawford was not instantly killed, but died while being borne back to the border on a litter. He was a brave, modest, efficient, and much-beloved officer, and his death in such a manner caused profound indignation throughout the army. The act of the Mexican troops was promptly disavowed by their government.

This was a truly remarkable incident. The troops of both nations, operating under a treaty, in the effort to kill or capture the hostile Indians came together and fought while the fiends they were seeking remained as observers of the battle. Strange to say, the Indians did not flee, but after the fight resumed the conference with the Americans and fulfilled their agreement to surrender.

After a conference with General Crook, in the *Cañon de las Embudos*, a day's march south of the border, Geronimo and Natchez, with about thirty-five followers, became apprehensive and fled again to the Sierra Madres. Chihuahua, his brother Josanie, the leader of the celebrated raid through New Mexico the previous autumn, and seventy-five bucks, women, and children surrendered, and on April

7, 1886, were sent east by train to Fort Marion, Florida. After being pursued and harassed for more than two thousand miles, Geronimo and his band were finally induced to come in by Lieutenant Charles B. Gatewood, Sixth Cavalry, who, at the risk of his life and without any assurance of a peaceable reception, rode into the hostile camp, accompanied by two friendly Apaches, and advised surrender. They formally surrendered at Skeleton Canyon on September 4, 1886, and were sent east to join those who had preceded them.

Mangus Colorado, Cochise, Victorio, and Geronimo were types of the Apache Indians who, under various local names—Chiricahuis, Mescaleros, Coyoteros, and others—scourged the southwestern territory for nearly three centuries. Predatory, brave, cruel, and rapacious, they would have been anomalies among Plains Indians such as Red Cloud and Spotted Tail. The warfare of Chief Joseph, the Nez Perce, was knightly in comparison with that of the average Apache.

Campaigning brings to light many traits of character which might otherwise remain unknown. While following one of the many trails made by the hostile Indians during 1885, Captain Chaffee's troop failed to receive their supplies and for a week in the Black Range were on less than half-rations. Captain Chaffee suddenly developed a violent antipathy to bacon, while his young second lieutenant continued to relish it until the day before rations reached the command, when the cook announced that the supply was exhausted. When the rations arrived and Captain Chaffee's appetite for bacon had returned, it transpired that the cook had notified him of the small supply on hand and that he had ceased eating bacon that his young subaltern might not suffer hunger.

Following the surrender of Geronimo's band, the troops were relieved from duty along the border. After an absence of a year and a half in the field Captain Chaffee rejoined his station at Fort Wingate by marching, arriving on October 19, 1886. In commenting, in an official report, upon the character of service against the Apaches in which Captain Chaffee had been engaged for more than ten years, one of the superior officers, a veteran of the Civil War, said:

> I am of the opinion that such service involved greater hardship, privation, endurance, more unremitting and unceasing vigilance, and more harassing difficulties of the march, and generally for longer periods of time, than any service experienced by me during the Civil War, with the possible exception of the Gettysburg campaign; this, too, with the chance of irretrievable disaster im-

measurably greater, and the hope of reward infinitely less.

Toward the close of this campaign Captain Chaffee was urged to avail himself of a leave of absence. His reply is typical of the man who through all the years of his arduous service considered duty first, safety last:

> Immediately after the close of the campaign will be a bad time for me to take a leave. After a campaign, things about a troop are pretty well worn, need overhauling, replaced by new and mended up generally. This can hardly be done as well by anyone as the captain of the troop. Then "I" troop has got to build a stable for its horses, the lumber for which is mostly ready now, I believe. There is no one who can get more work out of my men than I can, and besides, I am a good deal of a boss carpenter when once I set about such matters. In fact, I see a good deal of work which will need my attention after the campaign, and as I can only offer personal pleasure on leave, in opposition to doing my work, I think it best to stay with the latter.

Chapter 16: End of the Indian Wars

While in garrison at Fort Wingate, New Mexico, Captain Chaffee received his promotion to the grade of field officer, after more than a quarter of a century of exceptional service involving incredible hardships and danger. He was appointed Major of the Ninth Cavalry on July 7, 1888, and was directed to join that portion of his new regiment stationed among the Ute Indians in southern Utah. He reached his new station on August 28, 1888, remaining there two years, "building Fort Duchesne, Utah, with signal ability," as reported by his department commander. The new post was established not so much for defence against the Utes as it was to secure peace while the Indians were becoming accustomed to the new order of agricultural life, and to safeguard them from the encroachments of white men who had little respect for the rights of the Indians to anything desired by the superior race.

Major Chaffee now had one of the unusual experiences of his long career—two years of garrison life in the midst of Indians and no war parties to follow. He was detailed as acting inspector general of the Department of Arizona, serving in that capacity from October 6, 1890, until July 6, 1893, and in a similar capacity in the Department of Colorado until October 4, 1894, when he rejoined his regiment at

CHAFFEE IN UNIFORM OF MAJOR OF CAVALRY

Fort Robinson, Nebraska.

The Ghost Dance craze, encouraged by Sitting Bull and other medicine-men and chiefs, had culminated, during the winter of 1890 and 1891, in the last Indian war of the frontier, known in official history as the Pine Ridge Campaign. The close confinement to reservations, together with the increasing restrictions of the white man's game laws, bore severely upon the red men, accustomed to go and come when they pleased, and regarding the wild animals as the provision of the Great Spirit for the feeding and clothing of his children. From time to time, bands of Indians would leave their reservations to hunt in violation of laws they could not comprehend, and the result was always insistent demands that the army should be sent to punish them. It is to the credit of the service that in every instance the military arm restored the Indians to their reservations with utmost kindness and respect for their outraged feelings, without war.

Major Chaffee was sent upon duty of this character from Fort Robinson in July, 1895, and remained until the end of October, engaged in the operation of restoring to the Fort Hall Reservation the Bannocks, who had left and headed for their old hunting-grounds in and about Jackson's Hole, where the last of America's big-game shooting was being reserved for those Americans who were wealthy enough to penetrate that country with the necessary transportation and equipment. Major Chaffee conducted the operation to the entire satisfaction of the department commander as well as for the ultimate good of the Indians themselves.

It was hard for Major Chaffee to realise that the days of Indian campaigning had really come to an end. Year after year, during a quarter of a century, he had been called to the field, sometimes under tropical suns and sometimes in the land of blizzards, where the icy winds made life miserable alike to pursuer and pursued. With each recurring surrender the Indians had been restored to the tender mercies of the agent and his harpies, only to find their grievances multiplied. As years went by, the settlers with their wire fences closed in slowly but surely around the Indian reservations, and at last it was forced upon the minds of the red men that the wild, free life had been swept away by the march of civilization and that the remnants of once proud tribes were left stranded as driftwood along the shores of progress.

Encountering only the worst elements of the frontier, too often the mere outcasts of society, the unhappy warriors, shorn of the power wielded by their ancestors, turned trustingly for light as to their future to those with whom they had battled and at whose hands they had often suffered defeat. In many instances army officers were installed as agents and were instrumental in laying the foundations of lasting peace by showing the Indians the utter futility of contending against inevitable fate.

With the passing of the Indian wars efforts were made to improve and standardize the instruction of the army with a view to preparedness for normal campaigns. The service schools were put upon a better basis, and with increasing interest the improvement was rapid and progressive. Upon the recommendation of the *commandant* of the Infantry and Cavalry School, Major Chaffee was detailed as an instructor, and upon reporting on November 27, 1896, was assigned to duty in charge of the Department of Cavalry. At this time the student-officers comprised a group of young lieutenants who had come, at their own request, to receive the benefits of the instruction imparted by carefully selected instructors in the art of war and Allied subjects deemed essential to qualify officers for the higher staff duties and for the command of troops.

While Major Chaffee had not had opportunities for academic military instruction before undertaking the duties of actual war in 1861, his abounding experience in campaign and battle, his well-balanced mind, and his sterling character created a place for him immediately in the work of the school, for all its theory was but preparation for the practice of war. While serving as instructor at the school at Fort Leavenworth, Major Chaffee received his promotion to the next higher grade—Lieutenant-Colonel of the Third Cavalry—on June I, 1897. A few weeks later, on July 28, he was relieved from further duty at the Infantry and Cavalry School and transferred to the Cavalry and Light Artillery School at Fort Riley, Kansas. This mounted-service establishment was conducted as a school of application in which practice was the primary consideration.

Lieutenant-Colonel Chaffee had now served the nation for thirty-six years, and had taken part in half a hundred important battles and combats, and had not yet reached the grade of colonel of a regiment. Events, however, were shaping themselves for the inevitable war with Spain, in which Colonel Chaffee's military abilities were destined to receive generous recognition, leading ultimately to the highest professional advancement and the well-earned and gratifying expressions of confidence on the part of the government.

Chapter 17: War With Spain

The conditions in Cuba were most unsatisfactory during the winter of 1897-98. The efforts of our officials to preserve neutrality had been long continued, though not wholly successful. It was evident that a crisis was approaching, but neither the army nor the navy was prepared for war. While the legal strength of the army still remained on the statute books at thirty thousand men, nevertheless appropriations had been made for only twenty-five thousand for some years preceding 1898. Everything that could legitimately be done to make up for past neglect was urged with vigour; guns and ammunition, clothing and military stores, however, do not appear at the signal from a harlequin's wand. The President was well aware of our unpreparedness, but it required the co-ordinated statesmanship of all those in authority to delay the inevitable conflict, when, on February 15, 1898, the news of the destruction of the battleship *Maine* in Havana harbour was flashed over the cable.

For nearly thirty-five years the nation had devoted its energies to repairing the damage created by the Civil War and to the upbuilding of new states in our empire of western territory. There were no matured and accepted plans for the expansion of the Regular Army in the event of war, and it was evident that Congress would hark back to the expensive and unsatisfactory methods of the Civil War period.

The new Spanish minister, Senor Palo y Bernabe, entered upon his duties during March, yet early in April orders were issued for the concentration of nearly all the regiments of cavalry and infantry and the field artillery batteries of the Regular Army at southern camps, the major portion going to the famous battleground of Chickamauga, and the others to Mobile, Jacksonville, and Tampa. There is little cause for satisfaction with the methods employed in going to war in 1898, yet the Regular Army, led by veterans of the Civil and Indian wars, covered itself with glory and did much to save our pride of race—this with but meagre assistance from the Volunteer Army being brought into existence as rapidly as the machinery of the War Department could accomplish it.

The work of organisation—the task of putting a quarter of a million men under arms and equipping them for actual service in less than ninety days—was accomplished, but with much lost motion, for the efficiency of the War Department had been reduced to the lowest limit by persistent curtailment of appropriations. Every effort to perfect our military system before the war with Spain had met with discouragement and refusal. In making up for our past neglect and snatching victory from a brave and energetic enemy General Chaffee bore a leading part.

The following telegram started General Chaffee toward the theatre of preparation for the overseas expedition:

Washington, D.C, April 18, 1898

Commanding Officer
Fort Riley, Kansas
Major-General commanding army directs that Colonel Chaffee accompany your command to Chickamauga and there join his own regiment.   Carter
Assistant Adjutant General

The garrison of Fort Riley left promptly during the night of April 18, Colonel Chaffee going with the first section. Traveling with troop trains, when horses must be taken off each day, so that they may eat, drink, and roll in peace once in twenty-four hours, entails delay, but is necessary if they are to be fit for hard work at the journey's end.

Upon arriving at Chickamauga on April 23, 1898, Colonel Chaffee found that his own regiment, the Third Cavalry, was already in camp, and he at once joined it. There was some confusion pending the organisation of brigades and divisions, with announcement of commanders and staff officers for each. We have fought on many fields since the American people became a nation, but there has never been enough influence in behalf of correct military organisation definitely to create by law the composition of brigades, divisions, corps, and armies until the act of June 3, 1916, provided for such essential matters.

The Regular Army was below peace strength and when assembled was simply a collection of regiments, each short two companies under a scheme of skeleton organisations necessitated by failure of Congress to provide for the full legal strength of thirty thousand men. After looking over the situation at Chickamauga, Colonel Chaffee made some notes:

> We are not going to Cuba until an army is formed and organised; how long that will take I do not pretend to know. Order is out organising brigades; senior colonels command brigades. Colonel of Third is the junior here—he has no chance for a brigade, consequently I have no opportunity for a regiment—but it does not matter. I notice the state quotas of volunteers and that Kansas gets three regiments of infantry—one brigade—Ohio seven regiments—I don't suppose I could get a brigade if I were to try, so have concluded to make no effort. I don't believe the President will permit an "On to Richmond" cry to hurry him to Cuba before he is ready. It will take two months to organise and equip the army which will go to Cuba. This war must be popularized throughout the country by recognition of volunteer officers in high commands. The President is no doubt buried deep in requests; many will apply, but few can be chosen. We have several colonels richly deserving promotion before my claims can be considered. If the war lasts a year, changes must result, perhaps with me too, but changes will occur.

The notes jotted down by this modest veteran of more than half a hundred battles and combats are typical of him. Brave, self-reliant, physically and mentally fit for high command, he calmly surveyed the field of competitors and admitted to himself that others were more deserving, but that if the war should last his time for recognition might come. While he was committing his thoughts to paper, a group consisting of the Secretary of War, the Commanding General of the Army, and the Adjutant General were closeted at the War Department, endeavouring to do justice to the country and to the individual officers in the distribution of promotions to the grade of general officer in the new Volunteer Army.

The author, who was an assistant in the office of the adjutant general and had been placed in charge of the appointments, promotions, and commissions, remembers well the conference in the office of the Secretary of War, at the termination of which the adjutant general came out and handed him for execution the order for the promotions. Upon being asked what he thought of the list of promotions, the author promptly replied that the list was all right except for three names, the omission of which would be noticed by all the army from the Far West—Chaffee, Wheaton, and Randall. The adjutant general remarked that the three men were of the highest order of merit but were still in the grade of Lieutenant-Colonel; nevertheless, he went back to the Secretary and returned with authority for their promotions to vacancies following the list already agreed upon. The careers of the three admirable soldiers amply justified their elevation to the highest rank available for them. Colonel Chaffee was appointed Brigadier-General of the United States Volunteers on May 4, 1898.

Following the announcement of General Chaffee's promotion this application was received for his assignment with Missouri Volunteers:

St. Louis, Mo., May 7, 1898

President of the United States

Sir: We now have mobilised, in obedience to your instructions, Missouri's quota of volunteers. We earnestly request that you assign in command of our five thousand men, formerly Lieutenant-Colonel, now Brigadier-General A. R. Chaffee. We are like a ship at sea without a rudder. We need a competent man at once to assume control. We have our men at Jefferson Barracks awaiting your orders and trust you will give us General Chaffee immediately. Endorsed by our Missouri people.

Lon V. Stephens

The War Department had other plans for the employment of General Chaffee, and on May 9 he was ordered to report to Major-General Brooke for assignment to duty. The following day General Chaffee was directed to assume command of a brigade made up of the

Second and Seventh regiments of infantry and to proceed, as early as practicable, to Tampa, Florida. Upon arriving at Tampa, he was temporarily in command of the Second Division, Fifth Army Corps, but when that corps was finally organised for the Santiago expedition, he was assigned to command the Third Brigade of the Second Division.

General Chaffee's notes of May 15, 1898, state:

> We arrived here yesterday; last night I was tired; getting into camp and the worry I felt because we did not have water for our tired men made me tired too. Troops have been rushed in here the past week, finding no adequate provision made to supply the most dire necessities in a hot and sandy place. Water has to be piped to camping grounds and it takes a good deal of ground to camp a force of the size here. Everybody wants elbow room and must have it—takes a lot of pipe, and time to lay it down. And that is not all, for water is obtained from artesian wells and the quantity is somewhat limited because of the size of the outflow pipes. All in all, water is now our chief cause of complaint. The water is pronounced by the surgeons to be most excellent. I hear the troops longest on the ground about Tampa find it very healthy.
>
> I hear the President has called for 75,000 more troops. Doubtless it begins to dawn on the mind of the thoughtful man that Uncle Sam's hand has been made to reach far beyond the expectation of anyone three months ago, and that he cannot now withdraw if he would. Our people will now have to support an army of a hundred thousand men whether they like it or not. I think too that the government and Congress have learned a lesson regarding the National Guard which will not soon be forgotten—how woefully unprepared it was, yet asserted to be ready for war. No reserve supplies with which to go to war; ammunition, clothing, tents, transportation—all deficient in an enormous amount; this the fault of past Congresses. It is a rude awakening to a people who have heretofore talked foolishly about strength and readiness to do battle. The weakest power of Europe has called our bluff; what would have been our situation now had we gotten into a fracas with ———, for example, as many hot heads have talked about for several years. Present conditions make one think about what might have been.

The curiosities of statutes caused this comment:

It would really seem as though such unfortunate changes as have been made here might have been avoided. First General Wade was ordered here and Shafter to New Orleans. Then Shafter was ordered here and being the senior took command. Then both were made Major-Generals of Volunteers. Under the laws governing seniority Wade then ranked Shafter and ousted him. Now comes another change and Shafter takes this command and Wade goes to Chickamauga. All this must be mortifying to them as it makes the Tommy Atkins of the U.S. Army laugh.

To the American people Tampa became a word of reproach, but General Chaffee continued the even tenor of his way, getting his brigade ready for war and making frequent notes of his gratification at the smallness of the sick list and other matters which are of concern to men in the field. It is not strange to find in the notes of this old and experienced cavalryman the following:

The Fifth Corps goes with some artillery, the engineer battalion, and eight troops of cavalry from each of the five regiments in this vicinity—the cavalry go dismounted. The cavalry officers are all broken up about the matter and count their labour heretofore as lost. It is, any way we look at it, too bad, but I suppose an emergency must be met in any way possible. Our volunteer infantry is unfit to go into battle, hence the cavalry is taken. Events are now on which will cause to be made a large increase in the army. We shall soon have a Regular Army of 100,000 men, no less, probably more.

I don't know to what place we go, but the order calls for ten days' travel rations, which indicates to my mind either Puerto Rico or Santiago de Cuba. I hear the Fifth Corps is soon to go on transports, but I saw General Shafter this morning and he said nothing to me about it. One can hardly imagine the number of officers and others, old soldiers and civilians, who have written or asked me to aid them to office. It is not entirely agreeable to me to be great, for I dislike to tell men I don't think quite as they do sometimes.

The War Department endeavoured to limit general officers in the selection of aids to those on duty under their immediate command. Selection of an aid, hurriedly made, within the limits of a new command, is somewhat in the nature of a lottery chance. General officers will appreciate a note made by General Chaffee a few days after he had made a selection under such conditions:

> "I am greatly disappointed in my aid; not much force and I fear has not a very good comprehension of the duty he will have to perform; further, he likes to stand around, and talks too much. I made my choice too early, for I now see that I could have done much better had I waited and observed for a few days. *I hope he will soon be promoted.*

The days at Tampa were filled with the work of hurried preparation of an army for overseas service—something entirely foreign to our experience except that obtained during the Civil War, when troops were transported by sea to points along the South Atlantic and Gulf coasts. Events over which we had no control were rapidly forcing the crisis. There had been no time in which to organise and equip our Volunteer Army, or to fill the ranks of our skeleton regular organisations, when our secret service agent in Havana, obtaining the key of the cable instrument during the night, sped upon its way the message of assurance that Cervera's fleet was in Santiago harbour. Quick action became essential, and, notwithstanding the lack of readiness and the approach of the season of sickness, the army was destined to immediate operations against the enemy. Still uncertainty lurked in the air so far as General Chaffee's movements were concerned:

> General Shafter told me today that he hoped to put troops aboard transports Sunday. Still much to be done before that. General Shafter did not tell me that he would give Lawton my division, but I think he will have to do it. He is a great friend of Lawton's, and Lawton is extremely anxious to go on the expedition. He is also an excellent officer and ranks me.
>
> We are going, I now think, to Santiago to help in the capture of the Spanish fleet. General Shafter did not tell me this in so many words, but, while talking over matters, he drew a map of the bay and discussed positions of the batteries defending the harbour. There has been an attack made on the place by the navy, but results are not known here yet. It is probable our departure depends somewhat on results of the affair, yet to be reported. I think the fleet there. The proposition is to keep it in the bay. The number of troops to be encountered is not known. I doubt if we have transports here to take more than 16,000.
>
> I lose my division to Lawton and take the 3rd Brigade, 2nd Division, 5th Army Corps. I have already relinquished command

of the division and assumed command of the brigade.

We are aboard the *Iroquois*, the brigade on three boats. Left Tampa at 1:30 a.m. yesterday and was loaded at 9:25 last night; was up all night before last; on my feet all yesterday. Lawton is on the boat also; he has just come aboard and says we are to sail at once for Santiago, Sampson having telegraphed that he has reduced the fortifications and wants 10,000 men immediately. I never felt in better health than now. I have an idea I am to keep well and be able to hustle with the best.

The message from Admiral Sampson which hastened the movements of the army on its Santiago campaign was as follows:

Mole, Hayti, June 7, 1898

Secretary of Navy, Washington:

Bombarded forts at Santiago 7:30 a.m. to 10:00 a.m. today, June 6th. Have silenced works quickly, without injury of any kind, though stationary within 2,000 yards. If 10,000 men were here, city and fleet would be ours in forty-eight hours. Every consideration demands immediate army movement. If delayed, city will be defended more strongly by guns taken from fleet.

Sampson

Chapter 18: The Santiago Campaign

After the troops had embarked at Tampa a report of a mythical Spanish fleet was received in Washington, and the sailing of the expedition was suspended until the navy could ascertain whether any undue risk would attend the voyage under convoy of such warships as could be assembled for the purpose. The delay was very trying to the troops crowded between decks, during the heat of summer, without the benefit of the sea breeze. General Chaffee kept a very complete journal during the war. On the eve of departure from Tampa Bay he wrote:

Off Egmont Key Light, June 14, 1898

It is just a week today since my brigade came aboard ship. We left Tampa yesterday and anchored last night off Petersburg, about twelve miles from Tampa. Several of the ships were not ready to start yesterday, so another day of delay. We were in at Petersburg for water yesterday and went aground there; after three hours the tide helped us off. Unless something new turns up we will enter into the Gulf this p.m. At least such is the appearance of the situation now.

General Chaffee continued his journal during the voyage and filed with it a carefully drawn sketch of the disposition of the transports and naval vessels convoying the fleet. The voyage was not without interesting incidents. The conversations of brother-officers as to the effect of the expeditions to Cuba and the Philippines on the future of our government were most informing. Viewed from our present-day knowledge, they were remarkably accurate forecasts of the course of history.

After a week's voyage the fleet of transports, having passed around the eastern end of Cuba, arrived off Santiago on June 20, 1898. There was much of interest and excitement in the sight of the battleships and other war vessels cruising about the front of the harbour, alert and watchful to prevent Cervera's Spanish fleet from escaping. The troops had been on board the improvised transports two weeks and were eager to be off and at the enemy, but were still detained while plans were being devised for the disembarkation in the face of the Spanish troops, reputed to be both courageous and efficient. The ancient fort on the headland, Moro Castle, had become celebrated at the time. After viewing it General Chaffee noted in his journal its similarity in appearance to the "Navajo Church" and other steeple rocks well known to those who had followed the Indian trails of the Far West.

After forty-eight hours of delay General Shafter, on June 21, assembled the general officers on board his ship, the *Segurança*, and informed them that the disembarkation would begin next day, as soon as the navy ceased bombarding the coast in the immediate vicinity. The place selected for the disembarkation, Daiquiri, had no harbour and only one pier—a very high one for use in dumping iron ore from cars into lighters. There was a small dock extending only a few yards from shore. It was therefore necessary to make landings on the open beach, through the surf—a very difficult operation for men armed and equipped for immediate duty ashore. It was necessary to put the horses and mules overboard to swim ashore. Some of these turned back from the surf and swam out to sea and were lost.

About a thousand Cuban revolutionists had been detailed by their commander to operate in conjunction with the troops while they were effecting a landing. The army lighters had failed to reach Santiago. The men were landed in the surf from ships' boats belonging to the transports and the Atlantic Fleet, an operation with which the army later became very familiar in the Philippines.

General Lawton's division was assigned to the advance in the pending operations, being directed to begin disembarkation as soon as the naval guns ceased firing. As soon as the First and Second brigades had assembled on shore, General Lawton moved along the coast about two miles in the direction of Siboney. Some of the companies of the Third Brigade had not yet reached shore at 6:00 p.m., at which time General Chaffee with his command followed the other two brigades.

Early the following morning, June 23, General Lawton occupied Siboney, making the landing at that place available for further unloading of the transports. General Chaffee rode into Siboney at daylight, and on the way back to the bivouac of his brigade passed General Young's troops moving to the front. General Chaffee brought up his brigade and arrived near Siboney about 8:30 a.m., at which point he had been directed to put his brigade in camp. His journal recites:

> Heavy firing heard in front. Before camp had been made received note from General Lawton to march to the assistance of General Wheeler, who had gone forward with Young's brigade and attacked the Spanish troops in position at the junction of two roads. A very gallant fight by our troops, who suffered considerable loss. Enemy retreated, probably not much hurt. The battle had been won before I arrived. Moved forward and formed advance line. Posted one regiment, 7th Infantry, at Sevilla.

This entry in General Chaffee's journal does infinite credit to his generosity. He had been selected to lead the advance against Santiago, and his thunder, the honour of the first blow at the enemy, had been stolen by another, who quickly called for help and received it. The incident deserves more than passing notice.

General Shafter desired above all things to get his army on shore after the long confinement on board ship. He had no intention of moving against the Spanish forces until supplies could be landed and arrangements made for their distribution to the troops. His orders given to the assembled generals on board the *Segurança*, immediately following the disembarkation of the main body of his troops, establish this conclusively. General Shafter had planned to have General Lawton's division lead in the advance on Santiago, and General Lawton's plans placed General Chaffee with his brigade at the head of the division:

Headquarters 5th Army Corps
S.S. *Segurança*, off Daiquiri, June 24th

To Division Commanders:

Commanding General directs me to say it is impossible to advance upon Santiago until means to supply troops can be arranged. Take up strong positions, where you can get water, and make yourselves secure from attack and surprise.

General Lawton's division will be in front, Kent's division near Juraguasito, where he disembarked, Wheeler's near Daiquiri, then Bates.

General Shafter wrote to General Lawton, on the same date, saying:

I suppose you have received my orders by this time, which put you in front, a short distance in advance of other troops. I wish you to make a strong position there because we may have to hold it a week. I won't move until I can make provision to move rations and ammunition, so make yourself solid.

General Shafter's plans to get ready before moving against the enemy were disarranged at once by General Wheeler, who had passed around General Lawton's division and moved forward until the Spanish rear guard was encountered at Las Guasimas. Before the action had become serious the following message was dispatched:

24th June, 8:30 a.m.

General Lawton:

General Wheeler directs me to say that he is engaged with a bigger force of the enemy than he anticipated, and asks that any forces you may have be sent forward on the Sevilla road, as soon as possible.

W. D Beach
Captain Third Cavalry

General Lawton, the steadfast, sturdy, and loyal old warrior, was not blind to the trick played upon him and his division, but complied promptly with the request by sending General Chaffee with his brigade forward on the main road, and Colonel Miles with his brigade, by way of the trail on the northern side of the valley, to the assistance of General Wheeler's command. The effect upon the Spaniards created by the approach of General Lawton's division may possibly be determined by the impartial historian of the future.

We are not a military people, but are given to hero-worship. In all our wars individuals have sought to gain popular approval, knowing the advantages which come from our national tendency. General Wheeler had been long in public life and was by no means ignorant of the value of headlines. The overturning of the plans of an army commander cannot be indulged in without placing the general success in jeopardy.

In his autobiography President Roosevelt mentions this incident:

> General Young was one of the few men who had given and taken wounds with the sabre. He was an old friend of mine, and when in Washington before starting for the front told me that if we got in his brigade, he would put us into the fighting all right. He kept his word.
>
> General Young had actively superintended getting his two regular regiments, or at least a squadron of each, off the transports, and late that night he sent us word that he had received permission to move at dawn and strike the Spanish advance position. He directed us to move along a ridge trail with our two squadrons (one squadron having been left at Tampa), while with two squadrons of regulars, one of the First and one of the Tenth, under his personal supervision, he marched up the valley trail. Accordingly, Wood took us along the hill trail early next morning, till we struck the Spaniards, and began our fight just as the regulars began the fight in the valley trail
>
> Soon I learned that he (Wood) was all right, that the Spaniards had retreated along the main road, and that Colonel Wood and two or three other officers were a short distance away. Before I reached them I encountered a captain of the Ninth Cavalry, very glum because his troopers had not been up in time to take part in the fight, and he congratulated me—with visible effort!—upon my share in our first victory. I thanked him cordially, not confiding in him that till that moment I myself knew exceedingly little about the victory; and proceeded to where Generals Wheeler, Lawton, and Chaffee, who had just come up, in company with Wood, were seated on a bank. (Theodore Roosevelt, *An Autobiography*.)

On June 25 General Chaffee brought up the other regiments of his brigade, the Twelfth and Seventeenth Infantry, to Sevilla, and remained there until June 27, when he moved forward with his brigade about one and one-half miles on the road to Santiago, closely followed by the other two brigades of Lawton's division, which constituted the advance of the army. While in this position, General Chaffee entered in his notes on June 27, 1898:

> My command is in advance, four miles from Santiago. Effort is being made to close the army up and get rations to the camps.

Nature has resumed control of, at one time, cultivated fields, and with brush, vines, and high grass on every hand it is difficult to move off the trails. One-time roads are now mere trails, scarcely discernible. Often, we cannot see beyond a hundred yards unless on some elevated point. We hear of Spanish forts and wire entanglements to be encountered.

While occupying the position in advance of the army General Chaffee, on June 26, made a personal reconnaissance of the Spanish lines and prepared sketches of the intervening country, showing roads, trails, and obstacles to be overcome. These sketches, preserved with his journal, were used at the conference between Generals Shafter, Lawton, and Chaffee on board the *Segurança* on June 28, 1898, as a result of which General Chaffee was directed to open a road to the vicinity of El Caney and prepare positions for the artillery. This was accomplished on June 29, and orders were issued to the army for the advance and attack upon the Spanish works.

On June 30, 1898, the Second Division of the Fifth Corps left its camps, or bivouacs, to go into position preparatory to the attack on El Caney, the right of the American line. The position of the enemy proved to be much stronger than had been expected. The character and number of field guns available for the attack left much to be desired. Nevertheless, the assault was made and the action continued until victory was won. A general order was issued on July 4, from the headquarters of the forces in Cuba, stating:

> The Commanding General congratulates the army on the result of the first general engagement with the enemy. The strongly fortified outpost and village of Caney was captured after a most stubborn resistance, nearly its entire garrison being killed, wounded, or captured by the Second Division, Fifth Corps, Brigadier-General Lawton commanding. The heroic valour displayed by these troops adds another brilliant page to the history of American warfare.

The defence of El Caney deserves more than a cursory mention. The garrison consisted of 430 men of the battalion of the Constitution; 40 men of the Infantry of Cuba detachment, and 80 volunteers, making a total of 550 men under command of General Vara del Rey. The American plan of battle had in view the attack of El Caney by an entire division to overwhelm it quickly and permit the troops to close in on Santiago. The heroic defence of General Vara del Rey gave some unhappy hours to the American Army commander, besides inflicting a loss of 4 officers and 77 men killed, and 25 officers and 332 men wounded, a total of 438 casualties—almost as many as the entire number of the defenders. General Vara del Rey, his two sons and a brother, were killed in this battle. Three of the four American officers and forty-six of the seventy-seven enlisted men killed in this action belonged to General Chaffee's brigade.

GENERAL CHAFFEE AT EL CANEY

In writing of the fight at El Caney Captain Arthur H. Lee, R.A., British military *attaché*, said:

The strong post had been carefully reconnoitred by Brigadier-General Chaffee in person, and he had submitted a plan of attack which was afterward carried out almost to the letter.
I feel it is only just at this point to mention that however novel the absence of reconnaissance in other directions, nothing

could have been more enterprising or systematic than General Chaffee's exploration of his own theatre of operations. I had the pleasure of accompanying him on more than one occasion, and derived much profit from a study of his methods.

Leaving his staff behind, he would push far to the front, and finally, dismounting, slip through the brush with the rapidity and noiselessness of an Indian. My efforts to follow him were like the progress of a band-wagon in comparison, but I gradually acquired a fairy-like tread and a stumbling facility in sign language, which enabled me to follow the general without too loudly advertising our presence to the Spaniards. On one occasion we approached so close to the Spanish pickets that we could hear the men talking over their suppers, and until I began to speculate on the probable efficacy of the British passport that was my sole defensive weapon. In this silent Indian fashion General Chaffee explored the entire district, and was the only man in the army to whom the network of bridlepaths round El Caney was in any sense familiar. ("The Regulars at El Caney," *Scribners*, XXIV; October, 1898.)

During the progress of the battle Captain Lee in passing along in rear of the lines halted behind the Seventh Infantry, where General Chaffee was directing the action. Captain Lee says of this stage of the proceedings:

Wishing to see how they were faring, I crawled through the hedge into the field beyond, and incidentally into such a hot corner that I readily complied with General Chaffee's abrupt injunction, "Get down on your stomach, sir." Indeed, I was distinctly grateful for his advice, but could not fail to notice that he was regardless of it himself. Wherever the fire was thickest he strolled about unconcernedly, a half-smoked cigar between his teeth and an expression of exceeding grimness on his face. The situation was a trying one for the nerves of the oldest soldier, and some of the younger hands fell back from the firing-line and crept toward the road. In a moment the general pounced upon them, inquiring their destination in low, unhoneyed accents, and then taking them persuasively by the elbow led them back to the extreme front, and having deposited them in the firing-line stood over them while he distributed a few last words of pungent and sulphurous advice. Throughout the day he set the most inspiring example to his men, and that he escaped unhurt was a miracle. ("The Regulars at El Caney," *Scribners*, XXIV.)

General Chaffee had several narrow escapes at El Caney, one bullet cutting his coat on the left shoulder and another cutting in half a button on his left breast, leaving one-half on the coat.

Chapter 19: The Siege and Surrender of Santiago

After attending to the dead and wounded of his brigade at El Caney, General Chaffee moved with the division to join the forces along the line of hills surrounding Santiago and took position on the right of the dismounted cavalry division on the morning of July 2. The lines were extended gradually until the investment of the city of Santiago was complete, cutting off further communication with the interior of the island. The harbour had become untenable, and at 10:00 a.m. on July 3 Admiral Cervera proceeded to sea with the Spanish fleet. This was entirely destroyed by the American fleet, which had been guarding the entrance of the harbour since the Spanish fleet was known to have entered.

At 8:30 a.m. of that morning General Shafter sent the following demand for surrender:

Headquarters United States Forces
Near San Juan River, Cuba, July 3, 1898, 8:30 a.m.
To the Commanding General of the Spanish Forces, Santiago de Cuba
Sir: I shall be obliged, unless you surrender, to shell Santiago de Cuba. Please inform the citizens of foreign countries and all women and children that they should leave the city before ten o'clock tomorrow morning.
Very respectfully,
Your obedient servant,
W. R. Shafter
Major-General, U.S.A.

The following reply was received at 6: 30 p.m.:

Santiago de Cuba, July 3, 1898, 3:00 p.m.
His Excellency the General Commanding Forces of United States near San Juan River
Sir: I have the honour to reply to your communication of today, written at 8:30 a.m. and received at 1:00 p.m., demanding the

surrender of this city; on the contrary case announcing to me that you will bombard this city and that I advise the foreign women and children that they must leave the city before ten o'clock tomorrow morning. It is my duty to say to you that this city will not surrender and that I will inform the foreign consuls and inhabitants of the contents of your message.

Very respectfully,

José Toral
Commander in Chief, Fourth Corps

As illustrating the American methods of making war, the following messages are illuminating:

Adjutant General
    Washington

I do not know that these extreme measures which I have threatened be justifiable under the circumstances, and I submit the matter for the consideration of the President. The little town of Caney will not hold 1,000 people, and great suffering will be occasioned to our friends, as we must regard the people referred to, and it is now filled with dead and wounded, the dead still unburied. The consuls tell Dorst that there are not to exceed 5,000 troops in the city. I can hold my present line and starve them out, letting the noncombatants come out leisurely as they run out of food, and will probably be able to give such as are forced out by hunger food to keep them alive. I await your orders.   W. R. Shafter
Major-General United States Volunteers

War Department, July 4, 1898, 6: 10 a.m.

Major-General Shafter
Plaza del Este, Cuba

Telegram containing demand made by you for surrender of Santiago, the Spanish commander's reply thereto, and your reply to him, received. While you would be justified in beginning to shell Santiago at expiration of time limit set by you, still under the conditions named in your dispatch, and for humanity's sake, the postponement of the bombardment to noon July 5 is approved.   R. A. Alger
Secretary of War

The arrival of reinforcements from the United States enabled General Shafter gradually to extend his lines around the city and down to the bay. He therefore communicated again with General Toral with a view to bringing about a surrender without causing further loss and suffering:

Headquarters Fifth Army Corps
Camp Near Santiago de Cuba, July 11, 1898

To His Excellency

Commander in Chief of the Spanish Forces, Santiago de Cuba

Sir: With the largely increased forces which have come to me, and the fact that I have your line of retreat securely in my hands, the time seems fitting that I should again demand of Your Excellency the surrender of Santiago and of Your Excellency's Army. I am authorised to state that should Your Excellency so desire the Government of the United States will transport the entire command of Your Excellency to Spain.

I have the honour to be,

Very respectfully your obedient servant,

Wm. R. Shafter

Major-General Commanding

General Linares, the Spanish commander, lying seriously ill in Santiago, sent the following cable message to his government on July 12:

Soldiers without permanent shelter, their only food consisting of rice. Unfortunately, the situation is desperate. The surrender is imminent, otherwise we only gain time to prolong our agony. The sacrifice would be sterile, and the men understand this. The honour of arms has its limits; and I appeal to the judgment of the Government and the entire nation, whether these patient troops have not repeatedly saved it since the 18th of May—date of first bombardment. If it is necessary that I sacrifice them for reasons unknown to me, or if it is necessary for someone to take the responsibility for the issue foreseen and announced by me in several telegrams, I willingly offer myself as a sacrifice to my country, and I will take charge of the command for the act of surrender, as my modest reputation is of small value when the interest of the Nation is at stake.

It was not merely a question of starving out the Spanish garrison, for a few cases of yellow fever had appeared, and it was not desirable to disembark any more American troops. General Shafter expected heavy losses in event of an assault by his troops, already much weakened by sickness and exposure under a tropical sun. It was with intense satisfaction and a feeling of genuine relief on the part of General Shafter and the Washington authorities that the following cable message was sent and received:

Plaza, July 14, 1898, 2:40 p.m.

Adjutant General
Washington Have just returned from interview with General Toral. He agrees to surrender upon the basis of being returned to Spain. This proposition embraces all of eastern Cuba from Aserradero, on the south, to Sagua, on the north, *via* Palma, with practically the Fourth Army Corps. Commissioners meet this afternoon at 2:30 to definitely arrange terms.

W. R. Shafter
Major-General

For three weeks the American Army had been subjected to a great strain from hard work under most unfavourable conditions. General Chaffee had been seriously ill, and the number of men on sick reports was increasing by leaps and bounds. Release from the strain of watchfulness and anxiety gave the first opportunity to withdraw from the trenches and look after the welfare of the troops who had borne every hardship and danger in the most soldierly manner.

Chaffee's notes during this period of the siege recite:

We have a tremendous sick list, both officers and men. Malarial fever chiefly, while many are sick from exhaustion and want of a change of diet. As soon as the company kitchens can be got on shore the men will improve rapidly. Providence has been most kind to this army, it seems to me. Had not the Spanish Army surrendered before our own broke down physically, a very different condition of things would exist here today. We could not have maintained our hold before Santiago with our army sick as it is now, and with the enemy active in our front, and I think we may thank God very gratefully for this victory, gained in the face of many blunders and in spite of a woeful degree of unpreparedness for campaigning in this country. We are all so satisfied with results obtained that I dare say no one feels like complaining of inefficiency and deficiencies everywhere. At Tampa we saw the complete breaking down of the quartermaster and commissary departments, but all seemed to think the medical department would be efficient and adequate. Horrible disappointment—no one will ever know how great unless someone shall have the nerve to write a true history of this campaign.

Mail began to arrive after the surrender with considerable regularity, and one of General Chaffee's notes records:

> I receive a good many letters each mail from mothers, sisters, and friends of soldiers inquiring about them. War is an awful thing when we think of the extent of the range of its miseries. To every part of the land—our country—to the home of the poor, as to the home of the well-to-do and of the rich. All mothers' hearts cry out in the same sad voice: "Tell me something of my darling boy. Is he wounded; is he dead? The papers say he is killed but I will not believe it so." Fortunately, I can answer a great many inquiries and say your son is alive and well. I find it a wonderfully pleasant duty when I can do this in place of saying, "Your son is lost to you."

The condition of the army at Santiago was made known to the nation through the medium of a signed statement of those in authority and characterised by the press as a "round robin." General Chaffee's notes furnish evidence of his views in the plain-spoken manner characteristic of the man:

> Yesterday (August 2, 1898) all the general officers who were able met at Corps Headquarters to talk over the matter of health of the army and what should be done. Dispatches from Washington seem to indicate that we are to be left to chance in this place rather than make an effort to get us away from an impending and almost certain epidemic of yellow fever. Because a few sporadic cases have occurred, mostly at Siboney, where we landed, the purpose seems to be to let the whole army take its chances with the plague, rather than run the risk of infecting a transport, or landing a case on the shore of the United States. Had the withdrawal begun immediately after the surrender took place, two-thirds of this army might be today in the United States without the slightest danger to itself or our own people. Now our men are so weakened by malarial fever that they have not the power to resist yellow fever if it breaks out, and we shall lose many unless something be done at once. Washington theory about stamping out the fever, if it appears in our midst as an epidemic, is quite absurd to us who are here on the ground, and have examined with care all the country round about. Theory seldom works out practically in such matters. It is suggested

that we move camp frequently, and get to the high grounds or mountains. They do not seem to know that when we get there, we would not be able to feed our men; that the soil is a black loam, and at this season a quagmire because of the daily rains. Where we are—the first hills from the bay—the ground is hard and gravelly, and the heavy storms frequently pass us by.

It was the unanimous opinion of all the generals and the chief surgeons yesterday that the army should be sent home at once, and we strengthened General Shafter's hands with a paper to that effect, which he can use or not as he pleases. We feel very anxious, because of the condition of our men who are too weak to go through an epidemic of yellow fever.

It provoked me last week to see transport after transport leave the bay with hardly a soul on board besides the crew. All should have been loaded with troops. Probably all has been said here now that will be said and done. We shall submit to the decision. If we remain, God only knows what the result will be. We believe that more than half this army will never see America—the United States—unless it be moved without delay from here.

I think we have already lost by disease more than we lost in battle—a great many more than were killed certainly. Nearly every day one or two poor fellows are placed in the ground. Perhaps two hundred of the Second Division will be left; too sick to be moved now.

As fresh regiments were being sent to Santiago to take over the posts vacated by the Spanish forces it became necessary to select a commander for the new Department of Santiago, about to be established by orders from the War Department. The Adjutant General of the Army communicated an offer of the command to General Chaffee on August 8, 1898, to which he replied, on August 9:

Being allowed to express desire, answer in the negative in reply to your cable dated eighth.

In his notes concerning this matter he wrote:

I would not have the command unless absolutely forced on me by an order. This place would be the back door of all our military operations. I should be bottled up as effectually as was the Spanish fleet. I do not want to be so placed and I think my rank entitles me to an active command.

Two days later General Chaffee was directed to assume command of the Second Division in place of General Lawton, who had been assigned to the command of the Department of Santiago. In relinquishing command of the Second Division to General Chaffee, General Lawton issued the following order:

Headquarters, 2nd Division, 5th Army Corps

Santiago de Cuba, August 14, 1898

General Orders

No. 6

Having been ordered to other duty, the undersigned hereby relinquishes command of the 2nd Division, 5th Army Corps. In doing so he desires to express to the officers and enlisted men of the command his thanks for, and appreciation of, the gallant and soldierly manner in which the duties and labours required of them have been performed; the character of which has been almost unparalleled in severity, danger and importance. The 2nd Division, established a little more than two months since, proceeded almost immediately to embark for the expedition to Santiago de Cuba. Arriving off that coast, it was the first to disembark and the first military force to land on Cuban soil. Without delay, or waiting to secure rations, baggage, or other necessaries or conveniences of any kind, the division proceeded to Siboney, compelling the garrison at that place to retire and capturing the town.

From this point the division resumed the advance of the army on Santiago de Cuba; labouring almost day and night under trying conditions in its marches, reconnaissances and scouting while covering the advance. Fighting the decisive Battle of El Caney, unique in the character of its defences and importance of its situation; defended with a stubborn resistance permitting no surrender; it was carried by a charge such as could be made only by American soldiers, killing, wounding and capturing almost every Spaniard; moving thence within an hour, with but one man unaccounted for, toward the city of Santiago de Cuba, and taking up a position on the right of the Army. Hastily entrenching, it was engaged with the enemy on the 2nd of July. Extending to the right, covering the Bay of Santiago, and threatening the safety of the Spanish ships of war, they sought safety by flight to sea.

Fighting in daylight and digging at night, it pressed forward and to the right until the lines were at places within one hundred and fifty (150) yards of the enemy, and the right resting on the Bay of Santiago. The memorable 17th day of July came and with it the surrender of the city and the Spanish Army, and later the end of the war with Spain. When overtaken by the dreaded fever, your courage, cheerfulness and fortitude did not forsake you. When the history of the war for Cuban independence is written, the 2nd Division will deserve and receive a full page in every important occurrence which led up to its successful termination.

To my Staff, I desire to acknowledge a special obligation for most loyal and faithful duty well performed, under circumstances and conditions too trying to be described.

H. W. Lawton
Major-General, U.S. Volunteers

As fast as transports became available the regiments engaged in the Santiago expedition were embarked and sent to a large camp established for their reception at Montauk, Long Island. General Chaffee embarked on the *Harvard* on August 19, and arrived off Montauk on August 25, 1898. Here the returning troops were placed in detention camps until it could be observed whether any cases of yellow fever existed in the command.

Prior to General Chaffee's arrival the Adjutant General of the Army telegraphed to him that the Commanding General of the First Corps had requested his assignment to command the Second Division of that corps. The assignment was acceptable, but it was essential that General Chaffee should rest and endeavour to free his system from the fevers and disorders from which he had suffered severely while in the lines investing Santiago. The order relieving General Chaffee from duty with the Fifth Corps and assigning him to command the Second Division, First Corps, at Knoxville, Tennessee, was issued on September 26, 1898.

With the muster out of the volunteer regiments and dispersal of the regular organisations the historic Fifth Corps of the war with Spain ceased to exist. It was mainly a corps of Regulars, to whom honour is justly due for the splendid achievements of the brief campaign in Cuba. Hurried from widely separated posts on the frontier, put aboard transports in midsummer, disembarked in the surf of a tropical shore, without dependable reserves of men and supplies, the little army of highly trained men moved to the assault of an intrenched enemy, and, in face of theory and academic teaching, wrested victory from astonished opponents, received the surrender of an enemy larger in numbers, and materially hastened the downfall of Spanish power in the West Indies.

Upon the surrender of the Spanish forces at Santiago the following congratulatory order was issued:

Headquarters U.S. Troops in Cuba

Santiago de Cuba, July 19, 1898

General Orders

No. 26

The successful accomplishment of the campaign against Santiago, resulting in its downfall and the surrender of the Spanish Forces, the capture of large amounts of military stores, together with the destruction of the entire Spanish Fleet in the harbour, which upon the investment of the city, was forced to leave, is one of which this army can well be proud.

This has been accomplished through the heroic deeds of the army, and to its officers and men the Major-General Commanding offers his sincere thanks for their endurance of hardships heretofore unknown in the American Army. The work you have accomplished may well appeal to the pride of your countrymen and has been rivalled upon but few occasions in the world's history. Landing upon an unknown coast, you faced dangers in disembarking and overcame obstacles that even in looking back seem insurmountable. Seizing, with the assistance of the navy, the towns of Daiquiri and Siboney, you pushed boldly forth gallantly driving back the enemy's outposts in the engagement of Las Guasimas and completed the concentration of the army, near Sevilla, within sight of the Spanish stronghold at Santiago de Cuba.

The outlook from Sevilla was one that might well have appalled the stoutest heart; behind you ran a narrow road, made well-nigh impassable by rains, while to the front you looked out upon high foothills, covered with a dense tropical growth, which could only be traversed by bridle paths, terminating within range of the enemy's guns. Nothing daunted, you responded eagerly to the order to close upon the foe and attacking at Caney and San Juan, drove him from work to work, until he took refuge within his last and strongest entrenchments immediately surrounding the city.

Despite the fierce glare of a southern sun and rains that fell in torrents, you valiantly withstood his attempts to drive you from the position your valour had won. Holding in your vise-like grip the army opposed to you, after seventeen days of battle and siege, you were regarded by the surrender of nearly 24,000 prisoners—12,000 being those in your immediate front, the others scattered in the various towns of eastern Cuba; freeing completely the eastern part of the island from Spanish troops. This was not done without great sacrifices. The death of 230 gallant soldiers, and the wounding of 1,284 others, shows but too plainly the fierce contest in which you were engaged. The few reported missing are undoubtedly among the dead, as no prisoners were lost.

For those who have fallen in battle with you, the commanding general sorrows, and with you will ever cherish their memory. Their devotion to duty sets a high example of courage and patriotism to our fellow countrymen.

All who have participated in the campaign, battle and siege of Santiago de Cuba will recall with pride the grand deeds accomplished, and will hold one another dear for having shared great sufferings, hardships, and triumphs together. All may well feel proud to inscribe on their banners the name of "Santiago de Cuba.

By Command of Major-General Shafter:

E. J. McClernand
Official   Assistant Adjutant General
R. H. Noble
Aide

Chapter 20: El Caney—The Official Report

The following report of his reconnaissances of El Caney and of the battle itself is typical of General Chaffee's modesty as well as of his methods. No other commander in the army took such pains to inform himself regarding the strength and position of the Spanish forces. His sketches were used in the preparation of the plan of attack.

Headquarters 3rd Brigade, 2nd Div., 5th Corps
Near Santiago, Cuba, July 4, 1898

The Adjutant General
Washington, D.C.
Sir: In connection with the operations of the 3rd Brigade, 2nd Di-

vision, 5th Corps of July 1st, I have the honour to report that the road traversed by the Army from Siboney towards Santiago de Cuba, forks to the right about five miles from the latter place. The right-hand road runs a little west of north to a place called Caney, the distance in an air line being about four miles. The main road leads generally west to the city. Santiago and Caney are connected by a broad, well-marked road, and are about six miles apart. This road also is a main thorough-fare to Guantanamo. Thus, the point first mentioned (the fork of the road), Santiago, Caney, form a sort of triangle inclosing a vast thicket of brush and vines, the interior of which is only traversed by paths, although called roads.

About three miles from the fork towards Caney, a road branches to the left to the northwest, and intersects the Santiago-Caney road at about a mile west of the latter place. Further on towards Caney, about 600 yards, a trail branches to Caney, passing around on the south side of a ridge overlooking Caney. This ridge, which is short, is about 800 yards from the south-east corner of the town, where was located on a round and prominent knoll, a stone building used by the Spanish troops as a place of defence. Outside the building was sunk a trench about 3 feet deep, and covering the east, south, and westerly faces of the building. South of the town on lower ground, perhaps 100 yards from the houses, was located a small block-house, the structure being of wood, banked with earth on the outside about 4 feet high. On the northwest corner of the town was a similar and larger block-house. On the northeast face was a line of intrenchments close in to the town. The buildings and streets were also used by the Spanish troops for protection.

About one mile northeast of the town on the side of the moun-tain was located a block-house, its capacity being 15 to 20 men. This block-house was to the right of the line of march of the 7th & 17th Regiments of Infantry, to be explained. On the 26th of June I ex-amined this place from the ridge explained as being about 800 yards southeast of Caney, and reported the fact to the division commander. The main road to Caney continues on from the trail passing around to the eastward of a sugar-loaf mountain, and intersects the Caney-Guantanamo road about 2 miles east of the former place. This section of the Caney road, a mere trail, is extremely difficult for troops in single file to march over. Being authorised by the division comdr., I cleared the road for about three miles for the passage of artillery, also a position for a battery to the left of the road, this at the place where the first road branches to the left and intersects the main road Caney-Santiago. The position for the battery was about 2,000 yards from the town.

On the afternoon of June 30, I received verbal orders from the division comdr. to march on the Caney road and attack the Spanish position from the eastward. I marched at about 5 o'clock and assembled my brigade at the Sugarloaf Mountain after dark, passing on the way Capron's battery, supported by the 1st Infantry, of the 2nd Brigade. We camped without fires. I led forward on the Caney road Young's company of the 7th Infy., about one mile up to a point where it could seize a ridge at daylight. I also took forward by the trail, a company of the 12th Infy. about half a mile, and directed it to seize the ridge at daylight overlooking the town from the southeast. This ridge was the point on which the brigade was to base its left flank. Col. Comba commanding the 12th Infy. was given orders to march by this trail, base on this ridge and deploy to his right, and attack in the direction of the town.

I led the 7th and 17th, preceded by about 50 Cubans, by the Caney road to the Guantanamo road, following the latter towards the town. The head of the column came into connection with the right of the 12th at 7:50 a.m. and about ¾ mile east of Caney. At this point we received the enemy's skirmish fire, both from the town and from the block-house on the right before referred to. The 7th Infy. was deployed on the right of the road in an irregular way, because of the difficult nature of the terrain. Practically the 7th was on the right of the road and the 12th on the left, and formed a line of battle facing the town. The 17th Infy. was directed to proceed to the right of the 7th, the Cubans to attack the block-house to the right. The artillery, Capron's battery, opened fire on the stone building some minutes before my line was extended.

As we pressed forward the enemy's fire became very severe, and in the course of the action the 7th Infy. particularly met with heavy and severe loss in killed and wounded. The 12th also had losses, the 17th but few, owing to the fact that only the head of the column became exposed to the fire of the enemy. The action lasted nearly throughout the day, terminating at about 3:00 p.m., at which time the stone block-house was assaulted by Capt. Haskell's battalion of the 12th Infy. under the personal direction of Lt. Col. Comba commanding the regiment. The resistance at this point had been greatly affected by the fire of Capron's battery. A few moments after the seizure of this point, the key to the situation, my left was joined by Gen. Bates with a portion of his command. He soon after withdrew. This action was continuous throughout the day, with brief lulls for the purpose of quieting and resting the men, who were fatigued from their difficult march and broken sleep of the night previous. They marched to the field of battle without breakfast except a cracker and a drink of cold water.

The conduct of all officers observed by me, and I saw the most of them, is deserving of unlimited praise. The same may be said of the enlisted men with some few exceptions. All of the men were without battle experience, but the great majority went forward into action in a very soldierly and gallant manner. The reports of regimental commanders have been forwarded to Division Headquarters. These reports are unsatisfactory to these officers themselves, because of the limited time that has elapsed since the engagement, nearly all of which has been expended in fatiguing march or in the preparation of trenches for defence. They are also without proper means to render their reports in form to insure durability. I very cordially and heartily concur now and for the future in any special mention of distinguished conduct on the part of officer or enlisted man which commanding officers of regiments have now, or may hereafter submit.

The brigade is greatly indebted in its successful operation for the assistance rendered it by Capron's battery of artillery. Its fire on the stone block-house was accurate and very effective. The brigade is also indebted for assistance rendered by the command of General Bates, whose movements from the south on the town necessarily drew from me a portion of the enemy's fire. Immediately after the action ceased, I directed a thorough search of the field we had fought over, for our wounded and dead. These I think all collected before dark. After this I permitted the men to make coffee, detailed one company, Howell's 7th Infy., to remain with the wounded and bury the dead, and at 7:30 to 8 o'clock, marched for Ducoureaud House, a point of assembly of the division, previously directed by the division commander.

We arrived at about 11 o'clock p.m., officers and men exhausted of strength to the extent they were hardly able to walk. The brigade lay down on the road and rested till 3 a.m. At the Ducoureaud House I joined the Div. Commander who informed me he had sent me an order to leave a regiment at Caney. The courier had failed to find me before marching. The Division Commander concurred with my opinion that the return of a battalion would be sufficient strength. It was so ordered, Coolidge's battalion of the 7th Infy. being sent back, this in addition to Howell's Co. of the same regiment left behind, made 5 companies of this regiment on guard at Caney. Through a misunderstanding of my order, or the non-compliance therewith on the part of Captain Howell, one company of the 17th Infy. was left at Caney and is still absent at that place.

At 3:00 a.m. July 2nd the brigade resumed its march on El Pozo, thence on San Juan, and took position on the right of the Cavalry Division commanded by General Sumner, arriving on the ground at 7:30 a.m.

The losses of the brigade in battle from daylight July 1st to 7:30 a.m. July 2nd are as follows:

7th Infantry; killed, officer 1 (2nd Lt. Wansboro). Enlisted men 34. Wounded, officers, 4 (Major Corliss, Capt. Jackson, 1st Lt. Grisard, Adjt., & 2nd Lt. Lafferty). Enlisted men, 93. Injured, enlisted man, 1.

12th Infy. Killed, officer 1 (2nd Lt. Churchman who died of wounds on July 2nd). Enlisted men, 8. Wounded, officer I (2nd Lt. Dove). Enlisted men, 30.

17th Infy. Killed, officer, 1 (1st Lt. Dickinson, R.Q.M., who died July 2nd of wounds). Enlisted men, 4. Wounded, officer 1 (Lt. Col. J.T. Haskell). Enlisted men, 23. Missing, enlisted men, 2.

Total loss, killed, officers 3; enlisted men, 46,

Wounded, officers, 6; enlisted men, 146.

Missing, enlisted men, 2. Injured, enlisted man, 1.

Total loss 204.

Chapter 21: The Return to Cuba

Under the Treaty of Paris events were gradually shaping themselves, and the replacement of the Spanish garrisons in Cuba by American troops had progressed rapidly. In taking over the control of the island it became necessary to establish a military government to administer affairs, pending the final disposition of the island at the hands of Congress, under the provision of the act which declared our altruistic intentions in going to war with Spain.

After the return of the army from Santiago many changes of command had become necessary, owing to promotions and other shifting of personnel. On October 13, 1898, a general reorganisation of the several army corps in the United States was ordered, and General Chaffee was assigned, under the new arrangement, to the command of the First Division of the Fourth Corps at Huntsville, Alabama.

The following correspondence will explain General Chaffee's relief from his new command within a few weeks and his return to Cuba as Chief of Staff to the Military Governor:

Adjutant General's Office

Washington, December 13, 1898

Major-General A. R. Chaffee

Huntsville, Alabama

Confidential

General Brooke has just been assigned to the command of the Military Division of Cuba, and Acting Military Governor, with the power and duties heretofore devolving upon the Governor General. The President and Secretary of War are anxious that he should have a staff of high rank and first order of ability. To meet this requirement, General Brooke desires your assignment as his Chief of Staff. Inform me at once if it will be agreeable to you. If so, get yourself in readiness to leave for Havana as soon as possible. In my judgment this is a very important assignment, even for an officer of your rank. This, however, by way of suggestion only.

H. C. Corbin

Adjutant General

While a command commensurate with his rank was, in the nature of things, much more desirable to a soldier of General Chaffee's type, he sacrificed his wishes in the matter and, from a sense of duty, replied that the assignment would be agreeable. On December 19, 1898, he was ordered to proceed to Havana, Cuba, and report in person to Major-General John R. Brooke for duty as chief of staff.

There were no military operations of moment in Cuba at that time requiring an officer of General Chaffee's rank in the position of chief of staff. It was necessary, however, to reorganise the government of the island under American auspices with a view to its ultimate independence. The temporary arrangements for the government of Cuba, the Philippines, Porto Rico, and other islands taken over as a result of the war with Spain were giving the American authorities many anxious moments.

Our system of government, based upon a constitution applicable to United States territory on the continent of North America, did not lend itself readily to the administration of affairs under the Spanish system. The policy to be pursued became at once a bone of political contention between the two great parties, and there was also much of nonpolitical misgiving concerning the so-called imperialism involved in attempting to make the Constitution follow the flag. The administration of Cuban affairs was under observation and criticism from within as well as from without. Demands for more definite announcement of administration policies, and threatened and actual investigations, were the order of the day. There was neither glory nor satisfaction in the future outlook, but General Chaffee proceeded under his orders and arrived in Havana on December 26, 1898.

On December 28, 1898, General Brooke published a general order, by authority of the President, assuming the duties of Military Governor of the Island of Cuba and the command of the military division embracing the troops in the island. At twelve o'clock noon, January 1, 1899, General Brooke, accompanied by General Chaffee and the officers constituting the Division Staff, proceeded to the palace of the Spanish Governor General. The formal relinquishment of Spanish sovereignty in the island was then made by the Governor General, on the part of Spain, to the American commissioners, and immediately transferred by them to General Brooke as Military Governor. Immediately following the ceremonies, the retiring Spanish Governor General embarked on a ship for Matanzas, at which point and Cienfuegos about fifty thousand Spanish soldiers had been assembled for transportation back to Spain. The complete evacuation of Cuba by the Spanish Army was accomplished on February 6, 1899.

While matters were generally quiet in Cuba, the revolutionary army did not appear inclined to disband. Very few seemed disposed to return to their homes. Arrangements had been made for a conference between the Military Governor and General Gomez, as the head of the Cuban Army, which had maintained the revolution against Spain. The distribution of an appropriation of $3,000,000 awaited the adjustment and acceptance of terms involving the dissolution of the Cuban army. Matters were somewhat complicated by the sessions of a Cuban Assembly away from the capital, the members of which were for the most part officers of the Cuban Revolutionary Army. Having been advised, apparently, that by holding together the army would receive pay for its services during the entire revolution, the Cuban patriots were not inclined to disband.

It was fully realised that, as between the large business interests which would be relied upon to support the new government, as an independent nation, and the revolutionists who had kept alive the contest against Spain, some understanding and adjustments were necessary before Cuba could go far upon its road of constructive upbuilding. To add to the confusion there were numerous bands of outlaws and bandits who had availed themselves of the opportunity offered by unsettled conditions to commit murders and depredations against property. Their suppression called for the ungloved hand.

DEPARTURE OF GENERAL CASTELLANOS FROM HAVANA, JANUARY 1, 1899

The duties of army officers in all the new possessions were difficult in themselves, but were made intolerable in many instances by the lack of appreciation of their efforts at home. General Chaffee, although acting in the capacity of a staff officer, and not, therefore, responsible directly, felt keenly the conditions, but contented himself with recording his opinion:

> Of course, I recognise that politics is at the bottom of all the fracas and that the move is merely a scramble for advantage of position this fall, and that the course that has been adopted is to put the administration on the defensive.

Immediately following the taking over of Cuba from the Spanish authorities General Chaffee had become responsible for the financial affairs, with supervision and direction of much of the other business concentrated in the offices of the Military Governor and Commanding General of the American forces. Because of his responsibility in the matter, the Military Governor deemed it necessary that his headquarters should retain full control of the revenues of the island. This view was not pleasing or acceptable to all of the subordinates, and suggestions were made that collections at customhouses within the limits of a department should be made the basis of appropriations for such department, or that a specified percentage only of the collections within the limits of a department should be paid into the general treasury.

Matters drifted along for some time, with more or less recrimination, but the influences operating against the Military Governor eventually became strong enough to bring about his relief. As General Chaffee had been ordered to Cuba as chief of staff at the special request of General Brooke, he very naturally assumed that his own relief from duty at Havana would follow. He finally invited the attention of the War Department to the matter and was informed on December 21, 1899, by the Adjutant General, that:

> The Secretary of War desires that you remain temporarily in Havana. In the near future further provision will be made for you, probably in this country.

General Chaffee felt assured that his services had been appreciated by General Brooke, but he was very eager to be relieved from staff duty. To use his own language:

> In almost any other situation I could have broken my neck, ruined every chance for the future, or, not having done that, my prospects would have been improved. I would have kept pace with others, instead of falling so utterly into darkness. I do not object to the future of others, but I hold myself as in bad luck when so placed as to be out of the field of contest. Had I asked to be relieved, a construction detrimental to my future might be placed upon my act. I have, therefore, been very cautious not to give even the semblance of an utterance, by word or sign, as to the disgust that I feel because I came here a year ago last December, where I have been practically buried ever since that time.

While in Cuba General Chaffee had suffered, in common with other distinguished officers, a reduction in volunteer rank to the grade of Brigadier-General, owing to a reduction and general reorganisation of the army consequent upon the termination of the war with Spain. He recorded his determination to serve faithfully wherever the

Secretary of War believed the interests of the government demanded, but the position in which he now found himself was very trying for a veteran of half a hundred battles and combats. His new commander, whom he was serving as chief of staff, was a captain in the Medical Corps, who had been advanced within a few months from attending surgeon at the White House to Major-General of Volunteers, and substituted in command at Havana over the heads of all the tried and battle-tested generals in Cuba.

General Chaffee's dignified loyalty and faithfulness to every duty under these trying circumstances attracted the favourable notice of the President and led soon after to his assignment to command the China Relief Expedition. The Secretary of War, in announcing his selection for the China command, stated that in the opinion of the President a man who could rule his own spirit could take a city, and General Chaffee was therefore sent to take Pekin and relieve the besieged legations.

Soon after the relief of General Brooke an article by an officer formerly on duty at the headquarters at Santiago appeared in the *North American Review.* The publication was belated, but its intention, and apparently inspired character, offended General Chaffee in its references to the conduct of business at the headquarters, where, as chief of staff, he had been charged with the allotment of the revenues of Cuba for disbursement, and he took exception to the article, especially this paragraph, as reflecting on him:

> Another effective device of the Junta at Havana for increasing their power has been to make every municipality in the island directly dependent on the general treasury at the capital for the means with which to pay its way. No municipality is allowed to raise sufficient revenues out of its own resources and expend them for its own benefit. The custom house receipts and the greater part of the internal revenues are sent to the capital, there to be doled out to the cities and towns, for their local expenses, in sums deemed suitable for the purpose by functionaries who have no local knowledge whatever, and who may give or withhold as may suit their discretion or their personal or political interest. (Major James E. Runcie, "American Mismanagement of Cuba," *North American Review,* CLXX; February, 1900.)

General Chaffee kept his own counsel, but recorded his personal views that the new military governor should be privileged to select his own staff:

> General Wood needs about him very steady and cautious men—men who are not his tools—sycophants; but he does not want such material. It is necessary to serve him as he wishes, that his assistants think as he does, and believe in his infallibility. He is himself a quick thinker, a hard worker, but this does not necessarily imply that he is a correct thinker always. He is further impressed with the idea he has a mission—is charged with a great reformation.

Considerable time passed without action, and General Chaffee felt that his wishes to be relieved as chief of staff to the Military Governor should receive early consideration. He had continued in the performance of the duties of the office long enough after the change of military governors to prevent any misconstruction of his motives. He had never been able to shake off the effects of the fever which had troubled him periodically since the Santiago campaign, and the confinement of administrative work was having a depressing effect. Under the circumstances he regarded a summer in the north woods as essential to his complete recovery from the effects of malaria, and he therefore submitted a formal application to be relieved. In forwarding the application to the War Department the division commander remarked:

> I shall regret to lose the services of General Chaffee, and were it not that I believe it may be to his personal advantage, I would oppose his retiring from a position that he has filled with ability and assiduity rarely seen among public men. I trust he may be given a command commensurate with his ability.

Upon his relief from duty as chief of staff at his own request the following remarks were included in a general order of May 16, 1900, from the headquarters at Havana:

> In complying with this request the division commander desires to make known his high appreciation of the able manner in which the duties of Chief of Staff have been performed by General Chaffee, the constant, unremitting labour given to the responsible bureaus committed to his charge since the military occupation of the Island of Cuba in January, 1899, and the satisfactory results of that labour as shown by the records at these headquarters. General Chaffee bears with him the high esteem and best wishes of the Major-General Commanding, in this

separation of their official connection, and the hope that in his future field of action he may be assigned duties commensurate with his distinguished professional ability.

Chapter 22: China Relief Expedition

Grown restive under the long confinement incident to his administrative duties in Havana, General Chaffee had planned to avail himself of the summer months to go to Canada and travel westward to the Pacific, returning to the East by one of the American routes and spending the latter part of the period of rest and recuperation in the woods of Maine. After arriving home, and before he could put any of his plans into execution, he was directed to report to the Secretary of War in person. General Chaffee was then informed that he had been selected to command the American forces which were to march to the relief of the beleaguered legations in Pekin.

The progress of the "Boxer" uprising in China had caused much concern to all the nations having diplomatic representatives in China. As early as June 16, 1900, instructions had been sent to the commanding general at Manila to send a regiment of infantry to Taku, where the American fleet had assembled. It was intended that the regiment should proceed to Pekin and report to the American minister for the protection of the legation and of American citizens and property. The Ninth Infantry was chosen, but a violent typhoon in Manila Bay delayed embarkation, and the regiment did not sail until June 27.

In the meantime, the European squadrons in Taku Bay had opened fire on the Taku forts and captured them, clearing the way to Tientsin. The foreign legations in Pekin were already in a state of siege, and an expedition for their relief organised and commanded by Admiral Seymour, British Navy, had been attacked by Chinese troops and driven back to Tientsin with heavy loss.

The situation had gone beyond the power of mere landing parties from the fleets, and troops of several nations were immediately placed under orders to concentrate at Tientsin. Additional American troops were ordered from Manila and home stations to form a division of about fifteen thousand men. On June 26, 1900, General Chaffee was selected to command the American troops under orders to China and was directed to proceed to San Francisco and sail immediately under instructions which would be handed to him prior to his departure. He started westward without delay. While crossing the Middle West, so familiar during the quarter of a century when he was constantly engaged in Indian warfare, he pondered over the new task committed to him and made a note of his thoughts:

"I worry not a little for myself and reputation on this service because of its international character. A misstep or serious mistake might involve our country in a serious quarrel against its wish and to my everlasting undoing. On the other hand, if I am too cautious and lose an opportunity, I will be criticized at home."

Arriving in San Francisco, General Chaffee went immediately aboard the transport *Grant*, on which had already been embarked the Sixth Cavalry, the regiment in which he had spent the formative years of his military life, 1861 to 1888. The transport put to sea, but when a few miles out broke a steam pipe and was forced to return for repairs. Omens are always noticed by many soldiers in their undertakings, and such an accident would have appeared unfavourable to most men. Not so with General Chaffee, however, for after the final start he emerged from his cabin in the evening and saw the new moon over his right shoulder, an omen in which he took much satisfaction.

Before sailing General Chaffee received the following telegraphic instructions:

War Department, Washington, June 30, 1900

General Chaffee
  Care Transport *Grant*
    San Francisco, California

The Secretary of War directs that you proceed by the transport *Grant*, which will sail from San Francisco on or about the 1st day of July, to Nagasaki, Japan, there to receive such orders as may be telegraphed you at or about the time of your arrival, in view of the then existing conditions. In case such orders shall be to go to China, you will proceed with the transport *Grant*, and the officers and men whom she carries, to Taku, and will take command of the land forces of the United States in China. You will confer with the admiral in command of the naval forces of the United States on the coast of China; and it is expected that the two forces will, to the fullest extent, co-operate and assist each other.

The forces under your command are to be used for the protection of the life and property of American citizens and American interests in China wherever the Chinese Government fails to render efficient protection. You will communicate with the American minister in China and in general observe his wishes and answer to his demands in regard to his protection and that of the interests which he represents. You will confer freely with the representatives of the other powers in China, which are engaged in the protection of their citizens and interests, and wherever it shall appear to you that the American interests which you are to protect will be best subserved by that course you will act with the forces under your command concurrently with the forces of other powers. You will, however, avoid entering into any joint action or undertaking with other powers tending to commit or limit this government as to its future course of conduct, and you will avoid taking any action having any object except the protection of American interests hereinbefore charged upon you.   Corbin

It will be recalled that when the Volunteers of the war with Spain were being mustered out a number of Major-Generals of Volunteers were discharged and reappointed as Brigadier-Generals, General Chaffee being one of them. The term brigadier does not have the significance in other armies which it has in the United States Army, and, in any event, the American troops under orders to China constituted the units of a division. The President therefore again appointed General Chaffee to the higher grade on July 19, 1900, his full title becoming Major-General of the United States Volunteers.

While he was on his voyage to China the following characteristic letter was written to General Chaffee:

State of New York, Executive Chamber
Albany, July 10, 1900

My dear General Chaffee:

Like everyone else, I am delighted that you are to have charge of our destinies in China, for now I know that the honour of the country in that far-off land is safe. I only wish I were to have a regiment under you. It would double-discount the Vice-Presidency.

Faithfully yours,

Theodore Roosevelt

While General Chaffee was on the long voyage across the Pacific, events were moving rapidly in China to make his duty upon arrival very plain. The Ninth Infantry from Manila arrived on the transport *Logan*, off the Taku forts, at the moment when operations were about to begin against Tientsin. Colonel Liscum disembarked two battalions of his regiment, leaving the Third Battalion to bring forward the baggage, and marched to the camp on the German concession at Tientsin. On the morning of July 13, 1900, Colonel Liscum moved at three o'clock, with his two battalions, to attack the south gate of the walled city of Tientsin in a concerted action under the direction of General A. R. F. Dorward, British Army. The two battalions of the Ninth Infantry were assigned to a very difficult terrain in this action and lost heavily, among the casualties being the deeply lamented and gallant Colonel E. H. Liscum.

General Chaffee arrived at Nagasaki on July 24, 1900, and received these further instructions by cable:

Adjutant General's Office
Washington, July 19, 1900

General Chafee
     Care Hyde, Nagasaki

Secretary of War directs that you proceed at once with transport *Grant*, Sixth Cavalry and marines, to Taku, China, and take command of American land forces, which will be an independent command known as the China Relief Expedition. You will find there the Ninth and Fourteenth Infantry, one battery of the Fifth Artillery, and one battalion of marines. *Sumner* sailed from San Francisco July 17 with Second Battalion of Fifteenth Infantry and recruits to capacity of vessel.

Re-enforcements will follow to make your force in the immediate future up to 5,000 and very soon to 10,000. Full supplies, including heavy clothing, are on the way. After unloading at Taku, the supplies carried by *Grant* for your forces, send *Grant* immediately to Manila. Horses for Sixth Cavalry sailed as follows: *Leelanaw* from San Francisco, July 1, *via* Honolulu for Kobe; *Conemaugh* from San Francisco, July 1, direct to Kobe; *Lennox* from Portland, July 6, direct to Kobe. Do not wait for them, but direct that they follow you to Taku without delay. Manila will be your principal base. Arrangements have been made with the Japanese Government for using Nagasaki as secondary base and transshipment of stores coming from this country when necessary.

Immediately upon arrival at Taku, report arrival, and as soon as practicable thereafter cable your views of situation and supplies. Under one hundred and twenty-second article of war, your command will include marines on shore. Confer freely with admiral in command of fleet. Complete understanding and co-operation between the two services is enjoined by the President, and message to that effect has been sent admiral in command naval force. Reports now indicate that American minister with all the legation have been destroyed in Pekin. Chinese representative here, however, insists to the contrary, and there is, therefore, a hope which you will not lose sight of until certainty is absolute.

It is the desire of the government to maintain its relations of friendship with the part of Chinese people and Chinese officials not concerned in outrages on Americans. Among those we consider Li Hung Chang, just appointed viceroy of Chili. You will, to the extent of your power, aid the Government of China, or any part thereof, in repressing such outrages and in rescuing Americans, and in protecting American citizens and interests, and wherever Chinese Government fails to render such protection you will do all in your power to supply it.

Confer freely with commanders of other national forces, act concurrently with them, and seek entire harmony of action along the lines of similar purpose and interest. There should be full and free conference as to operations before they are entered upon. You are at liberty to agree with them from time to time as to a common official direction of the various forces in their combined operations, preserving, however, the integrity of your own American division, ready to be used as a separate and complete organisation. Much must be left to your wise discretion and that of the admiral. At all times report fully and freely to this department your wants and views. The President has today appointed you Major-General of Volunteers. Qualify and mail oath of office. Acknowledge. Corbin

As soon as the *Grant* had taken on board a supply of coal General Chaffee sailed for Taku Bay, arriving there at daylight on July 29. At eight o'clock he went aboard the *Brooklyn* and had a conference with Admiral Remey. He then went aboard the hospital ship *Solace* and visited the wounded from the Battle of Tientsin. As soon as a vessel could be provided, he went to Tongku, spending the night aboard the naval station ship *Monocacy*. Facilities for unloading the ships were inadequate, but, leaving matters in the hands of two energetic officers, he hurried to Tientsin as rapidly as possible on a houseboat which had been captured by the navy from the Chinese. General Chaffee arrived at Tientsin at 11:40 a.m. on July 30, 1900. He immediately called on the generals in command of troops of other nations, and a conference was arranged to be held on August 1 at the headquarters of Lieutenant-General Linivitch.

At this conference there were present Lieutenant-General Linivitch, of the Russian Army; Lieutenant-General Yamaguchi, of the Japanese Army, and his chief of staff. Major-General Fukushima; Lieutenant-General Gaselee, of the British Army, and his chief of staff, General Barrow; General Frey, of the French Army; Major-General Chaffee, accompanied by Major Jesse M. Lee and a marine officer, Lieutenant Little. The Germans were represented by an officer of the German Navy.

The purpose of the conference was to decide whether the armies were ready to make a movement for the relief of Pekin. It was disclosed that the Japanese, whose forces occupied the right bank of the river in and about Tientsin, where also were stationed the British and American forces, had by numerous patrols determined that the Chinese were in considerable force in the vicinity of Pei-tsang, about seven miles up the river from Tientsin, and that they were strengthening their positions by earthworks extending from the right bank of the river westward about three miles, and from the left bank of the river eastward to the railroad embankment. The enemy's forces were estimated at from ten to twelve thousand in the vicinity of Pei-tsang, with large bodies between that place and Yang-tsun, where it was reported that their main line of defence would be encountered.

At the time of the capture of Tientsin the most positive and circumstantial accounts of the massacre of all the ministers and members of the legations in Pekin had been published and almost universally believed. The general view then held was that the duty of the Allied forces was to avenge and punish, since any opportunity to rescue had vanished. On July II, however, the American Secretary of State had secured, through the Chinese minister at Washington, the forwarding of a dispatch in the State Department cipher to the American minister at Pekin, and on July 20 received through the same channels of communication an answer in cipher from Minister Conger, saying:

> For one month we have been besieged in British legation under continued shot and shell from Chinese troops. Quick relief only can prevent general massacre.

This dispatch was made the basis of urgent pressure by General

Chaffee for an immediate movement on Pekin without awaiting the arrival of the larger force previously deemed essential to success. The first question submitted to the conference was whether a forward movement should be made at once, and this being decided in the affirmative it remained only to determine upon the details of operations. The rough weather in the bay had impeded disembarkation, but on August 3 the Sixth Cavalry and marines had gone ashore and reached Tientsin. At a further conference held that day a decision was reached that the march should begin on August 5, about fourteen thousand men of the Allied forces being available.

AMERICANS WHO WERE AT PEKIN DURING SIEGE OF LEGATIONS

By arrangement of the Allied commanders the civil government of Tientsin was furnished with a mixed military force, the American contingent numbering one hundred marines. The Sixth Cavalry, being still without horses, was left to assist the Tientsin garrison. One troop mounted was sent to join the relief column as soon as the horses were unloaded, and reported to General Chaffee on the fifth day after his departure from Tientsin. General Chaffee reported his decision and movement on Pekin to the War Department and relieved much of the great strain and anxiety. The Secretary of War addressed this note to him in reply:

War Department
Washington, August 10, 1900

Dear General:
The Lord only knows what will have happened before you get

this letter of Corbin's, but I want to put in a word of congratulation and thanks for the start you have made. Your dispatches are most delightfully clear and your success thus far most gratifying. No American soldier since the Civil War has held a position of such responsibility and moment, and none was ever followed by more hopes and prayers among his people. We have every confidence in your judgment and nerve. God bless you.

Elihu Root

Chapter 23: The Capture of Pekin

The Allied troops moved out of Tientsin during the afternoon and night of August 4 and bivouacked in the vicinity of Si-ku arsenal. At early dawn on August 5 the Japanese moved pursuant to the plan agreed upon and commenced the attack at the powder house. They drove the Chinese from their entrenchments and, sweeping rapidly along both sides of the works to the river, left no space for the deployment of the American and British troops following in column. The Japanese commander sent messages to the American and British commanders, asking them to move northward. The British faced to the right and moved in the direction indicated.

It was necessary for General Chaffee to move his command around the British force, and before the Americans could join the Japanese, they had cleared the field of the enemy to the river at Pei-tsang and the action was practically closed. The American forces continued their movement and came upon the river about one mile north and west of Pei-tsang. They were now prevented from further advance along the river, the banks having been cut and the district flooded. The Russians and French encountered similar conditions on the left bank and crossed to the right bank of the river.

Being unable to march forward on the right bank, General Chaffee visited General Yamaguchi during the night and learned that the Japanese intended to construct bridges and continue on the right bank. They had already erected a pontoon bridge at Pei-tsang, and it was determined that the American, British, French, and Russian forces should cross on this bridge and march on Yang-tsun. General Chaffee began the march at four o'clock on the morning of August 6, proceeding along the line of the railroad, the Russians, British, and French crossing and moving along the river road. When they reached a point about two miles from Yang-tsun, the Chinese were discovered occupying a position in front of the bridge, to which point the railroad and river road converged.

After consultation with Lieutenant-General Gaselee, and at his request, General Chaffee placed the Fourteenth Infantry in position to attack along the west side of the railroad, where this regiment connected with the British line. General Chaffee then moved forward on the east side of the railroad with the Ninth Infantry, the marines, and Reilly's battery, deployed to conform with the advance of the British troops and Fourteenth Infantry. General Gaselee assigned a squadron of British cavalry to operate on General Chaffee's right flank.

While the Allied forces were in the act of deploying to advance, the enemy opened fire on their right flank with artillery. Soon afterward the commander of the British cavalry reported that eight companies of Chinese infantry and three guns occupied a village directly on the right flank. General Chaffee directed a movement against it, and the enemy's guns were soon silenced and the village set on fire. While engaged in this attack General Chaffee received two urgent messages by staff officers from the British commander stating that the Fourteenth was suffering from the fire from the embankment and village being attacked by that regiment and the British, and requesting that Reilly's battery be directed to open fire in that direction.

General Chaffee was loath to do this, as his immediate command was being subjected to both artillery and infantry fire from other villages on his right. However, he went into position to assist the operations of those on the other side of the embankment. Reilly's battery had unlimbered and was about to fire when General Chaffee observed men of the Fourteenth mounting the embankment in the line of fire and ordered Captain Reilly not to open with his guns. Immediately thereafter Reilly's battery was fired upon by Chinese secreted in the corn fields within short range. The battery replied with shrapnel and, aided by the marines, soon dispersed this opposing force. The Ninth Infantry coming up on the right of Reilly's battery mistook the Chinese flag for that of the French and lost an opportunity to inflict serious damage on the Chinese troops.

Several messages had been received from the Russians requesting that care be exercised not to fire on the Russian and French troops which were advancing on Yang-tsun and would turn in their march toward the American front. As a matter of fact, neither the Russian nor the French troops were at any time in advance of the American and British lines.

The Fourteenth Infantry, supported on its left by British troops,

GENERAL CHAFFEE IN THE FIELD ON THE CHINA RELIEF EXPEDITION

assaulted the position of the Chinese and carried it. After the position was in possession of the Fourteenth Infantry and some of the British who had mingled with the American troops in the contracted area over which they had advanced, they were opened on by British and Russian batteries and suffered severely at the hands of their Allies. The losses of the Fourteenth in this action were seven killed and fifty-seven wounded. General Chaffee estimated that at least half the loss was due to the mistake of the Allies in firing on the American troops. It will be remembered that General Chaffee himself had been wounded during the Civil War when through a mistake his regiment was fired on by the Harris Light Cavalry, a part of the command to which he belonged.

General Chaffee continued his advance northward through the villages lying to the east of Yang-tsun until all opposition was overcome. The troops were then assembled at the railroad bridge. The movements had all been carried out in excessively hot weather. The men suffered greatly from want of water, and many were prostrated by the heat, two of them dying on the field. The troops remained at Yang-tsun on August 7, burying the dead and arranging the transfer of the wounded by boat to Tientsin.

In the conference at Tientsin, it had been agreed that the first step of the advance on Pekin should terminate at Yang-tsun. During the forenoon of August 7, a further conference was held at the headquarters of the Russian commander, at which it was decided to resume the forward movement next day and continue the advance to Tung-chau, where final plans would be agreed upon for the attack on Pekin.

The position in the column of march held by the Americans prevented their movement at an early hour. Marching in the heat of the day, many of the American soldiers were prostrated and remained by the roadside, usually getting forward to their commands during the night. Very little opposition was encountered, and on August 12 all the Allied commands arrived at Tung-chau, which had been evacuated by the Chinese. After reaching this point the Russian commander sent a note expressing the opinion that the troops should be given a day of rest before proceeding. This did not meet the views of the other commanders, who assembled at the Russian headquarters and advised a forward movement to take place the next day. The Russian commander stated that he must rest his troops and could not move on the following day. Time was all-important, for the lives of the besieged foreigners in Pekin were hanging in the balance. It was finally agreed that the following day, August 13, should be devoted to reconnaissance and that on August 14 the Allied forces should be concentrated at the advance line held by the Japanese.

Pursuant to the agreement, General Chaffee, on the morning of August 13, reconnoitred the road assigned to the Americans, with M Troop, Sixth Cavalry, Reilly's battery, and the Fourteenth Infantry, up to a point about seven miles from Tung-chau. Meeting no opposition, General Chaffee brought forward the remainder of his command during the night. The reconnaissance was similarly carried out by the British and Japanese troops. The Russians did not play the game as Allies. Notwithstanding the alleged need for rest, the Russian commander moved his command during the night on the road assigned for reconnaissance, straight for Pekin, and attacked the Tung-pien-men gate of the city, where the Chinese wall joins the Tatar wall. Artillery and small-arms firing continued throughout the night. General Chaffee believed the firing to be due to a final effort of the Boxers to destroy the legations.

At daylight on August 14 a Japanese staff officer came to inquire of General Chaffee as to the whereabouts of the Russians. General Chaffee believed them to have remained at Tung-chau, but was assured by the Japanese officer that they were not on the opposite side of the canal. The British troops remained at Tung-chau until the morning of August 14, conformable to the agreement that the concentration on the line seven miles from that town should take place on that day.

General Chaffee had made no preparations to advance beyond the line agreed upon except a reconnaissance by a troop of cavalry, which moved forward at 5:00 a.m., leaving equipage in camp.

Soon after the departure of the cavalry a column of about two hundred French troops passed on the road, following the cavalry, the commander of which informed General Chaffee that he was marching to join the Russian force. General Chaffee replied that there were no troops in front, but the French commander had been operating with the Russians and knew the contrary to be true.

About an hour after the cavalry reconnaissance had begun a message was brought back that the cavalry was engaged with the enemy. General Chaffee moved forward with a battalion of the Fourteenth Infantry to its support, and brushed aside the Chinese who were firing from villages on both sides of the road. By this time, about 10:00 a.m., General Chaffee had become aware of the action of the Russians and could hear firing from the direction of the area occupied by the Japanese. He sent back orders for the American troops to move forward and join the advance force, which continued its march to the wall of the Chinese city. This was scaled at 11:00 a.m. by two companies of the Fourteenth Infantry, which unfurled the flag of that regiment, the first foreign colours unfurled upon the walls of Pekin. The two companies on the wall, with the assistance of the troops facing the wall, drove the Chinese troops from the corner to the east gate of the Chinese city, where the British entered without opposition later in the day.

The Russians had battered open the Tung-pien-men gate during the night and had effected an entrance there, but had their guns facing both ways and were in confusion when General Chaffee arrived at the gate with Reilly's battery and part of the Fourteenth Infantry. These two organisations gained entrance by tearing down a wall to the left, and then by enfilade fire of shrapnel and rifle fire cleared the wall westward to the Hait-men gate. The Ninth Infantry was directed to follow the movement to the Chien-men Gate of the Tatar city. By 3:00 p.m. the American advance had arrived opposite the legations, the fire of the Chinese having practically ceased. In recognition of its gallantry at Yang-tsun and during the attack on Pekin, the Fourteenth Infantry was directed to lead the way and entered the legation grounds.

Having communicated with the American minister, Mr. Conger, General Chaffee withdrew the troops from the legation and camped near the Tatar wall for the night. The work, however, was not yet over. The minister conveyed the information that a portion of the Imperial

UNITED STATES INFANTRY MOVING UP TO THE GATE, PEKIN

AMERICAN ARTILLERY IN ACTION AGAINST THE GATE TO THE
FORBIDDEN CITY

City directly in front of the Chien-men Gate had been used by Chinese to fire on the legations, and General Chaffee determined to drive the Chinese troops from that position and made his plans accordingly.

On the morning of August 15 General Chaffee placed four guns of Reilly's battery on the Tatar wall at the Chien-men Gate and swept the walls westward to the next gate. At about 8:00 a.m. the Chinese opened fire on General Chaffee's force at the Chien-men Gate from the second gate of the Imperial City north of the Chien-men Gate. General Chaffee directed an attack on the first gate, and in a short time a platoon of Reilley's battery under Lieutenant Summerall had battered an opening through which the infantry entered. They immediately came under a severe fire from the next gate, about six hundred yards distant. Fire was directed upon the second gate by the battery and such of the infantry as could be used effectively on the Tatar wall and side walls of the Imperial City. In the course of half an hour the Chinese fire had been silenced, and Colonel Daggett led his regiment, the Fourteenth Infantry, forward to the second gate. The same course was pursued with four gates, the Chinese troops being driven from each gate in succession, the fourth gate being near the palace grounds.

During the attack upon the gates Captain H. J. Reilly, the battery commander, standing at General Chaffee's left elbow, watching the effect of the fire from one of his guns, was shot in the mouth and killed.

When all opposition of the enemy had been overcome, a conference was held, at which the Allied commanders decided not to occupy the Imperial City. General Chaffee then withdrew his troops to the camp occupied the previous night, but retained the position held on the Tatar wall at the Chien-men Gate. The decision of the generals not to occupy the Imperial City was not concurred in by the ministers at a conference held by them. In consequence the imperial grounds were immediately reoccupied, the Americans resuming the position held at the conclusion of the fighting.

General Chaffee found time, when the fighting was apparently all over, to send this modest announcement by cable:

Pekin, August 15

Adjutant General
   Washington
We entered Legation's grounds at five o'clock last night with Fourteenth and Light Battery. Eight wounded during day's fighting; otherwise, all well.   Chaffee

Nothing of vainglory to be found there, nor in the next cable message, which followed at the close of the fighting on the same day:

Pekin, August 15

Adjutant General
Washington

Legation relieved last night. Purpose of expedition being accomplished, what is the further wish of government as regards use of troops? No more will be required as a relief force. Apprehend considerable difficulty supplying large force during winter about Pekin. The railway must be rebuilt if we stop here. Cannot get satisfactory answer about the matter yet. Suggest withdrawal of United States troops soon as practicable from China. Under present circumstances request full instructions for my future guidance and as basis for preparation of supplies. Henry J. Reilly, Captain Fifth Artillery, killed 9 this morning.

Chaffee

Before his dispatches, which had to go over a long and much-relayed cable route, were acknowledged he viewed conditions in a somewhat different light, and the result was communicated in the following message:

Pekin, August 18

Adjutant General
Washington

Conference today decided absolutely necessary to maintain troops in Pekin for winter; that railway be repaired at once; that this matter should be immediately reported to Governments interested by military commanders. The Russian commander will not push the work single-handed, and proposes that each nation repair a section of the road as a military measure. Could not consent to this, having no material or means to obtain any. Much trouble to keep telegraph working; cut frequently.

Chaffee

The policy under which the American government was acting was announced in this form:

Adjutant General's Office
Washington, August 23, 1900

General Chaffee
Commanding United States Forces
Pekin *via* Taku

Your dispatch of August 15 received. Secretary of War directs me to say no more troops will be sent you. Those under way will be ordered to Manila, leaving you about 5,000 effectives, including marines.

Following statement of American policy was communicated to all the powers by circular letter July 3:

"The purpose of the President is to act concurrently with the other powers: First, in opening up communication and rescuing the American officials, missionaries, and other Americans who are in danger; secondly, in affording all possible protection everywhere in China to American life and property; thirdly, in guarding and protecting all legitimate American interests; and fourthly, in aiding to prevent a spread of the disorders to the other provinces of the Empire and a recurrence of such disasters. It is, of course, too early to forecast the means of attaining this last result; but the policy of the Government of the United States is to seek a solution which may bring about permanent safety and peace to China, preserve Chinese territorial and administrative entity, protect all rights guaranteed to friendly powers by treaty and international law, and safeguard for the world the principle of equal and impartial trade with all parts of the Chinese Empire.

"We desire to withdraw all troops from China as soon as practicable, but attainment of ends specified requires that occupation of Pekin should continue for the present, and that you should with the troops under your command do your share toward maintaining the *status quo* and preserving order. We wish no aggressive action unless that be necessary for defensive purposes. We have no report yet of arrangements for bringing inmates of legation to the coast. It seems as if this should be done as promptly as consistent with safety to all women, children, and men not charged with official duties and in fit condition to perform them, but whether this ought to be done you and Conger can best judge. Give us timely notice to provide transportation for them from Taku to Japan or this country. Li Hung Chang, as plenipotentiary of China, now asks cessation of hostilities and appointment of envoy to conduct negotiations."

We have answered as follows:

"While the condition set forth in the memorandum delivered

to the Chinese minister August 12 has not been fulfilled, and the powers have been compelled to rescue their ministers by force of arms, unaided by the Chinese Government, still this Government is ready to welcome any overtures for a truce and invite the other powers to join when security is established in the Chinese capital, and the Chinese Government shows its ability and willingness to make on its part an effective suspension of hostilities there and elsewhere in China. When this is done, and we hope it will be done promptly, the United States will be prepared to appoint a representative to join with the representatives of the other similarly interested powers and of the authoritative and responsible Government of the Chinese Empire to attain the ends declared in our circular to the powers of July 3, 1900."

Show this to Conger.   Corbin

GENERAL CHAFFEE ENTERING PEKIN WITH ARTILLERY

From the day on which he had received his instructions to start on the long journey, nearly half around the world, to rescue the besieged legation from its perilous plight, General Chaffee had concentrated his mind solely upon the accomplishment of that purpose. The object achieved, he turned his attention to the solution of the many unfamiliar problems of the Orient, rendered doubly complicated by the entire absence of established civil government. Nevertheless, it was with genuine pride that he announced to the men who had followed and fought with him on the gruelling march from Tientsin the words of gratitude and praise which now came to him as the commander of the China Relief Expedition. The American minister wrote to General Chaffee:

From the moment of the arrival of the Allied relief column we have all tried personally to express our joy and gratitude for your timely coming. I am not satisfied, however, with this mere verbal acknowledgment. The patriotic purpose with which you hurried more than half around the world, the heroic courage displayed, and the tremendous sacrifices made in your victorious march from Tientsin to Pekin deserve a more fervent expression of our sincere appreciation and profound gratitude than can ever be given. But, dear general, I beg you, on behalf of all whom you saved, to accept for yourself, and to extend in large measure to the brave men who came with you, the sincerest thanks that grateful hearts can feel. We deeply deplore the loss of the splendid heroes who died that we might live, and our tenderest sympathies go out to the bleeding hearts never to be solaced by their return. We pray God to comfort them and to reward and bless you one and all.

The nation's rejoicing because of the relief of the besieged legations was communicated to the American minister by President McKinley:

The whole American people rejoice over your deliverance, over the safety of your companions, of our own and of the other nations which have shared your trials and privations, the fortitude and courage which you have all maintained, and the heroism of your little band of defenders. We all mourn for those who have fallen, and acknowledge the goodness of God, which has preserved you and guided the brave army that set you free."

Nothing in his official life gave the Secretary of War more satisfaction than the knowledge that General Chaffee had achieved the object of the expedition. He had selected him as the commander of the expedition solely because of his incomparable military record, and it was with sincere pleasure that he indited this message to him:

The President joins me in congratulations to you and the officers and men of your command on the brilliant achievement in which the courage, fortitude, and skill of the American forces in China have played so honourable a part. While mourning for your fallen comrades, the whole country is proud and grateful for your great success. The nation had waited in a state of feverish anxiety the result of the race of the Allied columns with death. When the message announcing the relief of the besieged legations was received, a wave of deepest satisfaction and pride in the achievements of General Chaffee and his command surged through the hearts of the American people.

Chapter 24: Allies Assume Control in Pekin

In an effort to burn out the Europeans all the buildings to the west of the American legation had been destroyed by the Boxers. They had ruthlessly applied the torch to every building in which Chinese merchants sold any kind of foreign goods. So numerous were the fires that they soon got beyond control, and the rich commercial portion of the Chinese city was almost entirely ruined. The sanitary conditions were indescribable. Unburied bodies, carcasses of animals, stagnant pools, and all that goes to make war horrible were in evidence on every hand. When the legation was entered, all the signs of a long and trying siege were visible. Many of the legations were in ruins.

The American legation remained and was occupied, but everywhere bore the scars of shot and shell. The children, white and wan from lack of proper nourishment, presented a pitiable sight. The legation had been reduced to a very limited diet, composed in the main of a small piece of horse or mule meat daily to each individual, all of whom were endeavouring to sustain life at the last only in the knowledge that General Chaffee and his brave soldiers were fighting their way to Pekin with the Allied columns.

At a conference of the Allied commanders on the afternoon of August 16 an agreement was reached for taking over the captured city of Pekin and the restoration and preservation of order. The territory was divided into sections and placed under control of the various Allied forces. The American troops were assigned to the west half of the Chinese city and to that section of the Tatar city lying between the Chien-men Gate and Shunchin gate of the south wall of the Tatar city, and north to the east and west street through the Tatar city, being bounded upon the east by the wall of the Imperial City.

The Chinese are a credulous and superstitious people. As long as there had been no demonstration of the complete fall of the Imperial City, they might consider that the occupation had been prevented by the interposition of the gods. A conference of the ministers and Allied commanders was held on August 25, when the question of a formal entry into the Forbidden City was determined upon by a vote of the Allied commanders, all of the Europeans voting in the affirmative. The American and Japanese commanders voted in the negative. In making a note of this action General Chaffee wrote:

> I opposed the performance as one based on curiosity merely and not one of military or political necessity, but was overruled. The city of Peking has been sacked; looted from corner to corner in the most disgraceful manner imaginable; such is my opinion. I had no idea that civilised armies would resort to such proceedings. It is a race for spoil. I have kept my own command fairly clean, thank God, but with all my efforts it is not spotless. It is only once in a lifetime, I can imagine, that one witnesses the march of foreign armies through the Heathen's reservation. It requires but one example of the sort I have witnessed to convince one that every nation's hand is against the Chinese Empire—innocent and guilty. The United States alone, of all the powers, may not wish to see the Chinese Empire destroyed, but she will not be able to stay the march of events.

The question of precedence—as to who should lead the entry—was discussed with some warmth. Precedence was desired by the Japanese for the very good reasons that they had the largest force and had done the greater proportion of the work. The Russians claimed first place because they were first in the city. Thereupon General Chaffee took occasion to remind the Russian commander that he was first at the gate because he had violated an explicit agreement not to start on the last day's march against Pekin until 8:00 a.m. by advancing secretly at ten o'clock the night before, and that even then the Russians were stalled at the gate until the Americans pushed forward and passed them. In view of his seniority, it was finally arranged that General Linivitch should lead the column, which comprised eight hundred Russians, eight hundred Japanese, four hundred English, four hundred Americans, four hundred French, two hundred and fifty Germans, sixty Austrians, and sixty Italians. The spectators were limited to a few reporters and photographers. No Christian had ever been permitted to enter the sacred precincts of the Forbidden City, and the procession of representatives of the foreign armies rent asunder the veil of mystery with which the Chinese had surrounded it.

As has been said, in the attack on Pekin General Chaffee's forces

AMERICAN BATTERY IN ACTION AGAINST PEKIN

AMERICAN TROOPS ENTERING THE FORBIDDEN CITY

entered on the eastern side and, after battering open the gates of three walls in succession, had arrived at the wall of the Imperial Palace. In a few minutes more the gate of the Forbidden City would have been blown down by the guns of Reilly's battery, but the Allied generals called a conference and operations were suspended to the great chagrin of the American troops, who not only were despoiled of the honour, but were compelled to withdraw under fire from the advanced position won by them. It was agreed that guards should be stationed at the gates and that the Imperial City should not be occupied. The agreement was violated by the Russians, whose commander could not be relied upon to keep faith. Duplicity and sharp practice are not uncommon in the history of diplomacy. The Russian commander seemed to mistake resourceful cunning for cleverness.

After one or two experiences with his military diplomacy General Chaffee lost faith and trusted no agreement thereafter. It was essential that no open rupture should occur among the Allied commanders, and General Chaffee managed to bear his disappointments with more equanimity than might have been expected of one of his character and temperament.

While the powers were exchanging views concerning the best plan for united action of the Allied troops, the Emperor of Germany offered to place at the disposal of the other governments concerned Field Marshal Count von Waldersee, who might be, in the capacity of commander-in-chief, intrusted with the direction of the operations of the international forces concentrated in China in the Pekin region.

The official Russian memorandum in reply stated:

His Majesty the Emperor, animated with the desire that the complications which have arisen in the Far East be settled as soon as possible, replied that, on his part, he saw no objection to accepting the proposition of Emperor William, considering that, since considerable international forces are concentrated on Chinese territory, unity of action becomes necessary as the essential condition of a successful completion of their task; also, that the high station of Count Waldersee, in his capacity of Field Marshal, confers upon him a paramount right to the direction of the operations of the various detachments called upon to co-operate in the same common object, and finally that considerations of a moral order, which may, in the present case, have inspired Germany, whose representative was heinously murdered at Peking, justify her in her desire to take the lead of the international forces operating against Chinese insurgents. It must be borne in mind, however, that by consenting to place the Russian detachment under the common to all and supreme command of the German Field Marshal, His Majesty the Emperor does not intend to depart in any manner from the political programme upon whose fundamental principles a complete agreement has been reached with France, as well as with the other powers. Russia is seeking no selfish end; she only aims at a general pacification and at restoring as promptly as possible relations of good neighbourliness with China, and she remains true to her historical traditions. Should more decisive military action become necessary by reason of the continuance of disturbances in the Chinese Empire, she would not forsake the humane principles that have at all times been the pride of the Russian Army.

Count von Waldersee was the chief assistant of Count von Moltke, who was at the head of the great General Staff of Germany. Upon the death of von Moltke, Count von Waldersee was assigned to command the Ninth Army Corps, At the time of his selection for the Chinese command he was one of five army inspectors with the rank of general field marshal. He had for years been looked upon as the man who would take charge in case Germany should become involved in a European war. At the time of his Pekin assignment, he was sixty-eight years old, thin, active, and a hard rider.

Japan and all the European nations represented by troops in China consented to Count von Waldersee's assignment to the command with direction of the Allied forces. The question was then broached to the American government and the views of General Chaffee were asked for:

Washington, August 7, 1900

General Chaffee:
State Department is advised by Berlin Embassy that Russia is willing to put Russian troops in China under Field Marshal Waldersee as commander-in-chief, and Japan also prefers Waldersee. German government asks views of United States as to chief command, and in which way it would be inclined to join American forces in China to army operating under Waldersee. Your views desired soon as possible.   Root
Secretary of War

The idea of joining forces for further operations in China did

GROUP OF OFFICERS OF ALLIED ARMIES IN CHINA. GENERAL CHAFFEE THIRD FROM RIGHT
SEATED ON LEFT OF LIEUTENANT GENERAL YAMAGUCHI

not appeal to General Chaffee. After Pekin had been captured all the
regular Chinese troops had been withdrawn out of reach and took
no further part against the Allies. General Chaffee communicated his
objections to further operations:

Pekin, August 22, 1900

Adjutant General
  Washington
Do not advise United States place its forces under chief command Count Waldersee. Suggest withdrawal of United States
troops soon as practicable from China.   Chaffee

General Chaffee amplified his views later:

Pekin, August 29, 1900

Adjutant General
  Washington
Military object accomplished, my opinion our troops should
withdraw from China, if possible, to permit. Supply of the army
during winter will be difficult, but the most serious aspect of
the situation is the terrible suffering of the million people in
Pekin and other millions about because of destruction of property and almost annihilation of commerce, trade, and business
in every form. The presence of the army for six months or
more will aggravate in the worst manner the woeful situation

growing worse each day.

In short time food supply will be exhausted Pekin. Population idle and hungry now. No government forage in the city; more than thirty thousand troops. Chaos and starvation inevitable throughout all the section have seen, if army remains. Conditions Tientsin no better Pekin. Hostilities certain to be resumed and make difficult for Chinese authorities to control situation if army remains. Japanese and English military commanders think with me that troops should be withdrawn, but they are without instructions from home. Seriousness of the situation more apparent each day to all the military commanders, and prompt decision whether or not armies are to remain during the winter very important.

Some prospect Prince Ching, uncle of Emperor, may come here in about a week with power to act. Minister Conger thinks negotiations should be hastened so that troops may be withdrawn before winter. Regards the outlook as most serious and only source of relief withdrawal of army or at least reduction to reasonable guard for legation if they remain. This is the general situation, but submitted with special reference to instructions respecting United States troops under my command. Have supplies Tongku and Tientsin to last to October first.

Chaffee

The Chinese government had abandoned Pekin before the entry of the Allied troops into the city. The primary object of the expedition, the relief of the besieged legations, having been accomplished, it had been expected that the Chinese government would resume control and that the Boxer revolution would terminate. General Chaffee communicated his views in this dispatch:

Pekin, September 4, 1900

Adjutant General
  Washington

Evidence accumulates diplomatic relations will not be resumed here for long time. Russian legation leave very soon for Tientsin. Appears to me certain Chinese Government will not return here whilst foreign army remains, and if this true our legation transact no business. My opinion Pekin to be merely camp foreign army pending settlement by powers at other points.

Chaffee

The Boxers had withdrawn from the immediate vicinity and were no longer aggressive beyond firing on scouting and foraging parties. The American troops took part in numerous expeditions to break up the bands of Boxers, but it was fully recognised that neither the insurgents nor the Chinese Imperial troops were in any condition for operations against the invading troops of the Allies. The American government finally decided to countermand all orders for the additional troops which had been directed to join General Chaffee's command, and approved his recommendation for a legation guard to include two regiments of infantry, the Ninth and Fourteenth, the Third Squadron, Sixth Cavalry, and Reilly's battery, all of which had rendered splendid service during the active operations in China.

When Count von Waldersee arrived in China, the Allied commanders, under instructions from their respective governments, reported their troops to him. General Chaffee was opposed to reporting the American troops, and his views had been approved. Before proceeding from Tientsin to Pekin Count von Waldersee organised a combined movement of troops from the garrisons of Pekin and Tientsin. In reporting his refusal to participate in the operations General Chaffee sent the following dispatch:

Pekin, October 4, 1900

Adjutant General
  Washington
Expedition about 4,000 strong leaves here for Pao-ting-fu today; co-operating force about 7,000 from Tientsin; ordered by Field Marshal Waldersee; purpose of movement not apparent; certainly not defensive proposition in my opinion.

★★★★★★★★★★

The following extract from Dawson, *Out of Their Own Mouths*, is of interest in this connection: "You know very well that you are to fight against the cunning, brave, well-armed and terrible enemy. If you come to grips with him, be assured quarter will not be given, no prisoners will be taken. Use your weapons in such a way that for a thousand years no Chinese shall dare to look upon a German askance." Speech made by William II to the German Expeditionary Force, July 27, 1900.

★★★★★★★★★★

United States troops will not participate in movement. Japanese troops from here probably move with Tientsin column, as Japanese minister is opposed to movement as being contrary instructions his government. Result is likely to postpone, for considerable time, arriving at condition for negotiation with Chinese representatives. My opinion to cause delay of negotiation is real object of expedition to Pao-ting-fu, although it is reported that there are three Belgian engineers in danger at Cheng-ting-fu, which is fifty miles south of Pao-ting-fu. Two American officers accompany expedition. There is unconfirmed report that Li Hung Chang has ordered Chinese troops to withdraw from Pao-ting-fu, if any foreign troops approach place. Have not heard of any hostile Chinese movement or force of consequence for a month.

All such reported have been found on examination to amount to practically nothing. Occasional shots are fired, if not at, to frighten foraging parties of two or three men by villagers. Do not hear of soldiers being killed or wounded by these real or supposed Boxers. Order has gradually improved along our line communication since indiscriminate firing by troops has been stopped. In Pekin Chinese are very orderly; returning to business where protected, notably in Japanese and American section. Under my instructions August 23, I cannot take part in any movement which, in my judgment, has tendency to promote rather than allay hostilities and unquiet in surrounding country. Have not placed my force under orders of field marshal for reason that from my instructions United States does not wish its troops to engage in offensive work. Li Hung Chang arrived Pekin yesterday; he calls on me this afternoon.

Chaffee

Upon receipt of the message in Washington General Chaffee was immediately informed that his entire course of action was fully approved by the Secretary of War.

The arrival of Field Marshal von Waldersee at Pekin was expected, and General von Hoepfner had several conferences with the Allied commanders, with a view to arranging the ceremonies contemplated at his reception by the troops. It was finally decided to have a cavalry squadron meet Count von Waldersee outside of the city and escort him through lines of troops from the Hait-men to the Emperor's Winter Palace, where the march should take place. In his notes of the ceremony one of General Chaffee's staff wrote:

On October 17, 1900, at 11:30 a.m. the boom of cannon announced the arrival of the commander-in-chief. At the Winter Palace the selected companies constituting the guard of honour executed a march past in column of fours. The Germans were all picked men, accurately sized, and executed an unusually high parade step, their knees going up as high as their elbows and their hobnailed boots coming down on the pavement with a whack. The march of the Americans at "port arms" without any ostentation was finely done, and made a good impression. The English and Japanese also did well. The French were a little better than usual; the Italians were disgraceful. It was a great opportunity to make notes of all the different kinds of uniforms. The field marshal looked well in his uniform of the Prussian *Uhlans*.

On December 11, 1900, General Chaffee wrote:

We have settled down to almost a dreary, monotonous life, pending operations of the ministers in their diplomatic fashion, which seems slow, but may not be after all. The subject is no doubt a weighty one when considered from all the points of view which can be, and no doubt will be, presented by eight or ten gentlemen when discussing the matter together. It must be a difficult matter to keep in the "middle of the road," when, as I fancy, there are several who wish to travel both sides as well, in order that nothing may escape. I have often thought that strict justice is not all that some have in view, but I may be mistaken. Poor, foolish old China will find her account a big one, and that foolishness costs dearly sometimes.

Chapter 25: Winter Quarters in Pekin

As the American troops were never placed under the control of Field Marshal von Waldersee, General Chaffee did not personally participate in any of the punitive expeditions sent out from Pekin and Tientsin. He established his headquarters in the Temple of Agriculture. This temple consisted of a number of detached buildings, more or less pretentious and elaborately decorated in the best Chinese temple style. The buildings stood in a vast park, wherein grew magnificent cedar trees unequalled outside of China and to be found there only in places under the special protection of the government. To make the temple buildings meet military needs certain alterations had to be made. These alterations were limited to ceilings and partitions, readily removed, which did not injure the buildings or their approaches in any way.

Upon the occupation of Pekin by the Allied forces it was found that the Chinese officials had left the city. No form of Chinese civil government remained. The city was at once divided into a number of administrative districts, and to each of the Allied forces was assigned one district. Most of the civilian population had fled. Valuable property was left in palaces, homes, and shops. The troops of some of the powers looted officially; others without official authority, but with equal facility. Chinese thieves operated industriously.

General Chaffee's orders against looting and cruelty to the Chinese were positive and admitted of no misunderstanding. Conditions, however, tended to demoralisation, and individuals belonging to the American forces did some looting, A sudden and minute inspection by the officers revealed a quantity of loot in the camps of the American troops. Wherever possible the property was restored to the owners; that not so disposed of was burned in the presence of the looters.

On August 26 two native Indian soldiers—sikhs—engaged in looting were discovered by an American patrol. They were ordered to halt, but sought refuge across the line of their own district and opened fire on the patrol. Two shots were fired in return, and both looters were killed. The members of the patrol were commended for their marksmanship and exonerated by a court martial; the good effect on the situation was marked. The measures of the American commander made it very clear that he intended that his men should protect the property and persons of the Chinese. His suppression of looting and the kind treatment accorded the Chinese brought about a return of confidence and the resumption of business in the American section long before it was resumed elsewhere, except in the portion of the city controlled by the Japanese.

At the time when the original division of the city was made no German forces were present. Upon their arrival, a few weeks later, a new partition of the city was made and an area carved out and turned over for policing and administration by the German troops. The area taken over by them embraced the Chinese Astronomical Observatory. With scientific precision the ancient astronomical instruments were dismantled and prepared for shipment to Germany as trophies. The instruments were of bronze, of curious design but of doubtful utility. Their chief value was that of curios. That this ancient observatory should be despoiled caused General Chaffee much indignation, which he expressed with so much more force than diplomacy, in a letter to Count von Waldersee, that a serious rupture of friendly rela-

GENERAL CHAFFEE AND STAFF AT PEKIN

tions with the German headquarters was threatened for a time. The instruments were shipped to Germany, but the indignation raised by General Chaffee's protest had much influence in causing their return to China.

Out of the government of the so-called American section of Pekin many difficult problems arose, in the solution of which General Chaffee habitually brought to bear equity rather than law. He endeavoured to secure justice to individuals rather than to construct a judicial system. After a time, the confidence of the Chinese in the security of life and property returned to such an extent that conditions again approached the normal state of affairs. Chinese policemen were then employed, and the Chinese courts were reestablished for the trial, under the Chinese laws and customs, of all cases arising between Chinese, the Allied commanders reserving to themselves only the power of final action in capital cases.

In all sections of the city except that under the administration of the Americans executions became a common occurrence. General Chaffee, however, steadfastly declined to approve the death sentences imposed upon criminals. While willing to use the fire action of his command against the Chinese in the most effective manner in battle, as a civil administrator he hesitated to sign a death warrant. His leniency soon caused criminals to seek refuge in the American section. A party of Chinese robbers made a bold attack with swords upon an old man and his daughter, and were captured by the American guard.

After long and serious consideration General Chaffee approved the death warrants. The offenders were beheaded on the following day, this action serving effectually to halt the wave of crime which had been making headway in the American section.

A vast amount of public property was captured by the invading columns of the Allies. That portion which came under American control included about thirty million dollars of bullion and hundreds of tons of rice in the Imperial granaries. A considerable quantity of rice was used to relieve hunger among the poor and needy, the remainder and all the bullion which had been held intact being delivered to the Chinese authorities upon the restoration of the Imperial Government in Pekin.

Delay in reaching a decision as to the further retention of General Chaffee and his command in China was very embarrassing as winter approached, and the date of freezing of the River Pei-ho was problematical. When the danger point was reached. General Chaffee felt constrained to ignore his instructions to hold his supplies at Tientsin and Taku awaiting a decision. He assembled a fleet of junks and rushed the needed stores to Pekin before ice closed the river. He knew that his instructions had been given during a parley of the diplomats on the other side of the world and that probably the urgency of the situation had been forgotten while the icy winter was forging the chains to cripple and starve his command. He therefore acted according to the dictates of his own wise judgment.

During the winter in Pekin General Chaffee spent much of each day in riding horseback. In one of his letters, he wrote:

Today I rode to the Lama Temple, where we saw the great wooden god seventy feet high and other wooden gods large and small. The priests are a sorry looking lot; unlike the Chinese generally, the hair is cut short. The temple is a place that may interest one to visit once—never a second time. This I can say for all the temples here, so far as I am concerned. All Imperial structures are disappointing to me; having seen one, the others can be mentally photographed, such is the sameness of construction and decoration. The Summer Palace grounds are really quite pretty, but only so in comparison with things Peking—no other place. If you have a map, note "Agricultural Temple" grounds, a large walled section near the south wall of the Chinese city. It is our "compound." A walled enclosure is a compound out here. Before the Emperor got into trouble with all his good friends, and cut their acquaintance by going "West," it was his custom to come out here once each year, plant a hill of corn, and pray for double ears per stalk. In his absence we find it a very good camping ground for the battery, squadron, and five companies of infantry.

Everything very quiet here. This is a good place to learn patience. We know that we must wait about six weeks before we can read the happenings in the States, of events which we get hints of as liable to occur, about which we want to read the details.

To relieve the monotony of garrison life the British, Germans, and others arranged race days at the course near Pekin. As no time records were kept, it may be readily understood that the horses entered would hardly be eligible for the Derby. There were many dinners and occasional military ceremonies. On the day following Christmas, 1900, General Chaffee wrote:

Today I was present at a review of the German troops by the field marshal, and presentation by him of new flags to the regiment. It was a very ceremonious military spectacle, and was executed with the precision of a clock. One would think the whole affair rehearsed and gone through with a dozen times before today, but not so. Once before the troops had been fitted to the ground—last Saturday—and I think that today each soldier knew exactly where he was to place himself and how to move from place to place. The German parade step and the carriage of head and eyes—the bold stare—would make you laugh, perhaps, but the next minute you would certainly applaud. One could read on the face of every man—"I am a German soldier—Hurrah for the Emperor and Fatherland—the world is looking and I am proud to show it what I can do. I took with me a hundred infantry and a hundred cavalry in order that our men might see how a military function is conducted by experts.

After the Germans had left the grounds, our troops marched by the marshal. The men looked well and marched well, but we have not the snap about us that is so marked a feature of soldiering with German troops.

Count von Waldersee occupied the Winter Palace as his headquarters. The buildings caught fire during the night and burned so rapidly that the count was barely rescued, being taken from his apartment through the window. His chief of staff, General Schwarzhoff, perished

149

in the flames. The count lost another of his superior officers in a peculiar way. He was on one of the punitive expeditions undertaken by the Germans and went to sleep in a Chinese house, leaving a charcoal fire in his room. He was found dead the next morning.

Upon the arrival of the mail, it was General Chaffee's custom to read carefully the American newspapers. One day Li Hung Chang with two secretaries and a retinue of servants made an unheralded social call and found General Chaffee surrounded by a pile of newspapers which he had been reading. After an exchange of greetings Li Hung Chang said:

"I see you have mail from America. Is there any news?"

"Oh, nothing much. I see we are having a severe drought and the preachers are praying for rain."

"Do the Christian preachers pray for rain?"

"Yes, when they need it badly."

"Do they get it?"

"Sometimes they do and sometimes they do not."

"Well, that is just the way the Chinese Joss God does," returned Li Hung Chang.

In writing of the visit General Chaffee said:

Li Hung Chang was out to call on me yesterday. I suppose it is not news to you that no power has any confidence in him except the United States, unless it be Russia, and it is the general idea that he is all too friendly toward Russia, hence the dislike of him.

The United States is far away, so the earl can, if not sincere, make expressions of friendship to stay her at a distance. But from my four conversations with him I think him entirely sincere in his expressions of friendship and appreciation by China for the course the United States has steadily followed in this matter. He never fails to express his great appreciation of the manner in which our troops have dealt with the people at large—refraining from indiscriminate shooting and having little part in the general looting of Pekin and none at all in the adjacent towns. There is excuse, and if the business had been confined to necessity, nothing could have been said. Many troops, ours in some respects, were hurried here inadequately supplied, and the country had to be drawn upon to make good the deficit; only in transportation were we deficient.

Earl Li was very inquisitive about our equipment, especially our rifle and carbine.

He witnessed the parade of the Ninth Infantry at retreat, and when the flag was lowered, the band playing the "Star Spangled Banner," he shook his own hands, Chinese fashion, very warmly.

LETTER FROM LI HUNG CHANG TO GENERAL CHAFFEE

When Washington and his brother-officers of the Revolution met together and organised the Society of the Cincinnati, they set an example which has been followed in our other wars. Out of the Mexican War grew the Aztec Society; out of the Civil War, the Loyal Legion; out of the Cuban campaign, the Society of Santiago. Following this custom, the officers of the China Relief Expedition assembled in Pekin during the early days of October, 1900, and organised the Military Order of the Dragon, provision being made for admitting to honorary membership the officers of foreign armies on service in China between June 15 and October 1, 1900. General Chaffee was elected president of the society and continued in the office until his retirement from active service, when he resigned.

Soon after this society was organised the commander of the Japanese forces in China, General Yamaguchi, called upon General Chaffee to inform him that the Japanese Government desired to bestow upon

151

him the "Order of the Rising Sun." General Chaffee wrote a letter of thanks and acquainted the Japanese commander with the restriction placed on American officials in the matter of receiving decorations and with the fact that our government had no reciprocal honours to bestow upon foreign officers.

During the winter of 1901 a reorganisation of the army was undertaken by Congress to meet the increasing demands of peace and to enable the President to discharge many thousands of Volunteers still on duty in the Philippine Islands. The act was approved on February 2, 1901, and two days later General Chaffee was advanced from Colonel of Regulars to Major-General in the permanent organisation. At that time, he held temporary rank as Major-General of Volunteers. The officers of the British force seemed quite as delighted with his promotion as were his own officers, A few nights later the British officers surprised General Chaffee with a genuine ovation. He endeavoured to express his appreciation, but was overcome with emotion and embarrassment. After his remarks were concluded, the enthusiastic British comrades actually carried him on their shoulders to his quarters. Altogether it was a most memorable occasion and is still mentioned with pride by American officers who had foregathered at the Temple of Heaven on that night.

In writing to the Secretary of War, Elihu Root, to express his appreciation of the promotion given him as a reward for his services, not alone in China, but during a long and exceptional military career, General Chaffee said:

> I am unable to pledge greater devotion and purpose to serve faithfully, to the best of my ability, my country, in the future than it has been my constant pleasure to do in the past—at times, too, when stars did not figure as tokens of reward."

General Chaffee's promotion, as well as his course in China, met with general approval. He had won the esteem of Colonel Roosevelt at Santiago, and in far-away Pekin it warmed his heart to receive this generous letter:

The Vice-President's Chamber
Washington, D.C, March 16, 1901
Major-General Adna R. Chafee
My dear General: I want one of my first letters as Vice-President to be a note of congratulation to you. I ought by rights to put it as a note of congratulation to our people and the army

upon your advancement. We are all your debtors for what you have done in China—for everything, from the way you fought, to the way you have done justice, and the stand you have taken on matters generally, including your letter to Waldersee. I got a glimpse of Mrs. Chaffee last fall and greatly enjoyed it. I look forward to seeing you again.

Faithfully yours,

Theodore Roosevelt

The letter to Count von Waldersee referred to by the Vice-President, and previously mentioned as endangering relations between the American and German headquarters in Pekin, was written under serious provocation connected with other incidents. General Chaffee recognised later that diplomacy called for gentler words, but his outspoken, blunt characterisation of the deed did not injure him in the least. The letter is as follows:

Headquarters China Relief Expedition

Pekin, China, December 3, 1900

Your Excellency:

Having heard that the astronomical instruments are being removed from the observatory, an officer of my staff went there yesterday and, on his return, confirms the report. I have the honour to inform Your Excellency that my government would vehemently denounce any officer of its service who might enter upon spoliation of this sort, and it will sincerely regret to learn that any nation with which it co-operated to relieve the besieged Legations in Peking authorises or permits its troops to injure or remove any instruments or other part of the observatory. As commander of one of the four co-operating columns which relieved the Legations on August 14, I make to you respectful protest in this matter, and shall inform my government of the fact.   With assurances of high esteem,

Very respectfully.

Your obedient servant,

Adna R. Chaffee

Major-General U.S.V.

Commanding U.S. Troops, China Relief Expedition

Field Marshal Count von Waldersee
Commanding Allied Forces

It was deemed advisable from a diplomatic point of view to rebuke

General Chaffee mildly:

Adjutant General's Office
Washington, December 5, 1900

Chafee
Pekin

Referring to your dispatch giving substance of communication to Count Waldersee regarding taking of instruments from observatory, the President regrets the severity of the language which appears to have been used.   Corbin

It should be borne in mind that the Germans did not participate in the movement from Tientsin to Pekin, but arrived after the armed resistance had ceased. They were enraged at the assassination of their ambassador by the Boxers, but General Chaffee regarded the aftermath of vengeance as murder and spoliation unjustified in the absence of organised resistance.

The garrison life at Pekin was full of interest, but General Chaffee was impatient at the delay in the re-establishment of the Chinese government and was continually incensed at the manner in which many of the Allies robbed and destroyed without reference to guilt or innocence of individual Chinese. He wrote at that time:

I presume the feeling is quite general that time is being unnecessarily consumed in the settlement of the Chinese question. It does seem so over here when one inquires from time to time regarding the progress made, and is informed that the day was spent in talking and that the next meeting would be a week hence. So far as my observation goes, the Chinese, heretofore regarded as being unequalled for procrastination, have been quite as prompt in compliance as have been their adversaries in determining what their demands shall be.

I suppose, however, that the funeral march cannot be avoided under circumstances where the strains of the music are so very discordant, as are the interests represented by the ministers here in council; especially, when backed by the purpose to advantage one over the other, for the future, is also a part of the program. The indemnity question, about how much for each, is under discussion now, and no doubt will be for a long time. China will then have to be given time to determine how she can pay. No doubt there are some creditors, should that necessity arise, who can be compensated with territory, and who are more than willing to be so recompensed. China seems doomed to disruption, to be divided up, before the nations will be satisfied; if not now, then later. But if this is done, the Chinese believe their time will come again, and China will be reunited, for they say, "Long united to be divided, long divided, to be reunited."

General Chaffee had been somewhat concerned over the anxiety of European contingents to lay hands on bullion and treasure. The American troops at Tientsin had rescued a considerable amount of bullion from the burned mint. The provisional government officials— Europeans, appointed for the temporary control of the city—were so eager and insistent about its transfer to them that General Chaffee caused it to be deposited to the credit of the United States Treasury, to be disposed of as a matter between the two governments. Millions of dollars secured from seizure of treasure and sale of property remained unaccounted for in any way to benefit the unfortunate Chinese in adjustment of indemnity.

The manner in which hands were laid upon anything bearing the semblance of Chinese Government ownership amazed General Chaffee. He grew sceptical of any future accounting by the Allies and was insistent that Americans should depart, when their stewardship ceased, with a fair name. He caused to be rendered a civil fund account, embracing property and treasure which had come into possession of the American forces and which could not be returned to the owners. Among other property found in the city were a hundred animals in a corral abandoned when the city was captured, and perishing for want of forage and water. General Chaffee had them cared for in the grounds of the Temple of Agriculture until the food supply was exhausted, when he sent the herd out of the city, turning the animals loose where they could forage for themselves until taken up by their owners.

Chapter 26: The Evacuation of Pekin

There had been no organised resistance since the Allied troops took possession of Pekin. It had become apparent that the Chinese governmental authorities would not return to take up the business of administration while foreigners remained in control of the nation's capital. The several governments of the Allied troops, therefore, began measures looking to an early reduction of strength of the forces in Pekin to the numbers deemed necessary to afford immediate protection to the legations. As early as February 26, 1901, the War Department had communicated to General Chaffee the fact that the Secretary of War expected that circumstances would permit an early reduction of the American forces to a legation guard of about two companies, and that about May 1 General Chaffee would be ordered to command the forces in the Philippine Islands.

Measures were promptly undertaken for transferring surplus stores to the seacoast. The first matter to receive attention was the removal of the bodies of those who had lost their lives in China. Other nations cremate or bury their dead on the field of battle. The American custom is to mark all places of temporary burial with a view to the ultimate return to their homes of the bodies of all who have fallen in battle or who have died in foreign service. This custom was inaugurated at the beginning of the war with Spain, and in 1899 was established as the policy of the nation by the following instructions of the President:

Executive Mansion, April 3, 1899

It is fitting that, in behalf of the nation, tributes of honour be paid to the memories of the noble men who lost their lives in their country's service during the late war with Spain. It is the more fitting inasmuch as, in consonance with the spirit of our free institutions and in obedience to the most exalted promptings of patriotism, those who were sent to other shores to do battle for their country's honour under their country's flag went freely from every quarter of our beloved land. Each soldier, each sailor, parting from home ties and putting behind him private interests in the presence of the stern emergency of unsought war with an alien foe, was an individual type of that devotion of the citizen to the state which makes our nation strong in unity and in action.

Those who died in another land left in many homes the undying memories that attend the heroic dead of all the ages. It was fitting that with the advent of peace won by their sacrifice their bodies should be gathered with tender care and restored to home and kindred.   William McKinley

In accordance with this policy a transport was started homeward, before the evacuation of China, with the bodies of two officers and fifty-seven soldiers and civilian employees.

Those who lost their lives or were broken in health by wounds and disease incident to the China Relief Expedition outnumbered those whom they were sent to rescue in the besieged legations. In the present state of pacifist sentiment there may be some who, weighing these facts in the balance, would have halted the columns fighting their way to Pekin. Whenever the American people, generally, reach such a state of mind that they are willing to discuss the cost in blood and treasure of protecting our citizens, the Republic is on the road to decay. A republic exists only by the virtue and courage of its citizens.

The withdrawal of the American troops was begun by transferring to Tongku the mounted organisations, thus making unnecessary the further shipment of forage to Pekin. On May 22 General Chaffee left Pekin with the Ninth Infantry to join the other troops which had arrived at the port of departure. The following report of the departure of the American troops was made:

Legation of the United States of America
Pekin, China, May 23, 1901

To the Honourable John Hay
Secretary of State
Washington, D.C.
Sir: I have the honour to report the departure today of Major-General Adna R. Chaffee, with his headquarters and the remaining United States troops at Pekin, nine companies of the Ninth Infantry, for Tongku and the Philippines. The Light Battery F, Fifth Artillery, and four troops of the Sixth Cavalry left some time ago and are now in camp at Tongku, awaiting his arrival.

The many expressions of regret on the part of all nationalities at his departure have been very gratifying. Nearly every British officer in Pekin, as well as many representatives of all the Allied forces, were present at the station to wish him, his officers, and men a "*bon voyage.*"

But his departure is still more regretted by the Chinese. Petition after petition has been sent into the Legation by the natives— from the Plenipotentiaries down to the poorest shopkeeper. His administration has been just and equitable, and while not as severe as the occasion may sometimes seem to have demanded, results show that his judgment has rarely been at fault. While the blunt, soldierly attitude of General Chaffee was misunderstood by some during the early days of the campaign, no general here is now more popular or is held in higher esteem by not only his colleagues in the military service, but by the Diplomatic Corps as well.

His relations with the Legation have been at all times most

pleasant, which cannot be said of the most of the military commanders and their legations. I have the honour to be. Sir,

Your obedient servant,   H. G. Squires

The occupation of Pekin by the Allies was rapidly drawing to a close. The punitive expeditions had degenerated into the taking of a few lives and the destruction of property without any compensating good whatever. The Chinese government was helpless, yet too proud to return to Pekin and resume the reins of authority as long as the foreigners remained in possession. Before General Chaffee sailed from China the German ambassador in Washington handed to the Secretary of State a memorandum announcing the recall of Field Marshal Count von Waldersee from his command in China:

In consideration:

That the anti-foreign movement, which broke out in the Province of Tschili, China, during the last summer, has been suppressed by the forces of the powers under the chief command of Field Marshal Count von Waldersee;

That the Chinese have been impressively shown the superior power of the Allies;

That, under the circumstances, greater military problems will, in the near future, not have to be solved in Tschili;

His Majesty the Emperor of Germany thinks that the time has come to put an end to the mentioned commander-in-chiefship, and to call it home.

The Imperial Government is convinced that this intention of His Majesty will coincide in the views of the United States Government. The Imperial Government will have no objection to the Allied contingent commander in Tschili deciding the future form of the military commander-in chiefship over the Allied forces which might be declared necessary by the respective generals in Tschili.

Washington, May 25, 1901

The Secretary of State thereupon communicated to the German ambassador the views of the United States government:

Department of State, Washington

The Government of the United States receives with satisfaction the announcement that His Majesty the Emperor of Germany, considering the anti-foreign disturbances in China to have been suppressed, thinks that the time has come for the termination of the existing military situation in China by the recall of Field Marshal Count von Waldersee.

The views of this Government upon the subject of the further military occupation of the territory of China by foreign troops have been signified by the entire withdrawal of its own forces, with the exception of a small legation guard for the protection of its diplomatic representatives in Pekin.

This Government is happy to avail itself of an opportunity to express the high personal respect and esteem with which Field Marshal Count von Waldersee has been regarded by the officers of the United States in China, and a grateful appreciation of the many courtesies they have received from him.

Washington, May 28, 1901

The territory of China has been invaded on numerous occasions, and each time the feeble resistance and entire lack of cohesion of the people amazed foreigners unfamiliar with the Chinese at home. As Americans know them in the United States, they typify capability, perseverance, tenacity of purpose, and great endurance. China is reputed to have a population of four hundred million people, yet fourteen thousand foreigners, under half a dozen separate commanders, operated with sufficient cohesion to brush aside all resistance and finally to assault the walled capital and subdue the defenders, mainly with infantry fire assisted by a few light field guns.

The Chinese at home are a peace-loving, thrifty race, possessing no form of militarism or desire to conquer other peoples. Their vast territory is disintegrating under the pressure of the more powerful and aggressive nations. It seems incredible that they do not mobilise their resources for national defence before they shall suffer humiliation and despoliation at the hands of those who seize and retain through superiority of force regardless of right. The awakening is long overdue; a little more delay and the opportunity for preserving the integrity of China's domain will have passed, so far as this generation is concerned. No conquering nation may absorb the Chinese, but it will take some generations before the conquerors will be absorbed, as they surely will be.

General Chaffee, upon his arrival in China, announced at the first conference of the Allied commanders that his instructions were to proceed to the relief of the legations in Pekin. When it was suggested that the obstacles to be overcome demanded delay until reinforcements could arrive, he informed the assembled generals that his instructions contemplated the rescue of the living in the besieged legations, not the execution of vengeance for their massacre, and that the American force would march on Pekin the following day; that the co-operation of all the forces was earnestly desired, but that if it was not to be had he was determined to proceed at all costs. Discussion instantly ceased when the British and Japanese commanders, who had previously conferred with General Chaffee, announced that their troops would march with the Americans.

When the object of their mission had been accomplished, General Chaffee took up the rehabilitation of plundered Pekin and the restoration of order as his most important duty. He set his influence and authority sternly against oppression and robbery of the Chinese in any form, whether by authority of superior commanders or not. He recognised that the mob had gained the ascendancy and that no permanent change could come until the lawful authorities could be restored to their functions. That civilized troops should vie with the oriental mob in looting shocked General Chaffee profoundly, and his outspoken condemnation of the wrongs being perpetrated materially improved the situation. That his course was humane and right he never doubted.

Nevertheless, it was a source of satisfaction to know that his course had met with the approbation of those whose lives and property he had endeavoured to protect from the spirit of vengeance so pronounced in some of the troops gathered in Pekin after the fighting was over. The following letter is a fitting close to the story of the China Relief Expedition:

Department of State, Washington

My dear General Chaffee:

The Chinese Minister called here the other day, and expressed, with great earnestness and deep feeling, the gratitude of the Chinese Government and the people of Peking for the humane, enlightened, and generous treatment they received at your hands and those of the officers and soldiers under your command. It was a personal and not an official dispatch. You know how we all feel about the matter here in Washington, that your whole administration of affairs in China was a source of the greatest credit to yourself and of honour to your country, and I am glad to be able to assure you that the same sentiment animates the people of China, with whom you were associated.

Yours faithfully,   John Hay

Chapter 27: Philippine Service

From the date of the occupation of the Philippine Islands by the army the commanding general of the forces, exercising also the functions of military governor, had been responsible for the civil and military control of the archipelago. Political opponents of the administration and those who were opposed to the retention of the islands, playing always for advantage, made it expedient, if not a matter of real moment, to hasten the inauguration of civil government. In his annual message to Congress, December 5, 1899, the President said, in reference to the Philippine Islands:

> As long as the insurrection continues, the military arm must necessarily be supreme. But there is no reason why steps should not be taken from time to time to inaugurate governments essentially popular in their form as fast as territory is held and controlled by our troops. To this end I am considering the advisability of the return of the commission, or such of the members thereof as can be secured, to aid the existing authorities and facilitate this work throughout the islands.

To give effect to this expressed intention the President appointed five commissioners to the Philippine Islands to continue and perfect the work of organising and establishing civil government already commenced by the military authorities. Honourable William Howard Taft was designated as president of the Board of Commissioners. In communicating his instructions to the Secretary of War the President said:

> It is probable that the transfer of authority from military commanders to civil officers will be gradual and will occupy a considerable period. Its successful accomplishment and the maintenance of peace and order in the meantime will require the most perfect co-operation between the civil and military authorities in the island, and both should be directed during the transition period by the same executive department. The commission will therefore report to the Secretary of War, and all their action will be subject to your approval and control.

On September 1, 1900, that part of the power of government in the Philippine Islands which is of a legislative nature was transferred from the Military Governor of the islands to the Commission. The Commission was directed to proceed with the establishment of municipal governments, in which the natives of the islands, both in the cities and in rural communities, should be afforded the opportunity to manage their own local affairs to the fullest extent of which they were capable. This was to be followed by the organisation of government in the larger administrative divisions corresponding to counties or provinces, in which the common interests of several or many municipalities, falling within the same tribal lines, or the same natural geographical limits, might best be subserved by a common administration. The Commission was instructed to report whenever its members were of the opinion that the central administration of the islands might safely be transferred from military to civil control.

Under an amendment to the act making appropriation for the support of the army, approved on March 2, 1 901, it was provided that all military, civil, and judicial powers necessary to govern the Philippine Islands should be vested in such person or persons and be exercised in such manner as the President should direct for the establishment of civil government and for maintaining and protecting the inhabitants of the islands in the free enjoyment of their liberty, property, and religion.

The President, by executive order, directed that the president of the Philippine Commission, with the title of civil governor, should on and after July 4, 1901, exercise the executive authority in all civil matters previously exercised in such affairs by the Military Governor of the Philippines. The Military Governor was, on the same date, relieved from the performance of the civil duties transferred to the Civil Governor, *but his authority was continued in those districts in which insurrection against the authority of the United States continued to exist, or in which public order was not sufficiently restored to enable provincial governments to be established.*

All the good intentions and loyalty of purpose in the world could not have prevented misunderstandings and friction under such provisions. It was thought that chances for disagreement might, to some extent, be eliminated by effecting a change of military governors coincident with the establishment of the new order of dual government. General Chaffee was thereupon assigned to command the Division of the Philippines and to serve as military governor of the Philippine Islands, his appointment to take effect on July 4, 1901, the date fixed for the inauguration of the new civil government.

While in China General Chaffee, as has been said, had been advanced from the grade of colonel to that of Major-General in the Regular Army—a very practicable exhibition of confidence on the part of the appointing power. This, with his assignment to command the Division of the Philippines, led him to record in all modesty:

"I could wish for myself the wisdom of Solomon, that I might make no mistake and cause my friends and those who repose trust in me a moment of regret. If I meet my responsibilities, God knows I shall be happy the day I die. I do not think for a moment that the Philippine matter is an easy task; it is, on the contrary, anything but easy. The natives do not love us or our ways. The Asiatic will never love the European or American. He may be, perhaps, put in a situation which will force him to say he does, but you may be certain he does not. The Japanese are very friendly, but they do not like Europeans or Americans when it comes to a matter of like or dislike; they tolerate us, so to speak, but the feeling is different from the feeling existing between Europeans and other Europeans, Americans and Europeans, and *vice versa*.

The Japanese smile when we tell them our affairs in the Philippines will soon be settled to our satisfaction; they do not believe us for the reason that they think they know the islanders better than we do. They talk of the time when it may be necessary to put a hundred thousand men in Formosa. They do not adopt our humane policy, but crush resistance. It has taken a great deal of killing and a long time to put the devil underneath. I fear the case is not so very different for our government in the Philippines. If our citizens would go there in numbers and make homes, it would help to solve the problem, but I do not hear of their doing so to any appreciable extent.

Conditions which confronted General Chaffee in taking over the command of the troops in the Philippines may be understood by some of the views expressed in the final report of his predecessor in command, Major-General Arthur MacArthur:

When the offensive action of the campaign became rapid, the native army, in order to avoid capture or destruction, was obliged to disband; but as the dissolution was accomplished in accordance with a deliberate and prearranged plan, it was not attended with large loss of life in battle.
The Filipino idea behind the dissolution of their field army was not at the time of the occurrence well understood in the American camp. As a consequence, misleading conclusions were reached to the effect that the insurrection itself had been destroyed, and that it only remained to sweep up the fag ends

of the rebel army by a system of police administration not likely to be either onerous or dangerous.

Acting on the assumption that the ascendancy gained over the concentrated armies of the insurrection had sufficiently demonstrated superiority in all the arts and policy of war, in all the resources of power and intelligence, the undersigned, on June 5, 1900, recommended a general and complete amnesty, the issue of which was directed by the President, and which was accordingly promulgated on the twenty-first of the same month.

The immediate result was not inspiring. In the light of the subsequently ascertained facts, referred to above, it is now apparent that it could not have operated directly to accomplish the end in view. In remote consequences, however, it is equally apparent to the reflective mind that the amnesty notice, and the memorandum published July 2, 1900, in connection therewith, proved to be most useful instruments in behalf of pacification, as, taken together, they effectively revealed to the natives the beneficent spirit of American institutions, and the determination of the United States to establish an essentially republican government attended with the largest amount of personal liberty.

The disbandment of the insurgent field armies was followed by a considerable period of comparative inactivity. At the time this was regarded as a favourable indication, and further encouraged the hope that the war might be terminated by general acceptance of American supremacy. These apparently favourable conditions, however, represented the time necessary to redistribute and adjust the insurgent forces to the new method of warfare. During this period, also, evidence came to hand which suggested that some of the Filipino leaders were willing to submit the issue to the judgment of the American people, which was soon to be expressed at the polls, and to abide by the result of the Presidential election of November, 1900.

This view obtained with considerable force within the American fines; but subsequent events demonstrated that the hope of ending the war without further effusion of blood was not well founded, and that, as a matter of fact, the Filipinos were organising for further desperate resistance by means of a general banding of the people in support of the guerrillas in the field. An entirely new campaign was therefore determined upon, based upon the central idea of detaching the towns from the immediate support of the guerrillas in the field, and thus precluding the indirect support which arose from indiscriminate acceptance by the towns of the insurrection in all its ramifications.

As a consequence of centuries of monarchical colonial administration, the people of the islands are suspicious of, rather than grateful for, any declared or even practiced governmental beneficence, and in this particular instance they undoubtedly looked upon the lenient attitude of the United States as indicating conscious weakness, which in itself was sufficient to induce grave doubt as to the wisdom of siding with such a power, especially so, *as the United States had made no formal announcement of an inflexible purpose to hold the archipelago and afford protection to pro-Americans by proclaiming a legal and constitutional right, as well as a determined purpose, to act accordingly.* (Annual Report of Major-General Arthur MacArthur, Commanding Division of the Philippines and Military Governor of the Philippine Islands, July 4, 1901, in *Report of War Department*, 1901, Vol. 1.)

Within a few days after taking command General Chaffee found it necessary to resume military operations, all efforts to induce a general surrender having failed. It became a matter of great importance to have in advance of operations a clear and comprehensive understanding and agreement with the civil government of the islands in order that no conflict of authority should arise. General Chaffee, on July 6, 1901, addressed a communication to the civil governor of the Philippine Islands, Honourable William Howard Taft, requesting detailed information as to the use of the army in provinces not yet pacified, and remarked:

I think it important to the end that harmonious relations shall exist between the civil and military authorities, and that the officers of the army may know where and judge of the time for and method of action, that you name to me the provinces—if not whole provinces, then municipalities—which in your opinion are now in a satisfactory state of pacification and have the necessary civil organisation for administration of affairs, maintenance of law and order, and protection of life and property without assistance from the troops.

In his reply the Civil Governor stated the understanding of the

Commission to be that under the President's order of June 21, 1901, the civil executive jurisdiction of the Civil Governor extended only to those provinces organised by legislative act of the Commission, and remarked:

> The Commission is further of opinion that all territory in the archipelago in which the Commission has not organised civil government is subject to the civil jurisdiction of the Military Governor to exactly the same extent and in the same manner as before the order of June 21, 1901, but that as the Commission shall organise provincial governments, in accordance with the instructions of April 7, 1900, such governments and territory embraced within their jurisdiction will pass under the civil executive jurisdiction of the Civil Governor."

All efforts to effect the general surrender of those in insurrection had failed. Many bands operating in Southern Luzon had brought about a condition which demanded severe measures. The majority of the people undoubtedly desired peace, but they had been terrorized by lawless bands which contained some Filipino patriots, intermingled with a large number of bandits and former *ladrones*. Fear of assassination prevented the people from giving aid to the American troops and from refusing contributions to the *insurrectos*. The operations of the *insurrectos* extended to the islands of Samar, Mindoro, Cebu, Bohol, and Mindanao.

A rearrangement of commands and a general movement were inaugurated to disperse the roving bands, as well as to break up the guerrilla methods of many communities, the members of which were friend and foe as the occasion demanded. Every act in the Philippines was watched by the so-called anti-imperialists, and it was essential that good order be restored in all the islands so as to permit the experiment of civil government to have a fair trial without embarrassment from political partisans in the United States. The army has always found, when its acts come to be judged by American citizens, that patriotism is merely a state of mind, not steadfast and immovable in the light of political advantage.

That General Chaffee loyally and faithfully endeavoured to divest himself of all preconceived ideas of the Philippine situation, and to execute the tasks before him in the interest of the nation he served, the records establish beyond cavil. That he could not avoid complications was a foregone conclusion in the mind of every responsible officer familiar with conditions. The troops under his command were quartered at more than four hundred stations. Economy of administration and supply dictated a concentration, but General Chaffee held to the opinion that the municipal and provincial governments being organised were in an experimental stage, and that the continued presence of the army would afford moral support by making evident to the Filipinos that the armed power of the nation was there to aid and support the civil power.

Within a few weeks after he assumed command at Manila a massacre of troops unexcelled in horror and duplicity in the annals of the army awakened the isolated garrisons to a realisation that the entire body of natives had not yet accepted the sovereignty of the invader. Lulled to a sense of security by the friendly attitude of the inhabitants of the village of Balangiga, Samar, the officers and a majority of the men of C Company, Ninth Infantry, a regiment which had formed part of General Chaffee's command during the operations against Pekin, were foully attacked while at breakfast and, being cut off from their rifles, were butchered with *bolos* and knives.

In all the military operations in the Philippines the American troops had suffered much from Malay duplicity. They had encountered hidden dangers on many trails—traps with lances, poisoned bamboo, *lantakas*, and an infinite variety of ingenious methods of slaying one's enemy without danger to one's self. The polite native of daylight hours fired into the American camps by night and thus involved the peaceably inclined Filipinos in the general suspicion. Americans are straightforward and generous fighters, little imbued with personal hatred. To warn them against the evils of overconfidence General Chaffee sent out this order:

> The division commander calls the attention of all officers and enlisted men of this command to the loss of comrades at Balangiga, Samar, September 28, last, due to unwatchfulness and unwarranted confidence in the professed loyalty and friendship of the inhabitants of the town where the troops were located. For these reasons too much reliance should not be placed on professions of faith and friendship as yet unproved. Military vigilance should never be relaxed, and every precaution must be taken to guard against a recurrence of disaster as at Balangiga.

The subsequent military operations in Samar were conducted with a view to convincing the natives that treachery and assassination would not bring peace and order to their island. Much criticism in America resulted from the course pursued by some of those in authority in Samar during this campaign. General Chaffee maintained his characteristic balance of mind throughout and upheld his subordinates as long as they executed their orders in full accord with the rules of warfare, but unsparingly enforced the army regulations when they were at fault. That some grave wrongs to individuals occurred there was never any question, but that the provocation was great there was no doubt whatever.

With the Balangiga massacre and its consequences uppermost in his mind and demanding immediate attention, General Chaffee found himself confronted with the inevitable conflict of authority which none could long avoid under a dual government with some radical partisans on each side. Inasmuch as General Chaffee credited his views in this conflict of authority with some disagreeable features of his later service, it is deemed desirable to enter somewhat into the details of the incident. The following letter will give an idea of the character of the contention concerning the limitations of authority of the military governor:

Manila, October 2, 1901

Adjutant General
  Washington

On August 25, pursuant to writ of *habeas corpus*, case Calloway ordered deported, I declined to produce prisoner Court of First Instance, making return that prisoner was held by authority United States, that Court had no jurisdiction in such case. Court decided no jurisdiction; man was deported.

Yesterday, Supreme Court served writ for Brooks, Civil Service Messenger, who violated his contract, deserted, went to Iloilo for employment private firm. Man arrested and ordered deported as disciplinary measure; offered make return as before, prisoner not produced in court. Court refused to hear, and demanded presence prisoner. I have declined to produce. Until peace in these islands, authority Commanding General Division Military Governor must not be subjected to review by courts which I hold to be analogous to State courts; have acted accordingly, being careful to show respect by giving heedful attention to its demands. The influence of army on which life of civil government depends in these islands, no matter whose opinion to contrary, will be seriously impaired if action of

Commanding General Division is reviewable by civil courts. A respectful return will always be made. The only course that should be permitted is appeal from his decision to Secretary of War for final decision as to right or wrong of his action.

Chaffee

The Civil Governor then presented his views of the matter to the Secretary of War. In a public statement made several months later on the general subject Governor Taft said:

It must be understood that as the head of the civil government in the islands, under a form of dual control, my interests and sympathy are more with the civil government than with the military, and that the inevitable friction which must exist under such a government between the two branches does not incline me to partiality in favour of military methods, however necessary or inevitable, but I believe that justice requires that both sides should be heard before judgment is given.

The Civil Governor having expressed his views of the particular case under consideration, a copy of his statement was sent by cable to General Chaffee, and he made reply:

Manila, October 4, 1901

Adjutant General
  Washington

Taft dispatch Secretary of War received. Principle involved is more far-reaching and of more deadly importance to stability United States Army authority these islands, until better sentiment masses obtains, than put by Taft. Complied with following results: *habeas corpus* for any deserter who may employ lawyer; any person now held for trial rules of war; inquiry into cases adjudged by military commissions. . . . . The principle is so far-reaching that efforts of army, its influence will be jeopardised, and beg to say, in a state of insurrection authority over prisoners should not be questioned by civil court. . . . .I have always given courtesy and support to court. This conflict is not my seeking. Principle involved is that when court is informed that prisoners held by military authority of the United States for crime, court shall not discharge prisoner nor shall he be taken into court, *nor is trial by authority of military law reviewable on habeas corpus by court.*

Chaffee

The matter was laid before the President, who directed a settlement of it in the Philippines:

Executive Mansion
Washington, October 8, 1901

Taft

Manila

Desire you see Chaffee at once and come to agreement with him. Am deeply chagrined at the disagreement which aside from unfortunate results in the Philippines may also have unfortunate results here. I most earnestly wish to have this question settled in the Philippines.   Theodore Roosevelt

The wishes of the President could not be ignored. General Chaffee produced the prisoner, and the Supreme Court of the Philippines set aside the action of the Military Governor and restored Brooks to liberty.

Matters drifted along during General Chaffee's incumbency of the command in the Philippines, but the broad question of jurisdiction as between the civil and military authorities had yet to be settled. The adjustment of the question of jurisdiction was later made Imperative by the action of the civil government in the case of Private Homer E. Grafton, Twelfth Infantry, who was acquitted by a general court martial of the charge of killing two Filipinos while he was performing duty as a sentry on post on a military reservation. Subsequent to the acquittal a demand was made by the Court of First Instance for the delivery of Grafton for trial by that court for the same offense under a different name.

The surrender of the prisoner was refused by the department commander, but at the request of the Civil Government of the Philippine Islands orders from superior authority directed that Grafton be turned over to the civil authorities. The Court of First Instance proceeded with his trial, found him guilty, and sentenced him to prison for twelve years and one day. An appeal to the Supreme Court of the Philippine Islands was taken and the judgment of the lower court was affirmed, three of the seven judges rendering an opinion that, under the facts proved at the trial, the accused should have been acquitted. The case was then appealed to the Supreme Court of the United States, the expenses of the appeal, between ten and fifteen thousand dollars, being paid by contributions from officers and soldiers of the Regular Army. The decision of the court of last resort included the following statement:

Of such offenses courts-martial may take cognisance under the 62nd Article of War, and, if they first acquire jurisdiction, their judgment cannot be disregarded by the civil courts for mere error or for any reason not affecting the jurisdiction of the military court.

But we rest our decision of this question upon the broad ground that the same acts constituting a crime against the United States cannot, after the acquittal or conviction of the accused in a court of competent jurisdiction, be made the basis of a second trial of the accused for that crime in the same or in another court, civil or military, of the same government. Congress has chosen, in its discretion, to confer upon general courts-martial authority to try an officer or soldier for any crime, not capital, committed by him in the territory in which he is serving. When that was done the judgment of such military court was placed upon the same level as the judgments of other tribunals when the inquiry arises whether an accused was, in virtue of that judgment, put in jeopardy of life or limb.

"The Government of a State does not derive its powers from he United States, while the Government of the Philippines owes its existence wholly to the United States, and its judicial tribunals exert all their powers by authority of the United States. The jurisdiction and authority of the United States over that territory and its inhabitants, for all legitimate purposes of government, is paramount. So that the cases holding that the same acts committed in a State of the Union may constitute an offense against the United States and also a distinct offense against the State, do not apply here, where the two tribunals that tried the accused exert all their powers under and by authority of the same Government—that of the United States

We adjudge that, consistently with the above act of 1902 and for the reasons stated, the plaintiff in error, a soldier in the army, having been acquitted of the crime of homicide, alleged to have been committed by him in the Philippines, by a military court of competent jurisdiction, proceeding under the authority of the United States, could not be subsequently tried for the same offense in a civil court exercising authority in that Territory. (*Grafton v. U.S.,* 206 U.S. 333, 1906.)

Military operations continued in Samar during the winter of 1901-2 under great disadvantages. The enemy were not numerous, but the character of the country was entirely in their favour. The ease with which they could escape in the jungle made capture most difficult. The scattered remnants of insurrecto organisations were gradually isolated, however, and the damage they could commit greatly limited.

During the year all parts of the archipelago except the Moro country were formally organised for civil government, and the army was relieved from all supervision or control over the inhabitants or their affairs, except the non-Christian tribes.

In the execution of the governmental policy General Chaffee continually expressed in orders his anxiety to avoid bringing on conflicts with the Moros, especially those of the Lake Lanao region, but it finally became necessary to send troops into the country about the lake to separate the friendly from the unfriendly natives. To this end a road was opened and Camp Vickars was established, but not without severe fighting. The operations against the well-defended *cottas*, or forts, of these fierce Mohammedans constitute a story of the mingling of the bitter realities with the romance of war. Before the operations began against the Lake Lanao Moros they were fairly warned as to the consequences of their hostile acts by a message from General Chaffee, dated April 13, 1902, which recited the wrongs complained of and expressed the hope that the friendly *datos* and *sultans* would continue their peaceful attitude. General Chaffee, as military governor, then specifically proclaimed:

> Therefore, in the discharge of my office as military governor and commanding general of the army in the Philippines, I now call publicly on Dato Adta, of Paigoay, the Sultan of Bayan, and the Dato Amanitampugu, of Tubaran, to deliver to me or my representatives at Malabang or Paran-paran the assassins referred to in this proclamation, who are known to them, and to make restitution of the government property which has been stolen by their followers, within the period of two weeks from this date, or suffer all the consequences which such refusal, if persisted in, will certainly bring upon them. With the other *datos* about Lake Lanao the government has no cause of complaint, and it is earnestly hoped they will continue the friendly relations now existing.

There were no organised armies in insurrection at any time during the period of General Chaffee's command in the Philippines. He did not assume personal command in the minor warfare which prevailed, but by instructions and personal directions he guided the widespread operations to a successful conclusion. He never struck a useless or unnecessary blow. His sense of humanity did not desert him for an instant, yet, in the state of partisanship which prevailed at that time concerning the question of the administration's policy in the Philippines, he did not escape harsh and unjust criticism. His few detractors in the halls of Congress have passed on and joined the great body of the unknown. It is no longer profitable to revive either their names or their foolish and insincere charges. That he had not lost any of the confidence of the President was made known to him in this form:

White House
Washington, January 15, 1902

My dear General Chaffee:

Your letter gave me real pleasure. I thank you for it, and I thank you still more for the admirable work you have done for our country and the honour you have reflected on our flag. Believe me, my dear general, I feel very safe about the Philippines while you command our troops there. I do not expect impossibilities and all that can reasonably be expected I know full well you will do.

With warm regards to Mrs. Chaffee, I am,

Sincerely yours,

Theodore Roosevelt

The army in the Philippines grew restive and discontented under the criticisms and lack of understanding or appreciation of the difficulties and dangers of service there. This will probably be the case in all our military operations until the nation definitely adopts universal service in the creation of its armies. Criticism has always been generously bestowed by those who do not serve. The careers of all our fighters, from the days of Miles Standish down to those involved by the last raid on the Mexican border, amply attest this freedom of speech, and yet, if our statues and monuments give evidence of real American appreciation, our heroes have been found among the fighters rather than in the ranks of the critics and calumniators. Nevertheless, the critics demanded victims, and several officers were brought before courts martial to defend their courses in various military operations during this period. General Chaffee's action in all these cases challenges criticism.

Insurrection had become a thing of the past, so far as the army was concerned, but the presence of a military force to co-operate with the constabulary when necessary was deemed advisable. To determine what were the needs in that regard occupied General Chaffee's close attention, for the expense of the large and widely dispersed force in the islands was very great. He was planning for the concentration and reduction of the forces when he received the following message:

Washington, July 9, 1902

Chaffee
  Manila
Confidential

Before a reassignment stations department commanders, incident to retirement John R. Brooke, the Secretary of War desires to know whether you wish to remain there or be assigned New York City or Chicago. He feels your two years of trying and most successful service in the Orient entitle you to return or remain as you prefer. Corbin

Forty years had elapsed since General Chaffee enlisted at the beginning of the Civil War. During this long period no other officer of the army had been more continuously in active service. In one of his letters from Pekin, to his wife, recalling that they were nearly always engaged in correspondence and seldom together, he wrote:

One of these days you will be satisfied for me to retire and keep house with you, going no more to war."

The conditions in the Philippines had assumed a quietude beyond the hopes and expectations of the most optimistic. The constabulary had been organised and dispersed widely through the islands. Upon that body and the municipal police would eventually fall the duty of ridding the country of ladrones and organised outlaws. There remained no serious or important work which demanded the presence of any particular general, and there were a number of capable and efficient officers of that grade in the islands available if needed.

General Chaffee therefore signified his desire for assignment to the command on the Atlantic Coast, with headquarters at Governors Island, New York. A few days later, on July 14, 1902, orders were issued relieving him from the command of the Division of the Philippines and assigning him to the command of the Department of the East, these orders to become effective on September 30, 1902.

Many incidents occurred during the period of General Chaffee's command in the Philippines to mark his *régime* as one requiring high ideals and definite performance of duty. Accustomed, as he was, to death in all its horrible forms, on and about the ragged edges of battlefields, the dastardly shot which terminated the life of President McKinley struck a note often observed in men of the Ironsides type. Instead of issuing the usual formal order for draping the colours in mourning upon the death of a president, General Chaffee assembled the troops in and near Manila, and at twelve o'clock noon read to them in person the announcement of the assassination of President McKinley. Then followed a funeral dirge, during which the colour-bearers of all organisations advanced and formed three sides of a hollow square; the troops presented arms and the colours were then draped in mourning. The troops then stood at ease and all joined in singing:

My country, 'tis of thee,
Sweet land of liberty.
 Of thee I sing;
Land where my fathers died,
Land of the Pilgrim's pride.
From ev'ry mountain side
 Let freedom ring!

Our father's God, to thee,
Author of liberty,
 To thee we sing.
Long may our land be bright
With freedom's holy light;
Protect us by thy might,
 Great God, our King.

Then followed the President's salute of twenty-one guns, the benediction, and, at the last, three salvos of cannon, the muffled drums of each band sounding the roll during the firing.

Not an American soldier present on that day will ever forget the deep and solemn impression made upon him by this patriotic and dignified ceremony. Patriotism of the kind that rises and shouts when the stars and stripes are waved from the vaudeville stage, or that contents itself with standing at the curb and applauding other men marching away to war, is not of the type that makes possible the perpetuation of the Republic. This gratuitous remark really has no fitting place in connection with the story of General Chaffee's life, but, having been injected in the hour of a new and greater war's alarm, it is permitted to stand.

General Chaffee sailed upon the homeward voyage on the transport *Sumner* on October 2, 1902. His home-going was attended by a generous outburst of affection and regret on the part of those who had shared his service, as well as of the many civilians who had learned to admire his rugged manhood and sterling integrity. When the parting ceremonies and farewells at his headquarters had been concluded, he passed out from the portals of ancient Fort Santiago to go aboard the waiting vessel, but turned, walked back, extended his hand to the young soldier on guard at the entrance, and said: "Goodbye, my man; I have gone over the road from private to general and so may you."

Chapter 28: Homeward Bound

Sailing on the transport *Sumner* with General Chaffee and his party were the Civil Governor of the Philippines and the usual complement of army people, some going to Japan to visit that interesting country, while others who had completed their sightseeing took the vacant places aboard ship. In its many voyages to and from the Philippines the army has grown accustomed to the long and dreary waste of waters between San Francisco and Manila, and learned by hard and dangerous experience how very often the name Pacific is belied by that vast ocean.

All went well until the vessel left Yokohama on October 15, 1902. At noon the following day the barometer began to fall rapidly. The wind increased and by six o'clock had become frightful. Suddenly it died down, and just as the passengers were congratulating themselves on the fact that the typhoon had passed, the gale returned with cyclonic force and continued for some hours. During the worst of the typhoon a huge wave came aboard, smashed a lifeboat, carried away the chain lashings of the steam launch, and threw it out of the chocks and on beam ends afoul of the cabin, in which General Chaffee's wife was lying ill. Porthole covers were smashed and cabins flooded.

At one moment the transport appeared as if in a crater, surrounded by mountains of water, then was lifted on the crest of a great wave with water gone from under bow and stern. During the storm one of the most beautiful lunar rainbows ever seen by those aboard appeared a few feet above the ocean. The storm abated slowly, but the wind and high seas did not die down until noon on October 18. Water on the promenade deck rose at times as high as a man's head and flooded all the cabins. The experience was altogether fearful and can be comprehended only by those who have sailed close to the vortex of the oriental typhoon.

Upon his arrival in San Francisco General Chaffee was met by a delegation from the Union League Club of Chicago with a private car to convey him to that city. On November 12, the day following his arrival in San Francisco, he was tendered a banquet by the Merchants' Association, which was given at the Palace Hotel, covers being laid for nearly five hundred guests. He left for Chicago after numerous receptions and arrived in that city on November 17.

General Chaffee's views on Philippine conditions were eagerly sought. Such interviews as were authorised were tactful statements well within the limits of truth and good taste. At the moment of his arrival in the United States the returns of the recent election were being interpreted. It was generally accepted that the people had grown impatient with the group of politicians who had systematically criticized the conduct of affairs in the Philippines, especially in the line of detraction of the army and its achievements. The army had triumphed by its courage and patience in the distant islands and had now won another victory at the hands of American voters, who had returned some of the most violent and virulent of its detractors to private life.

It was generally recognised that when the American Army took over the Philippines the archipelago was in a state of disorder verging upon chaos. In the fighting, and in the restoration of order sufficient to admit of the establishment of civil government, the army had done yeoman service. Substantial progress had been made, and in all the beneficent work the army had borne a conspicuous part. As the true story of the operations in the islands was unfolded by the returning volunteers, criticism was silenced and followed by amazement that our soldiers should have remained, in general, so humane in the face of such grave provocation.

When the purpose of the continued attacks upon the army was comprehended by the people, the effect was just the reverse of that planned. In the West, where so many survivors of the Civil War had taken up their residence, a movement of condemnation of those engaged in traducing the army increased rapidly, and the tide of criticism was stemmed when the Grand Army men began passing resolutions in this form:

Resolved, That the survivors of the war for the Union heartily approve the conduct of the United States in the war with Spain, the insurrection in the Philippines, and China. We denounce as uncalled for and unjust the attack upon our army in the

Philippines which has sustained so efficiently and gallantly the honour of our nation, and we extend to that army our congratulations for its uniform success and the assurances of our hearty support.

Upon reaching San Francisco General Chaffee was greeted with enthusiasm as the warrior who had led the China Relief Expedition to the succour of the besieged legations in Pekin. In the Philippines he had been no less successful. He had borne hard upon the lawless element while he extended the hand of kindness to the law-abiding and worthy. Several months before his relief from command in the islands General Chaffee sent out invitations to the more prominent people of Manila to meet the officers of the army at his quarters. In commenting upon the function, a Filipino newspaper said:

> Shortly after eleven o'clock numerous carriages passed up Calle Real, Malate, to the residence of General Chaffee. In the vestibule the guests were received by army officers who, with the frankness of the soldier, combined the amiability and manners of the courtier.
>
> Serious without suspicion, cordial, spontaneous, and eminently frank, without descending to the level of familiarity, such was the reception at the palace of the general where were met together all who are of consequence and significance in the land. We saw there the Honourable Commission, Supreme Court, Consular Corps, Most Excellent Administrator of the Archbishopric of Manila, Most Illustrious Dean, Heads of the religious corporations. Rectors of the University of Santo Thomas, of the Ateneo, and of the Normal.
>
> Well satisfied may be the brave and distinguished General Chaffee with the favourable impressions received by all his guests. The conquest of the Philippines may be accomplished in this way rather than by arms; by the latter the physical man may be overcome, but by the former are won the heart and good-will essential to the real victory."

General Chaffee's successor in command at Manila, after some months of intense application, wrote:

> The burden you left to me has not been an easy one to carry, I mean for *me* to carry. I heard Colonel Hall say once that you were able to work more hours and play longer than any general, he had ever known. That you did not find the work light as air

I am sure, but you have a faculty I envy, that of great concentration and a memory like a printing press.

As General Chaffee journeyed to his station at New York he had every reason to feel that the services he had rendered beyond the seas were valued at their full worth by his countrymen. While the train to which his car was attached was standing in the station at Chicago the Chinese minister, Mr. Wu-Ting-Fang, arrived in the station. When General Chaffee, standing upon the rear observation platform of his car, was pointed out. Minister Wu approached and made a profound bow to the general who had been just to China.

Soon after reaching his station General Chaffee was invited to address the Cleveland Chamber of Commerce, as were also Generals Corbin and Young, the occasion being the fifty-fourth annual dinner. General Chaffee was asked to speak about his services in China in 1900. His remarks are of more than ordinary interest at the present time, when we have been perilously, near the vortex of war for more than two years and a half, and, notwithstanding all our efforts to keep out of it, are now forced by the untoward and barbaric course of events to engage in it.

General Chaffee in his address said, in part:

Soon after returning from Cuba that summer, I was hastily summoned by the Secretary of War, who desired that I start for China immediately, as there was a possibility of trouble there. On three days' notice I left Washington and hurried to San Francisco to catch the transport *Grant*, accompanied only by a single *aide-de-camp*, a young officer in the service, Lieutenant Harper. Before leaving Washington, I requested assistance in my undertaking; that is, I desired a staff, for I was uninformed as to Chinese affairs except that I had read in the newspapers some reference to the dangerous situation of our minister at Pekin. The mention of this brings forcibly to mind my embarrassment in hurriedly starting off on an undefined mission to a practically unknown country. The bill introduced in Congress to establish a General Staff Corps is intended to correct a serious omission in our service, which forcibly thrust itself forward on my departure for the expedition to Pekin. The Chief of Staff, with his assistants, is to be prepared on call to submit to the Secretary of War full information regarding troops and material, which the genius of military men may formulate to meet emergency events as well as the ordinary ones that may arise in the future affecting, in a military sense, the government of the United States.

Now, supposing that the General Staff Corps to be created in the proposed bill had been in existence, it would have been its duty, at the first sound of alarm in China, to have devoted attention to that subject and to have formulated some method or plan to meet the situation that would unfold as the volume of the alarm increased. It should have specified with exactness the force and material which the government could assemble at a selected landing in a specified time; the specification to go to the third degree—advance, support, reserve.

It is not necessary to quote General Chaffee's story of the expedition. It was an isolated incident, in a distant part of the world, which we were enabled to participate in, not without some honour and credit, solely because we had troops available in the Philippine Islands. The General Staff Corps has been created, but its existence has not been a path of roses, and we continue to walk blindly up to each emergency expecting Providence, our isolation, and the spirit of '76 to pull us through in some way.

General Chaffee's new command included the harbour defences of the Atlantic and Gulf coasts. His previous experience had been almost wholly with mobile troops. His diary recites in detail the steps taken to familiarize himself with the defences, their operation, their condition, and their needs.

The General Staff act was passed early in 1903, General Chaffee being selected as a member of a board of general officers to recommend the names of officers of the several grades to comprise the initial detail for the organisation of the new corps.

There were many things to be considered in inaugurating this new corps, not the least being the desirability of its peaceful entry into War Department affairs, where the powerful bureau chiefs had succeeded during more than half a century in repressing every effort of the commanding general of the army to broaden the scope of his control of military affairs. The real necessity for general staff work had been generally recognised within the department, but in the nature of things the tendency of any bureau system is to create resentfulness at presumed interference in legalised or accustomed prerogatives.

The substitution of a chief of staff, acting in the name and by authority of the Secretary of War, and the elimination of the office of commanding general of the army, were changes deemed essential to relieve the administration from never-ending conflict, both annoying and detrimental to the public interests.

Chapter 29: Chief of Staff

When the General Staff was organised in 1903, the President appointed Lieutenant-General Young as chief of staff and a few weeks later made known his intention to appoint General Chaffee to succeed General Young upon his retirement. At this time General Chaffee was subjected to some rude awakenings. He had not solicited any of the promotions which had come to him in recent years, and was deeply chagrined to learn the extent to which envy and ambition had affected some of those who had looked forward to preferment and power. His notes record a sense of sincere regret that some of those whom he held in high esteem could not have been advanced and saved from that wounded pride which attends the closing days of so many army careers.

On October 2, 1903, General Chaffee was detailed as a member of the General Staff Corps, relieving General Corbin, who was assigned to command the Department of the East, the command vacated by General Chaffee. The duties of the assistant chief of staff had not yet been standardised, for the new corps was still groping for the best system of accomplishing the objects for which it was created and was without any available precedents for action. General Chaffee was entirely familiar with the employment of troops and the administration of their affairs. His reputation as an experienced and brave soldier inspired men of similar type to lend their efforts to the successful accomplishment of his projects and plans. It was not a simple matter for him to take up his new duties, for he was without experience in War Department administration. He did not spare himself, but concentrated upon the new duties with the energy and power of application for which he was well known throughout the army.

About three months after General Chaffee joined the General Staff Corps the retirement of General Young became effective through the operation of law, and on January 9, 1904, General Chaffee was promoted to the highest grade in the army, lieutenant general, and was detailed as chief of staff. He made many notes of his observations of the methods in vogue in and about the War Department, and promptly reached the conclusion that some in authority, who had not agreed entirely with the retiring secretary of war, Elihu Root, in the reforms introduced during his administration, were determined upon a reactionary campaign.

General Chaffee underestimated neither their influence nor their power, but set himself sternly against the current of reaction and aroused much hostility. He was convinced that the small group had planned a course of action that would deprive the nation of the benefits contemplated by the establishment of the General Staff Corps unless the scheming was stopped. The detail system also met a determined opposition which boded ill for its survival unless the President and Secretary of War could be warned and induced to announce their convictions in favour of it. General Chaffee had to fight from the start to the finish of his service, as chief of staff, concerning these and other bureau activities which monopolized much of his time and attention and prevented consideration of the grave questions involved in the development of the General Staff Corps. The fact that the President was known to favour both the General Staff and the detail system is believed to be all that prevented a successful combination of interests against their continuance except in a mutilated and ineffective form.

During the year 1904 a statue of Frederick the Great, presented to the nation by Emperor William, was unveiled at the Army War College. The official and social society of Washington assembled for the ceremonies. The presentation on behalf of the German Emperor was made by his adjutant general. Lieutenant-General von Loewenfeld. The unveiling was performed by Baroness von Sternberg. The address of welcome was delivered by President Roosevelt. General Chaffee then gave the formal address of the occasion. Nothing can better illustrate General Chaffee's growth and development, along with high command and its requirements, than the forceful and attractive manner in which he delivered his well-chosen remarks. One of the most popular of the many public speakers of Washington of that time took occasion to send him a note:

> Allow me to offer my congratulations upon your admirable address at the unveiling of the statue of Frederick the Great. It could not have been better.

A well-known public official wrote:

> You made a good speech on Saturday. There are not many military men that can get up and look at an audience and talk straight at them as you did. You very much pleased the group where I sat.

One who observed him at close range wrote of the occasion:

One has only to stand near General Chaffee, the Lieutenant-General of the United States Army, to note the effect of years of discipline furrowed in his face. Without exception, I think he has the strongest features of any man whom I have ever met. The high forehead, deep-set eyes, prominent cheekbones, and determined mouth, all denote the commander of men. Surely here is a man of whom our country should be proud.

Nearly twenty years prior to the appointment of General Chaffee as chief of staff a group of distinguished officers comprising the Endicott Board considered the questions involved in our coast or harbour defence system. Their report enunciated sound military principles and recommended the application of these principles to the conditions then existing. During the intervening years so many conditions had been modified, and the engines and implements of war had been so materially improved, that it was determined early in 1905 to convene a new board to consider the subject and determine upon the most economical and advantageous methods of completing the fixed and floating armament, mobile torpedoes, submarine mines, and other defensive appliances essential to harbour defence.

The Secretary of War was detailed by the President to preside over the investigations of this board, General Chaffee becoming the senior of the army and navy members. The business was most important and occupied the careful attention of General Chaffee. He had availed himself of an opportunity, while department commander, to inspect carefully the harbour defences of the Atlantic and Gulf coasts, and preserved a volume of detailed notes on the subject which served him to good purpose as a member of the board.

As the Senior General of the Army General Chaffee was requested to perform the functions of grand marshal of the inaugural parade on March 4, 1905. Among his *aides* on that occasion were Cadets Adna R. Chaffee, Jr., Sherman Miles, and Charles B. Gatewood.

During the summer of 1905, at the invitation of the French government, President Roosevelt sent General Chaffee, with a party of five other officers, to attend the army manoeuvres held in the vicinity of Brienne-le-Château. It was between this town and the neighbouring one of La Rothière that, on February 1 1814, Napoleon, with 37,000 men and 128 guns, held back the Allies—Austrians, Prussians, and Bavarians, totalling 102,000 men and 286 guns. General Chaffee sailed from New York on August 19, arriving at Brienne on September 7, 1905. Here the American party was met by the commander of the manoeuvres, General Brugère, and his staff, and escorted to the *château* of the Prince de Beauffrement, which had been courteously placed at the disposal of General Chaffee's party as the specially invited guests of the French nation.

General Brugère had been sent to the United States on a mission a few years previously to represent the French government upon the occasion of the dedication of the Rochambeau monument opposite the White House in the park, which also contains the monuments erected to commemorate the services in the Revolution of Lafayette, von Steuben, and Kosciusko. General Brugère had a keen sense of appreciation of the hospitable manner in which his mission had been welcomed to our shores, and took occasion to manifest it by extending every courtesy to the American visitors. This was particularly gratifying, as General Chaffee was aware of the then very strained relations between France and Germany, due to the attitude of the latter in the Morocco incident. The Americans were the only foreign officers who were permitted to witness the cavalry engagement which opened the manoeuvres and the only foreign officers who were allowed to be present at the critique following each day's manoeuvres.

At the conclusion of the manoeuvres General Chaffee entertained General Brugère and a number of French officers at dinner in Paris. During the years which had elapsed since the beginning of the war with Spain General Chaffee had found himself, on many occasions, in the role of speaker at functions at which were present guests of other countries. His remarks on the occasion when the French generals were entertained were most felicitous. As head of the mission General Chaffee had to speak at nearly every function attended in France. He was credited by his comrades as having shown remarkable talent for saying just the right thing on each occasion without taking sides in any way in the acute international situation then existing. His sincerity of manner and of speech made him many friends among the French officers with whom he came in contact.

Concluding his mission in France, General Chaffee proceeded to England, where he was the guest of Colonel Arthur Lee, Civil Lord of the Admiralty, who, it will be remembered, was the British military *attaché* in Washington in 1898 and accompanied General Chaffee in his reconnaissances prior to the battle of Santiago, being with him also during the bloody encounter at El Caney. General Chaffee was later entertained by the American ambassador, Mr. Whitelaw Reid, at his country residence. Among other guests invited by the ambassador

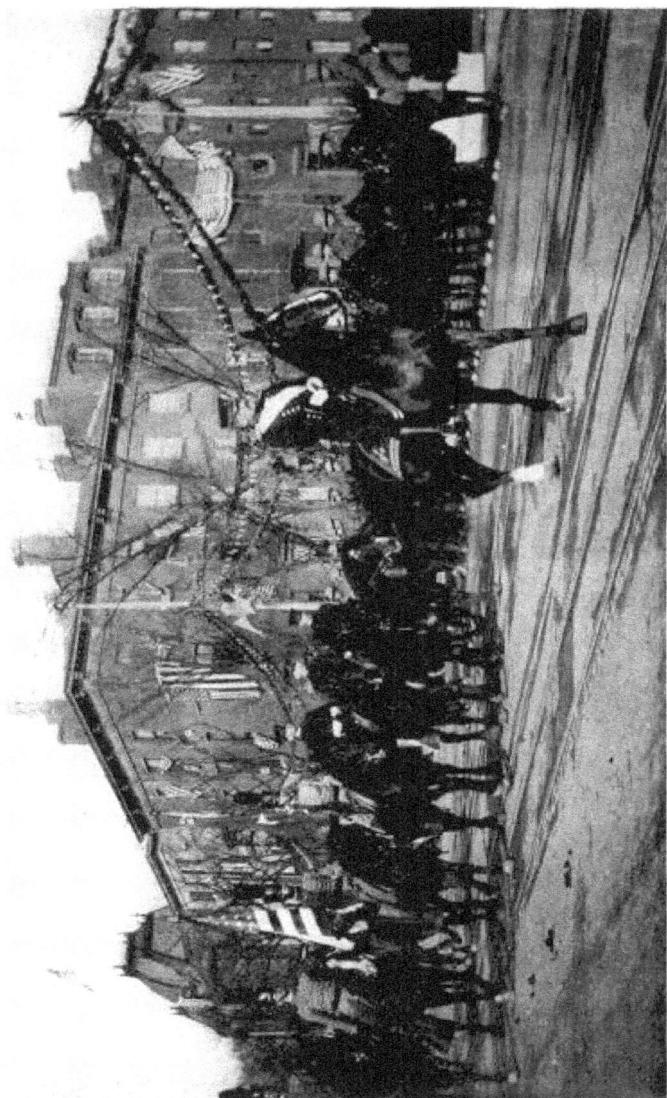

By permission of George Grantham Bain

GENERAL CHAFFEE, GRAND MARSHAL, AND STAFF AT INAUGURATION OF PRESIDENT ROOSEVELT IN MARCH, 1905

was General Earl Roberts, from whom General Chaffee received the following note:

Balmoral Castle, 3rd October, 1905

Dear General Chaffee:

I am much concerned at not being in London while you are there, the more so as I was unable to accept Mr. and Mrs. Whitelaw Reid's invitation to pay them a visit to have the honour of meeting you.

I hope to be passing through London on Monday next, and would call at the Metropole about 12 noon if you would be at home then.

Perhaps you would very kindly let me know by telegram.

Believe me

Yours very truly, Roberts

The meeting of these two battle-scarred veterans of many campaigns was full of interest. During their interview a question was asked as to what was done for General Chaffee by his government in recognition of his success in China in comparison with the honours and emoluments showered upon successful British commanders. The pathetic picture of our most renowned soldier, General Grant, commander of all our armies and twice President, spending his dying hours in writing a book that his widow might not be left in poverty, was all that needed to be recalled to answer the question. A modest pay in life for services of a high order, followed in death by pensions more noted for numbers than for individual value, is the measure of the nation's gratitude. Republics are not wholly ungrateful in the mass, but when the rewards of exceptional service are considered in comparison with what prevails abroad one is led to think the nation is to be congratulated upon being always able to command the services of her bravest and best men.

General Chaffee had made many friends among the British officers in China, and his visit to England was filled with incidents pleasantly remembered in afteryears. Joined by others of his mission who had remained longer in France, General Chaffee sailed for New York on October 7, 1905.

During the period of the occupation of Pekin by the Allies General Chaffee was furnished with a large fund to meet the expenses of official entertaining. It subsequently transpired that he had expended his own funds for the purpose in the most liberal manner, returning to the Treasury nearly all the amount placed to his credit by the government. This having come to the knowledge of the President prior to the departure of the mission to France, he sent the following letter to General Chaffee:

White House
Washington, July 3, 1905

Personal

Dear General Chaffee:

The enclosed letter is for you in your capacity as Chief of Staff. This note is to tell you personally that while at the French manoeuvres you are not to spend your own money. You are sent out to represent the Government, and I do not intend thereby to penalise you. So, my dear general, understand that my *orders* are that all your expenditures for reasonable entertaining and the like should be credited to this Government. You are one of the men who if not closely watched insist upon charging to their own slender salaries matters that should properly be charged to the Government.

With all good wishes,

Sincerely yours,

Theodore Roosevelt

While he was at the head of the American military mission in France the French government conferred upon General Chaffee the order of the Legion of Honor:

Embassy of the French Republic to the United States
Washington, November 14, 1905

General

The Government of the Republic has sent me a commission as Grand Officer of the National Order of the Legion of Honour, the insignia of which was sent you while you were at the head of the American military mission to the last grand manoeuvres of the French Army.

I find particular pleasure in transmitting to you, in compliance with instructions from my government, this diploma, which is intended to recall to you the visit that you made to France, which our army will hold in pleasant remembrance.

Believe me, General, with assurances of highest consideration,

Jusserand

General Chaffee was unable to accept the decoration without authority of Congress. This was requested, as shown by the following letter, but no action was ever taken upon the request:

Department of State
Washington, December 21, 1905

The Honourable
    The Secretary of War

Sir: In reply to your letter of the 8th instant, I have the honour to advise you that under date of the 16th instant, application was made to Congress for permission to enable Lieutenant-General Chaffee to accept the decoration of Grand Commander of the Order of the Legion of Honour conferred upon him by the French Government.

I have the honour to be, sir.
Your obedient servant,

Elihu Root

Soon after his return to Washington General Chaffee was elected an honorary member of the Society of the Cincinnati.

One of the highest functions of the Chief of Staff is that embraced in the legal requirement that he shall make recommendations from time to time concerning the promotions and assignments of officers where selection is involved. General Chaffee was of the opinion that Major-General Bates, by long years of excellent service, had earned promotion, and early in 1905, as chief of staff, he had recommended that General Bates should succeed him in the office of lieutenant general, a recommendation approved by the President.

At the time of General Chaffee's promotion to the grade of Lieutenant-General it had been in contemplation that Major-General Corbin should succeed to the office upon General Chaffee's retirement, and that Major-General MacArthur should succeed General Corbin. The approval of General Chaffee's recommendation for the promotion of General Bates would have operated to reduce the period during which General Corbin would serve as Lieutenant-General to a few weeks. Upon General Corbin's presentation of his views it was arranged, with the approval of the President, that General Chaffee should retire a few weeks before reaching the age limit and that General Bates should thereupon be promoted to serve until the date at which General Chaffee would have retired for age.

In this way the period of General Corbin's service in the grade of Lieutenant-General was not curtailed. In the execution of this arrangement General Chaffee requested, on January 15, 1906, to be re-lieved from duty as chief of staff, and on February 1, 1906, was retired after over forty-four years of service.

In following General Chaffee through his long military career, the closer the investigation the greater he becomes in the character of sol-dier and leader. He never had the opportunity to display the qualities of a Washington, a Grant, or a Lee, but not one of those masters would have failed to rejoice in having a Chaffee to lead his forces in battle or to carry to completion distant and dangerous enterprises.

With all his accredited sternness of manner on duty his first thought after every battle was of the anxious ones at home. His affec-tion for his own family and concern for their well-being and comfort became comprehensively understood by the author during forty years of friendship and intimacy.

General Chaffee had now passed the allotted three score years and ten. Considering the infinite vicissitudes, exposure, and hardships which he had ever shared with his men without thought of shield-ing himself, the sands in the glass of life had run long. The end was now approaching. During the autumn he became seriously ill with a complicated case of typhoid pneumonia and died at his home in Los Angeles on November 1, 1914.

It was a distinct shock to the community to learn of the passing of its most respected and distinguished citizen. From all parts of the world came messages of affection and grief. Privates and teamsters vied with generals and presidents in making known their sense of the nation's loss. As his body was escorted to the station to begin the long journey across the continent, the most profound evidences of sorrow were evident on every hand.

He was buried in America's Valhalla—Arlington Cemetery—with the high honours due his military rank. When a soldier of the type portrayed in the life and services of General Chaffee passes to the great beyond, and his mortal remains are laid away among those of the leaders and heroes on that beautiful crest overlooking the capital of the nation, imagination pictures the spirit host assembling at the sound of muffled drums from the land of perpetual dreams and hover-ing tenderly above the grave of one who never missed a battle except when laid low by wounds of a previous one, and who went to his God unabashed and unafraid.

Some Observations on the Pekin Relief Expedition

By Captain William Crozier, U.S.A., Chief Ordnance Officer on the Staff of General Chaffee, Commander of the American Contingent in the recent expedition for the relief of Pekin

The readers are familiar with the history of the Pekin Relief Expedition. It will be recalled that the advance to Pekin was commenced on August 4th, having been preceded by the failure of the Seymour relief column, the capture of the Taku Forts and the battle at Tientsin. The nations represented in the advance were Japan, Russia, England, France and the United States. The French force which started with the expedition was small and was left on the fourth day out at Yangtsun, to guard the railroad crossing of the Peiho at that place. At Tung Chow, thirteen miles from Pekin, a mountain battery with about a hundred infantry, commanded by a Major General, again joined the column.

The combatant force available was composed of approximately 8,000 Japanese, commanded by General Yamagutchi; 4,000 Russians, commanded by General Llinevitch, and 3,500 each of British and Americans, commanded respectively by Generals Gaselee and Chaffee. No common commander was chosen; the different contingents cooperating whilst retaining their independence. It fell out that the British, Japanese and Americans usually acted together, as did the Russians and the French. That this not very military arrangement resulted in no compromise of the success of the expedition was due probably to the fact that as a fighting task the job was not a hard one, there not being an active and courageous enemy to confront.

The principal concern of each general was to keep his troops supplied and to get them into efficient condition through the hardships of the trying march. The Japanese being the most numerous force, and being composed of troops of the three arms of the service in good proportion, and having a properly organised staff, lacked nothing necessary for independent action; their reconnaissances were always the most extensive and their information the most complete. Without the least tendency toward assumption, they thus fell naturally into a position of initiative, and took a leading part in arranging the order of march and of battle.

The British force also comprised infantry, cavalry and artillery; that portion which remained continually with the expedition consisted entirely of Indian troops. The Americans had the 9th Infantry, the 14th Infantry, a battalion of marines and Light Battery F of the 5th Artillery. Without cavalry they were deprived of tactical eyes and ears, and being thus dependent on others for information, and having too small numbers to act otherwise than as a compact unit, their only course was to fall in with the plans which were made for them. These always assigned to them a dignified part and involved a full share of the fighting. The Russians had with them infantry and artillery and a small number of cavalry; the French, infantry and artillery.

The first engagement was at Peitsang, and was fought, practically, by the Japanese; the others would have been glad to take a more effective part, but the nerve of the Chinamen was not sufficient to provide fighting enough to go around, and the Japanese, being in advance, got it all. On the following day occurred the combat of Yangtsin, at which the supply of fighting was again short, and the Americans and British, having the advance, got practically all there was. Pekin was entered on August 14th, when all the forces were engaged except the British, who, after all, were the first to enter the legation enclosure; and on the 15th the Americans took the Imperial City, carrying the five successive gates leading through it into the Forbidden City. A fortnight afterward the Forbidden City was formally entered.

Knowing the salient facts of the expedition and something of the manner of their accomplishment, the reading public is now in position to take an interest in a comparison of the attributes and methods of the different forces. Comparisons have already been begun by different observers and are characterized by a mixture of praise with some very sharp blame. Most of the praise, as well as a small portion of the blame, is given to the soldier, and perhaps by inference to his officer in the line, while, as is the fashion, the staff, in most accounts and current comments, comes in for tremendous rating in which there is no admixture of praise. Blame is wholesome, but in order that profit shall be taken from it, it is necessary that it be bestowed with proper, not to say expert, discrimination, else we shall fail to make the right corrections.

To begin with the Subsistence Department, it is borne in upon the campaigner that the eatables and drinkables, if not the most important, are at least the most continuously insistent, of the indispensables. Of these there was an ample supply at Tientsin from the time of the arrival there of the first American troops; and they included not only the ordinary components of the ration but most of the delicacies classed as fancy groceries. Ginger ale and bottled waters were in abundance, and plenty was the order of the day. The food of our soldiers exceeded in quantity, quality and variety that of any of the allied forces, as was the comment of all foreign officers under whose notice it fell. When the march to Pekin was taken up, however, the fare was less generous.

All supplies directly accompanying the troops had to be carried in wagons or on pack mules, and of these means of transportation the command was very short, having sufficient only for carrying three days' rations and one hundred rounds of reserve ammunition per man; but, in common with the other contingents, we had a reserve supply of rations and ammunition following upon *junks* by the Peiho, of which the course was in the general direction of the march as far as Tung Chow, within thirteen miles of Pekin. Such luxuries as tents, however, were out of the question, officers and men sleeping in the open air and taking the rain as it came.

The ration thus carried was reduced to about three pounds per man—the full ration in bulk with its packing cases weighing about five pounds per man—and comprised the staples: bacon, hard bread, sugar, coffee, rice, beans and condiments. Even so, it was better than was carried for the troops of any other nation; the Japanese had only rice and dried fish, the Indian troops mainly rice, the others a variety and quantity approaching, but not equalling, those of the Americans. No provision was made for supplying the United States troops on the march with water other than the canteen which each man carried. Other troops were better off in this respect; the British Indians carried water in skins on pack mules, and some had barrels upon carts. But there are wells in all the Chinese villages, and these, along the line of march, were not more than a mile and a half apart; and, with the column properly halted, it is as easy to fill canteens from a stationary well as from a stationary cart or mule.

The water in the wells was always cool, and, though seldom perfectly clear it was never revoltingly turgid, as was that of the river and canals; it was drunk freely by all the troops of the expedition. No other troops made such a time about water as the Americans, who had orders to drink none without boiling it, and had special utensils provided for the purpose. These orders could not be enforced, however, as thirsty soldiers will not wait, even when arrived in camp, for water to boil and cool. Portable filters were provided and were used in the hospital service; one also I observed in the Light Battery and one was in the headquarters mess. The characteristic ailment of north China, however, seems to come independently of the water; it attacks nearly all Europeans and Americans during their first summer, not sparing even those who drink nothing but imported waters. With careful inquiry I was unable to find a medical man who could assign a satisfactory reason, other than that it was "in the air."

I have neither heard nor read any criticism of the operations of the Subsistence Department other than, as these were affected by lack of transportation, which suggests inquiry as to the character and quantity of the latter. The Americans had thirteen four-mule army-wagons and one pack train of forty freight mules, besides two or three ambulances and a Dougherty wagon. The four-mule wagon is considered to be distinctly superior to the means of transportation of supplies employed by any other nation. Loaded with 3,000 pounds of freight, and often with more, it made light of everything in the way of obstacles which the roads offered, and was much more economical, in both men and animals, than the two-wheeled, one-horse carts of the Japanese and Russians, with a driver for each vehicle.

The latter would have been overloaded with more than 600 pounds each, of which, for a ten days' march, 150 pounds would have to be reserved for the food and baggage of the horse and man, leaving only 450 pounds of useful freight; whereas the four-mule wagon carries 2,580 pounds of useful freight, so that transporting power in carts equivalent to that of one wagon, four animals and one man would require five and three-quarters vehicles, animals and men, costing much more and occupying twice the space on the road. The Japanese pack trains were organised with a man for each pony, who led him on the march; in the Indian pack trains, one man riding a mule led three other mules; the American train had one man to four mules, all of the loaded animals being driven in a bunch with a bell mare leading.

Here also was economy of men, although perhaps the Japanese provision of a man to each animal was a necessity, as their ponies are all stallions, and their train, at a halt, was a bedlam of flying heels and wild snorts; it was more dangerous to pass than a Chinese outpost. A large proportion of the Japanese transportation consisted of pack animals; the British Indians had nothing else; the inferiority in economy, when contrasted with the American system, is striking when it is noted that it requires the same number of mules to carry 1,000 pounds on packs as will haul 3,000 pounds in our army-wagon.

The American pack train carried ammunition only, for which purpose it could not have been replaced, as it afforded the only means of maintaining a first reserve supply in constant readiness for immediate distribution to the firing line. The pack saddles of the different nationalities were, in their effect on the animals, of about equal merit. Occasional sore backs were noticed in all the trains; but the American required the most skilful packer.

The indispensable *impedimenta* of troops in the field are always the occasion of delay in active operations. All the American troops which started for Pekin on August 4th were at Tientsin by July 27th, except the Light Battery, which arrived on August 3rd; but the only vehicles for transportation were those which had been sent over in June with the Ninth Infantry. Others which followed the Fourteenth Infantry from Manila on the transport *Wyfield* were still aboard that vessel in Taku Bay, awaiting unloading and shipment up the river by the scanty means which, in the keen competitive press for them, had only been secured by energy and enterprise on the part of the Quartermaster's Department.

The pack train arrived on the morning of August 4th, was loaded at the railroad station from the accumulation which it had been impossible to transport to the camp, and started with the expedition in the afternoon. Investigating the reasons for the lack of transportation, the facts show that the first troops sent over, the Ninth Infantry, had been abundantly supplied, but that this supply was subsequently stretched to take care of two regiments of infantry, a battalion of marines, a light battery and the headquarters. If it be asked why the additional troops did not have their own means of transportation immediately after their arrival, it must be remembered that an improvement in transportation conditions could have been insured only by the maintenance at Manila of a thoroughly provided depot for the dispatch of military expeditions, regarding the Philippines as an outpost for guarding the interests of the United States in the far East and equipping it accordingly.

The shortness of the American transportation, however, was at no time the cause of delay; while the advance to Pekin from Tung Chow, the place where connection with the *junks* was finally broken, was delayed from the 12th till the 13th because of the plea of the Russians that their transportation had not yet come up. The large numbers of missionaries' families and other refugees and entrapped visitors, especially the ladies, who were sent down from Pekin a day or two after its relief, owed the comfort of their journey to Tung Chow to the American ambulances and other vehicles, which were the only ones in that part of the world fit to ride in. Within three days after the arrival at Pekin fancy groceries and bottled waters began to make their appearance in the American commissary, and within a week there was abundance of these for all.

A radical feature of the Japanese and British Indian organisation is the employment in large numbers of auxiliary troops, or *coolies*, approximating fifty *per cent*, of the fighting force. Most of these accompany the baggage train and are used in drawing carts or as bearers, and they do the general work of the camps. Their employment may be justified in countries where men are cheap, and good animals and vehicles scarce, but it does not make for economy; their own rations and baggage have to be carried along, and if used as bearers they are more fatigued upon arrival in camp than the fighting troops, and, therefore, not in condition to work for the latter.

During prolonged rests, it is well for soldiers to take care of themselves; the considerable number of *coolies* employed by the American forces in China and the Philippines, as litter bearers, etc., were believed by the officers to exercise a demoralizing effect upon the men, who were apt to develop an inability to carry a bucket of water or clean a gun. If a sufficient number of four-male wagons, the most rapid and economical transportation yet devised for countries in which they can go at all—and with a little help they can do marvels in the way of trail covering—be supplied to carry all the men's baggage except their arms and canteens, and in addition a sufficient number of armed men to act as train guards, riding either on the seats with the drivers or on others provided, these men would be sufficiently fresh to do the loading and other extra work, and the whole organisation would be much more economical and serviceable than one provided with *coolie* corps.

From a competitive criticism of arms and personal and horse equipments, the American force comes out well; the infantry rifle, with some instances of remarkable endurance, sustained the reputation which it had acquired in Cuba and the Philippines. At Tientsin, when the troops crawled through the mud and lay in it for hours, the rifles became completely clogged; but, by taking them by the muzzle and swishing them through the water for a few seconds, they were restored to perfect action. The thimble belt, used only by the Americans, is still preferred to the cartridge pouches of the others. Our field artillery was as good as any there, although there was none of the most modern design, with its special effort to increase rapidity of fire by reducing the recoil of the carriage to a minimum.

The McClellan saddle would fit anything from the largest sized American horse in good condition to a Chinese donkey, three feet high, in the last stages of emaciation; and allow either to be ridden without producing a sore back. No other hospital corps was provided with such means for transporting sick and wounded as our ambulances; the British *doolies*, or heavy, curtained litters carried by four men, were a poor substitute, and, considered as litters, were only half as economical of men as ours, which required only two.

In United States base and temporary hospitals, the patients were on cots; in the Japanese, they were on the floor, an illustration of the greater requirements—and their supply—of the American soldier. No other hospitals, either, had women nurses.

The shoes, hats, uniforms of the American troops, were not such as any would wish to exchange for those of the patterns used in other services, and no failure in their serviceable qualities was developed. The horses were coarse brutes compared with the high-class animals ridden by the English officers and the Bengal Lancers, but in regard to its other war material the United States has learned no lesson of inferiority.

In regard to military organisation, the same cannot be said. The other forces showed evidence of preparedness and readiness, resulting from the fact that each unit, as well as the general command, was complete with its transportation, drilled auxiliaries and staff assistants, all organised and accustomed to act together; while the American troops had to be sent as small independent units to China, to be there brought into relations with their staff and organised as a mobile force. It was again proved that our staff departments are of inadequate numbers. General Chaffee had to take his adjutant-general from one of his line regiments, his inspector-general from another, also his chief quartermaster of the expedition, as well as other officers for various staff duties; thus, robbing the line, as we always do at the time when it can least spare its officers, depleted as it now is also by the officers required for the volunteer army.

I do not think I am mistaken in saying that, of the two infantry regiments which marched to Pekin, not one company possessed its full complement of officers, and that the majority had only one of the three allowed. We have no organised staff for purely military purposes disconnected from supply, such as collecting and disseminating information, arranging the details of movements, supervision of the condition of the forces, etc. The Adjutant-General's and Inspector-General's Departments and the Engineer Corps have, scattered among them, many of the elements of such duty, and there is nothing in our organisation to prevent the first department from taking it up; but its officers are far too few for the purpose, even if they were selected with special reference to it; and in the field they, or the ones detailed for their work, speedily find all their time required to keep the orders, correspondence and records from hopeless confusion.

When the hampering conditions under which it worked are appreciated, credit should be given by the country to the administration of the War Department for putting into the field, as promptly as it did, a force of respectable numbers, which was able to give a good account of itself. What could have been done without the Philippine base, forms a fit subject for reflection, when it is understood that every soldier, every pound of ammunition and supplies, and every wheel of transportation which reached China in time to start on the relief expedition, came from that possession; lacking which, we would have been unable, like the Germans, to render effective co-operation in the relief of our people.

Another respect in which the United States force does not well bear comparison with the others, is that of the smartness and soldierly conduct of the troops. Both in China and on the way there, at Nagasaki, the men in going about were utterly careless as to their dress and bearing. The Japanese and Sikhs, at the rendezvous, in the camps and at Pekin, whenever seen in public, wore their uniforms complete and properly put on, carried themselves with military bearing and were careful in saluting officers; and the heavy and somewhat awkward Russians, while not presenting so trim an appearance, were particular in these respects. American soldiers off duty walked around or rode in *rickshaws* without blouses, belts or leggings; with shirts open at the throat and breast, the sleeves unbuttoned and rolled up to different heights, or perhaps one flapping, and with the military-looking campaign hat worn in every shape and at every angle. Such sights were common.

The American soldiers were the slouchiest of all, except the French. At Nagasaki, in addition to disregard of the arrangement of such portion of the uniform as they might have on, many were to be seen wearing travellers' caps of various shapes and styles. Their carelessness as to saluting officers must have caused some wonder among the people of the military nation considered to have recently emerged from barbarism, and among the Indian soldiers of lower civilization. The horse equipments of the British officers and of the Bengal Lancers were always cared for and neat, the leather having good surface and the metal shining. Let an American officer try to imagine one of our soldiers polishing a steel bit on a campaign! The belts and shoulder-pieces of the British officers were of uniform pattern, made to carry certain articles which they all had.

American officers carried what they liked—usually a field glass and a pistol, the latter on such belt as suited their fancy. It is not intended to convey the impression that the American troops constituted anything like a mob; their control was never in the least degree out of hand, and they showed themselves, as heretofore, perfectly subject to such discipline as was exacted. They were the most intelligent of all the troops forming the expedition, as was strikingly apparent from observation of their faces at the good opportunity afforded by the march past the staff at the entry of the Forbidden City, on which occasion also their neatness and fine appearance were most gratifying.

For such slackness as is here noted, the fault lies with the officers, the men being in this respect what the officers make them. They come from a people who are not in the habit of considering smartness as a necessary accompaniment of efficiency, but who, having only recently gone through the process of reclaiming a wild country, in which much bad to be accomplished with little, have a high appreciation of the rough and ready, which they reflect. Americans have a tendency to stand up and fight, for which we are to thank God; it is for military training to give this quality its best chance of successful exhibition, by adding to it every feature which the best talent of the world judges useful in the composition of the soldier. Elements of the training are evidently lacking in our soldiers, and it is pertinent to ask why.

Every regular regiment has now among its officers a good proportion of graduates of West Point, who, alone, would represent the knowledge of what constitutes a soldier's duty and contributes to his efficiency. Why is this knowledge not applied? In China, it certainly was not because of indifference on the part of the commander, whose own impulses are all the other way—but it would have been impossible for him, with the responsibility of the expedition upon his shoulders, to produce an excellence of detail of which the spirit did not pervade the commissioned mass. I believe the answer to be, that the constant thought, attention and effort required cannot be secured without stimulus, and that stimulus is lacking in our service. It may not be generally appreciated how little power exists, under our laws, to reward meritorious officers, or to place subordinate command in the hands of the most efficient.

The President selects general officers and the appointees to some of the staff departments; there his power stops. All promotion in these departments and throughout the line is strictly by seniority; the efficient and the inefficient, the careless and the attentive, the sober and the intemperate advancing equally; if an officer avoids a court-martial the rest follows. There is no effective process of elimination of the inefficient; officers are examined for promotion, and if they cannot pass are supposed to go out of the service; but in the ten years of the operation of the law upon the subject, there is no single instance of an officer having been deprived of his commission by its application, except for physical incapacity. Not only has merit no influence in the advancement of officers, but in normal times the natural rate of promotion is so slow that all officers become too old for their grades, and are apt to lose interest in the duties.

This results from the small proportion of high to low officers in a military organisation, and can be corrected only by artificial elimination, i. e., the application of a method by which a sufficient number of officers, preferably the least efficient, shall retire from active service—such a rule as exists in every military and naval service of the world, with the sole exception of the army of the United States. The table below shows the ages at which officers can hope, under existing laws, to attain the various grades:

First Lieutenant	at 31.1 years.
Captain	" 43.5 "
Major	" 57.1 "
Lieutenant-Colonel	" 60.9 "
Colonel	" 62.25 "

The figures show the average ages for all officers of the staff and line; their discouraging character is apparent, and receives illustration in the ease of Captain H. J. Reilly, the commander of the American Light Battery, who was killed while directing the fire of his guns at the taking of the Imperial City. He was of the class of officers who can ill be spared; under his efficient command the battery had achieved a reputation in the Philippines, and during this expedition it had always been found where it was wanted, ready to do what was expected of it. His death as a Captain, after thirty-three years of service, was an honour to himself, but was a discredit to the system which kept an officer of his well-known merit in low grades for such a length of time.

I believe the material of our army, both officers and men, to be the best in the world. No other nation has company officers of the average ability and education of our own; but the superiority shades away as their service progresses, and they get farther away from the rigorous system of stimulus and selection which spurred and winnowed them at the Military Academy, and which in other services is continued through all grades.

At the instance of the War Department, a bill was introduced in Congress at its last session designed to correct some of these evils; it provided that one promotion out of every three in the line should be made by selection, and that the selection should be primarily in the hands of the officers themselves of the branch of the service concerned, a board of whom would submit three names to the President, who would from these make the promotion. The latter feature was to meet the objection of the Army, that selections made, as have been most of those for the staff departments, would be through political influence and not for merit. Another provision was that appointments for service in the staff departments would be made by boards of officers of those departments, without the feature of the submission of three names to the President. The subject of artificial elimination was not dealt with.

Administrations confronted with military difficulties are usually embarrassed by the insufficient number of troops, and, being themselves temporary, have strong reason for devoting their attention to the increase of the size of the army rather than to the introduction of reforms of permanent though slower benefit; the more especially as the augmentation itself carries a transient improvement in quality by promoting younger officers and affording, usually, occasion for the exercise of selection—the patched-up machine will tide over the emergency, and the unremoved deteriorating influences will not produce their old effect until it shall have become the instrument of other hands.

But here was a case in which an administration made its first concern quality and not size, as far as the measure it recommended affects the greater part of the army, and it should have received corresponding encouragement. Far be from me the Cassandra task of attempting to persuade my countrymen that an army of any given size is a necessity for the Republic; if the views of certain persons upon this subject be correct, events will demonstrate it, and if the demonstration be accompanied by a lesson, I have no doubt that it will be pluckily, if not good naturedly, received. But I believe that the people strongly desire that the military establishment which they are willing to pay for shall be of good quality, and I make this my apology for my representing that, unless reforms embodying principles similar to those above outlined be instituted, full efficiency will not be attained, and our army will continue to compare unfavourably with those of other nations.

There are many minds to which, in looking over the progress of the campaign, will be suggested the inquiry: What valuable contribution has its conduct made to the cause of humanity in warfare? With so many nations acting together, what examples have they been able to afford each other of the successful use of methods designed to cause the distress of war to bear only on the combatant forces and governments, to the exclusion, as far as possible, of peaceful inhabitants? Immediately upon arrival it became necessary to employ largely native labour; this labour was always impressed, if not to be had voluntarily, but from the beginning it was paid for by the Americans at a satisfactory rate—twenty Mexican cents, ten cents American, with rice ration, per day. This practice was eventually adopted by all, but was said not to be followed for some time by several of the Powers.

Private property, horses, carts, provisions, &c, were taken for public use, sometimes with compensation, oftentimes not, at least in the earlier stages. But in regard to the general matter of payment for value received, it is to be believed that, after the initial disorderly period was passed and a certain regularity and order had been established, the principle was quite generally observed. In regard to the personal treatment of noncombatants and wounded, much good cannot be said. The circumstances of the expedition were not such as to predispose the troops to a feeling of consideration toward the Chinaman, whose barbarous treatment of missionaries and their families was well known throughout the force; and the more or less popular character of the society guilty of it tended to involve the population in the detestation justly provoked, so that personal hostility prevailed to a much greater extent than in the case of an ordinary war between States.

The majority of the natives had no other desire than that of safety for themselves and their belongings, and were willing to do anything to placate whatever party might be in local power; but this disposition, while saving them from continued cruelty, did not induce careful discrimination in the heat of an exciting situation. With all the explanation that can be made, stories of inexcusable brutalities were current throughout the camps, some indicating the loose rein to passions, others mere brutishness. None of the worst class of cases came under my personal observation, and all stories should be received with caution. One was told me by a fellow staff officer of the American commander and is as worthy of complete credence as any testimony can be.

He related that, while riding by a Russian column on the march, he saw a soldier violently kick a child of some eight years, who was sitting on the edge of the road; and, as the blow of the heavy boot turned the child's body, he kicked him again in the face, sending him over backward into the corn. The assault was murderous, and could scarcely have had less effect than the permanent loss of the boy's eyesight; it was seen by the rest of the Russian column without other mark than of amusement, although from the formation there must have been officers near enough to have witnessed the act.

At Tung Chow, while riding with a group of officers, one of them exclaimed: "Look at that dreadful thing!" Glancing up, I saw a commotion among a small group of Russian soldiers about seventy yards away, and it was explained that they had just dragged a Chinaman from the grass and stabbed him with bayonets. I did not see the act itself nor investigate it further, and am not a good witness as to the murder, the occurrence of which, however, I do not doubt.

While riding alone about Tung Chow on the day of its entry, I found in an empty compound a Chinese *coolie*, lying face down, bound hand and foot, with his head brought back by his queue, which was tied to his hands, and his hands then tied to a fence. He was unconscious and breathing, but with a bullet through his body and no chance for his life. I cut him loose and arranged him so that he might die comfortably. Returning sometime after, I found him apparently gone, but with some Japanese soldiers poking him with sticks to see if they could prod him into a sign of life. I, of course, knew nothing of the circumstances under which he got into the state in which I found him; he may have been guilty of the exasperating offense of "sniping." During the entire advance, and for a fortnight after, dead bodies of *coolies* floating in the river and lying about in odd places gave evidence of killing which must have been unjustifiable.

Crimes against women were told of, including one instance of horrible cruelty to a husband who had interfered; but there is no reason for believing that these cases were more numerous than is inevitable under the circumstances, or that there was toleration for the offenses. One American soldier was brought to trial and conviction, and received a sentence of twenty years' imprisonment, and there were reports of just punishment in other commands. As to the wounded on the field of battle, there was general expectation of no quarter on either side; but, as none of the foreign wounded fell into the hands of the Chinese, and as the latter usually got off while the invaders were far enough away to give them time to remove theirs, there was not much opportunity for the application of the pleasant principle.

One instance came practically under my observation. At Peitsang, I was at the Chinese outpost at the powder depot almost immediately after its capture by the Japanese; Chinese soldiers apparently dead were lying about. As I rode along the embankment, I saw a Japanese soldier ahead hastily putting a cartridge into his gun, and after having passed him, I heard the discharge. Calling back to my orderly asking what he had fired at, the reply was that he had fired down into a trench; for which there could have been but one object, although neither of us saw it. The justification for this was held to be that the Boxers and their sympathizers were fanatics whose dearest object was to kill foreigners, and that they would do what they could toward its accomplishment as long as life was left in them. Riding over the field a few minutes after this occurrence, I passed two wounded Chinamen in the grass, but their bloodthirsty enthusiasm, if they had had it, had waned, as they made no hostile demonstration.

Of looting there was much. Tientsin was thoroughly looted. At Pekin there were no guards to prevent it until the day after the hands of the American force had been freed by the capture of the Imperial City. The earliest and most persistent looters were the Chinese themselves, either the soldiery and Boxers or the inhabitants. As soon as they considered the proper period to have arrived, they commenced operations and were willing to take high risks in carrying them on. The British looted openly and systematically, the plunder being turned in to a common store from which auction sales were held each afternoon at the British legation, under the direction of an officer; the proceeds to be used for the benefit of the soldiers.

Other nationalities were believed to have imposed little check. When the city was divided up, the Americans placed guards over the portion assigned to them and quickly put a stop to disorderly proceedings. Their commanding general was strongly opposed to looting, as to all other forms of abuse of the natives; and he issued stringent orders in regard thereto, in the spirit of which he was supported by the officers, whose duties were lightened by the fact that robbery and cruelty are not found in the grain of the American soldier. Although some looting was done by Americans, it is believed to have been very much less than that by any other troops of the expedition.

Incendiary fires were common, and the route to Pekin can be said to have been marked by burning villages. No instance is known of Americans starting these fires; and, in general, it is believed that the record of the Americans for humanity is indisputably better than that of any other troops.

On the whole, the campaign cannot be said to have marked for the foreign powers an advance in the diminution of the horrors of war, but must be recognised as rather a step backward; notwithstanding which, its conduct was so far better than Chinese standards that the tendency of its teaching must be for them in the right direction.

I arrived at Tientsin with the 14th Infantry from Manila on July 26th, as Chief Ordnance Officer of the expedition on the staff of General Chaffee. I was much of the time near the American commander and available for general staff purposes; and he honoured me by making such use of my services. In this manner I had good opportunity for general observation. Like all officers, I was intensely interested in the showing made by the different forces; and, in the comparison, I found cause, as an American officer, for both congratulation and dissatisfaction.

Removal of the reasons for dissatisfaction is not apt to result from much of the criticism which has been printed; it has been apparent to the critics that something has been wrong, and, in casting about for underlying causes, they have been misled by too ready acceptance as facts of unverified rumours, and in some cases of mere guesses. The harshest critics have been those organs of public opinion which, in their disapproval and discouragement of the whole military institution, have contributed most to the unsatisfactory conditions of which they wrongly appreciate the manifestations. The inadequate though perhaps wearisome detail of the preceding pages can be summarised as follows: In the character of their material, animate and inanimate, the

troops of the United States excelled; in all the results of liberal organisation, training and stimulus, the product of national interest in and
fostering encouragement of the military arm, they were outclassed by
the forces of the other nations.

William Crozier.

www.ingramcontent.com/pod-product-compliance
Lightning Source LLC
Chambersburg PA
CBHW032057080426
42733CB00006B/319